METALLICA S

Original orchestrations by Michael Kamen
Transcribed by Jeff Jacobson and Paul Pappas
Front cover photography and inside color photography
by Anton Corbijn

ISBN 1-57560-369-1

METALLICA S&M
HIGHLIGHTS

Left to right: James Hetfield, Kirk Hammett, Lars Ulrich, Jason Newsted

Photography by James R. Minchin III

To find out what's up in the world of Metallica, check out the Metallica Club, the worldwide fan club that's completely guided, controlled, and overseen by the band. Send a self-addressed stamped envelop to:

The Metallica Club
P.O. Box 194
369-B Third Street
San Rafael, CA 94901-3581

(from outside the United States, please include an International Response Coupon)
Or e-mail your full name and address to:

METCLUB@aol.com
Metallica Worldwide Web Address:
www.metallica.com

MICHAEL KAMEN

Michael Kamen has an illustrious musical career as a composer, artist, arranger, and collaborator with the leading pop and classical performers of our day. Fusing traditional and modern genres in his diverse yet always recognizable voice, Kamen's work showcases his innate ability to break down musical barriers. In addition to orchestrating Metallica's classic "Nothing Else Matters" from their 1991 *Metallica* (the "Black" album), Kamen has worked with numerous artists including Sting, David Bowie, Eric Clapton, Pink Floyd, Pete Townshend, Bryan Adams, Aerosmith, Bob Dylan, Pavarotti, and many others. As a producer/writer/arranger, he has been nominated for nine Grammy Awards, winning three, and two Academy Awards for his songs "(Everything I Do) I Do It for You" and "Have You Ever Really Loved a Woman." His numerous film credits include *Mr. Holland's Opus* (which won a Grammy for best instrumental composition); *Robin Hood, Prince of Thieves; Brazil*; all four *Lethal Weapon* films; and all three *Die Hard* movies. From Kamen's lifelong love of music came the Mr. Holland's Opus Foundation. A believer of music in our schools, Kamen founded the non-profit organization dedicated to music education by providing new and refurbished musical instruments to schools and individual students across the country. For his work, he won a NARAS "Hero of NY" Award.

Kamen is currently composing a millennium symphony entitled *The New Moon in the Old Moon's Arms* commissioned by Leonard Slatkin for the prestigious National Symphony Orchestra. The work will debut at Washington, D.C.,'s Kennedy Center in January 2000.

Kamen's adventures in music, in all its forms, from film scores to hit singles, from ballets to symphonies, leave pop and classical audiences alike eager to hear what Kamen will achieve next.

THE SAN FRANCISCO SYMPHONY

The San Francisco Symphony gave its first concerts in 1911 and over the years has grown steadily in acclaim. In recent seasons, the San Francisco Symphony has won some of the world's foremost recording awards, including the Grammy and the Grand Prix du Disque. Today, Michael Tilson Thomas—Music Director since 1995—and the San Francisco Symphony record exclusively for RCA Red Seal. The Orchestra tours Europe and Asia regularly and performs throughout the United States. The San Francisco Symphony Chorus has been heard around the world on recordings and on the soundtracks of three major films: *Amadeus, The Unbearable Lightness of Being,* and *Godfather III*. Through its radio broadcasts—the first in America to feature symphonic music when they began in 1926—the San Francisco Symphony is heard across the country.

SAN FRANCISCO
SYMPHONY

PERFORMING METALLICA COMPOSITIONS
ARRANGED & CONDUCTED BY

MICHAEL KAMEN

UNDER THE DIRECTION OF BILL GRAHAM PRESENTS

THE CALL OF KTULU

Words and Music by
James Hetfield, Lars Ulrich,
Clifford Burton and David Mustaine

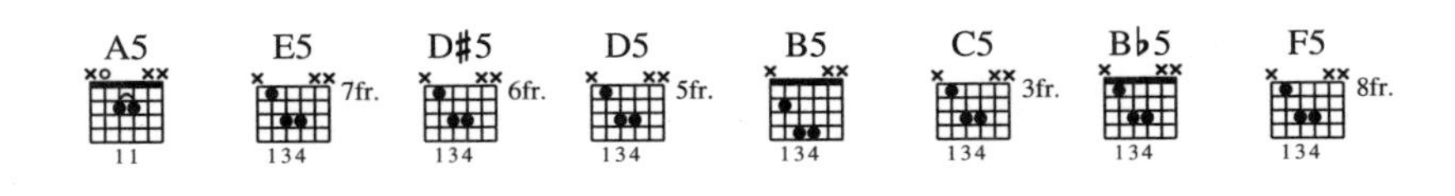

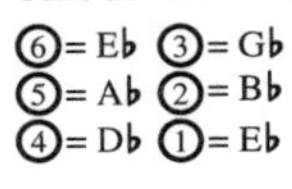

*Orchestra arr. for gtr.

*Orchestra arr. for gtr.

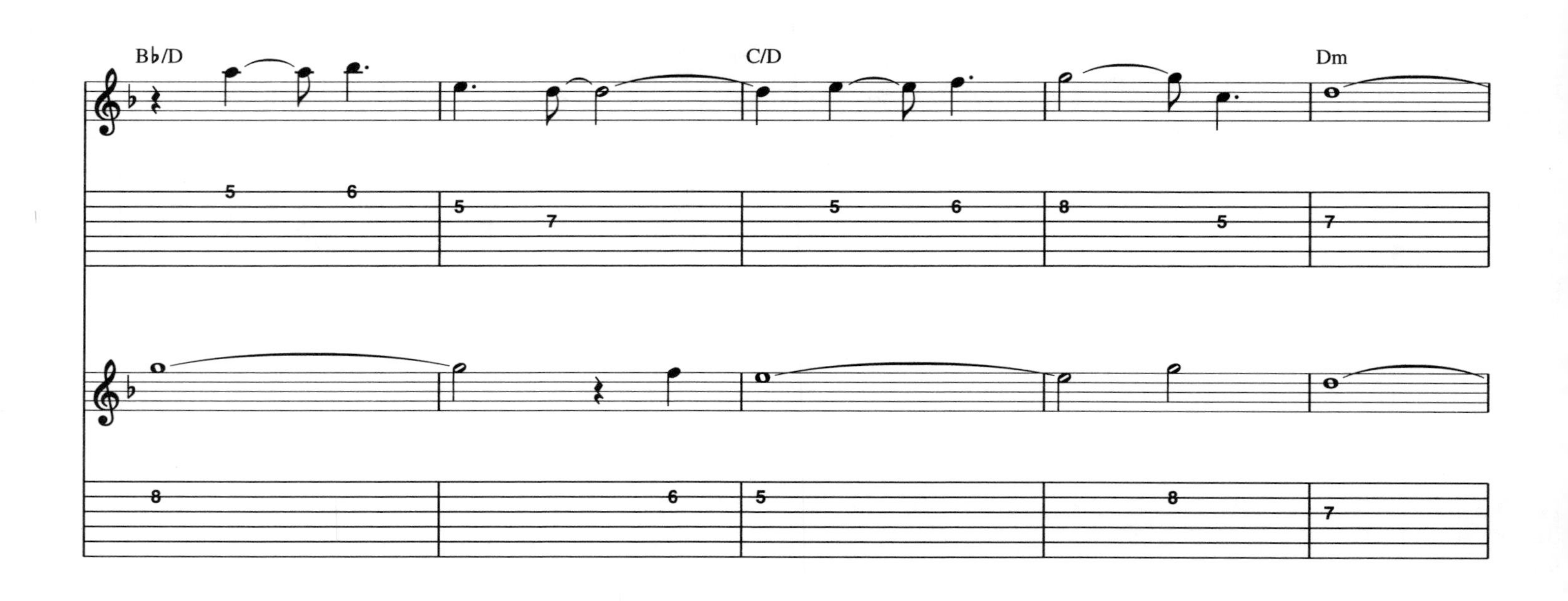
B♭/D
C/D
Dm

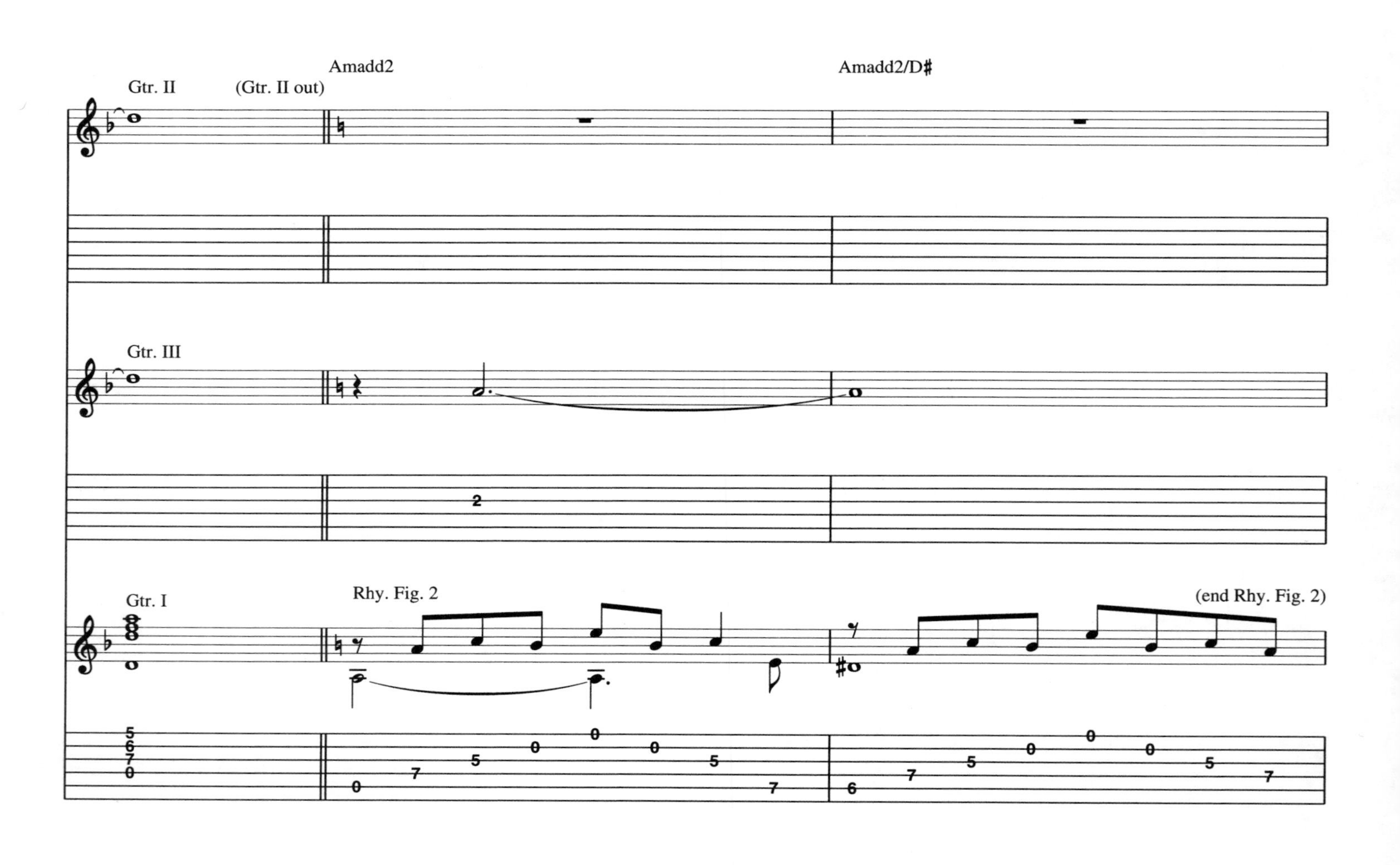
Amadd2
Amadd2/D♯
Gtr. II
(Gtr. II out)
Gtr. III
Gtr. I
Rhy. Fig. 2
(end Rhy. Fig. 2)

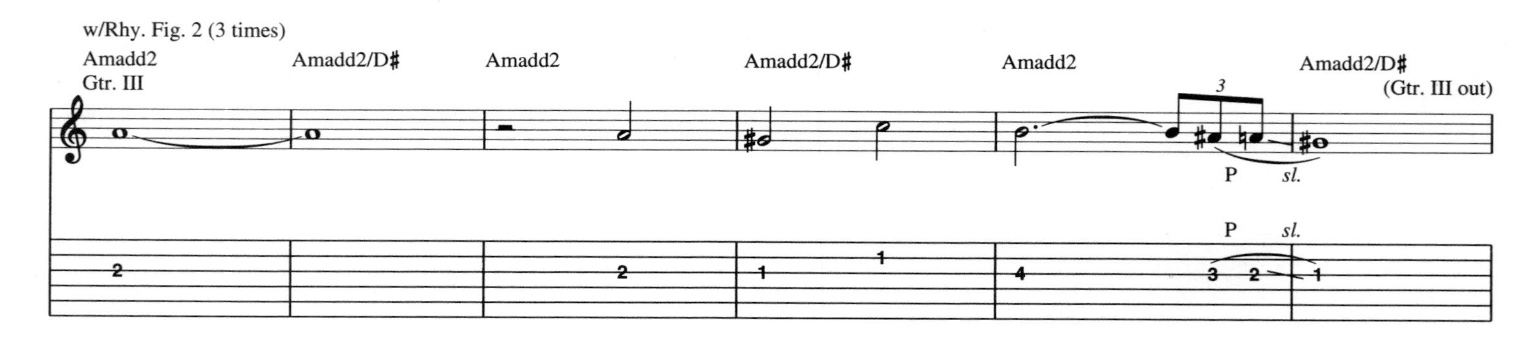
w/Rhy. Fig. 2 (3 times)
Amadd2
Gtr. III
Amadd2/D♯
Amadd2
Amadd2/D♯
Amadd2
Amadd2/D♯
(Gtr. III out)
P
sl.

w/Rhy. Fig. 3 (3 times)
Dm
Dm(#5)
Dm6
Dm7
Gtr. II
Rhy. Fig. 3 (Gtr. I)
(end Rhy. Fig. 3)
w/Rhy. Fig. 2 (4 times)
Amadd2
Riff A
Amadd2/D#
(end Riff A)
w/Riff A (3 times)
Gtr. III
(Gtr. III out)
w/Rhy. Fig. 3 (4 times)
Riff B (**Gtr. IV)
(end Riff B)
w/Riff B (3 times)
*Vol. swell
**Clean elec.

Half time feel
w/Rhy. Figs. 4 & 4A (both 3 times)
A5
E5
D♯5
E5
F♯5
A5
E5
D♯5
E5 F♯5
A5
E5
Gtr. II
f
Rhy. Fig. 4A (Gtr. I)
(end Rhy. Fig. 4A)
w/dist.
P.M.
Rhy. Fig. 4 (Gtr. IV)
(end Rhy. Fig. 4)
w/dist.
P.M.
P.M.
sl.
sl.
D♯5
E5
F♯5
A5
E5
D♯5
E5
F♯5
Dm
Dm(♯5)
Dm6
Dm7
Rhy. Fig. 5A (Gtr. I)
(end Rhy. Fig. 5A)
P.M.
Rhy. Fig. 5 (Gtr. IV)
(end Rhy. Fig. 5)
P.M.

w/Rhy. Figs. 5 & 5A (both 3 times)
Dm Dm(#5) Dm6 Dm7 Dm Dm(#5) Dm6 Dm7 Dm Dm(#5) Dm6 Dm7
Gtr. II
w/Rhy. Figs. 4 & 4A (both 4 times)
A5 E5 D#5 E5 F#5 A5 E5 D#5 E5 F#5 A5 E5 D#5 E5 F#5
Gtr. III
Gtr. II
(Gtr. II out)
A5 E5 D#5 E5 F#5
w/Rhy. Figs. 5 & 5A (both 4 times)
Dm Dm(#5) Dm6 Dm7 Dm Dm(#5) Dm6 Dm7
(Gtr. II out)
*Gtr. II to left of slash in TAB.
8va
loco
(Gtr. III out)
w/Rhy. Fig. 4 (4 times) (Gtrs. I & IV)

w/Rhy. Fig. 5 (4 times) (Gtrs. I & IV)
A5 E5 D♯5 E5 F♯5 Dm Dm(♯5) Dm6 Dm7
sl.
Dm Dm(♯5) Dm6 Dm7 Dm Dm(♯5)
8va
P
loco
sl.
Dm6 Dm7 Dm Dm(♯5)
w/Rhy. Fig. 4 (4 times) (Gtrs. I & IV)
Dm6 Dm7 A5 E5 D♯5 E5 F♯5 A5 E5 D♯5 E5 F♯5
Gtr. III
(Gtr. II out)
Gtr. II
sl.
A5 E5 D♯5 E5 F♯5 A5 E5 D♯5 E5 F♯5 Dm Dm(♯5)
w/Rhy. Fig. 5 (4 times) (Gtrs. I & IV)
Gtr. III
sl.

Dm6
Dm7
Dm
Dm(#5)
Dm6
Dm7
sl. H H
sl. H H
P P
P P
P
Dm
Dm(#5)
Dm6
Dm7
Gtr. III
*Gtr. V
(Gtr. V out)
Gtr. II
*Orchestra arr. for gtr.
Dm
Dm(#5)
Dm6
Dm7
*A5/E
(Gtr. III out)
Gtr. II
(Gtr. II out)
sl.
Riff C (Gtrs. I & IV)
P.M.
P.M.
*Chords are implied till Guitar solo.
F
F#°
Gtr. II
G5
(end Riff C)
P.M.
P.M.
P.M.
P.M.

w/Riff C
A5/E
Gtr. II
F
F#°
G5
8va
w/Riff C (Gtr. I) (2 times)
A5/E
Gtr. II
loco
F
F#°
1.
G
2.
G
mf
f
Gtr. IV
sl.
C5/G
Gtr. II
Ab
A°
Bb5
Riff D1 (Gtr. IV)
(end Riff D1)
Riff D (Gtr. I)
(end Riff D)
P.M.

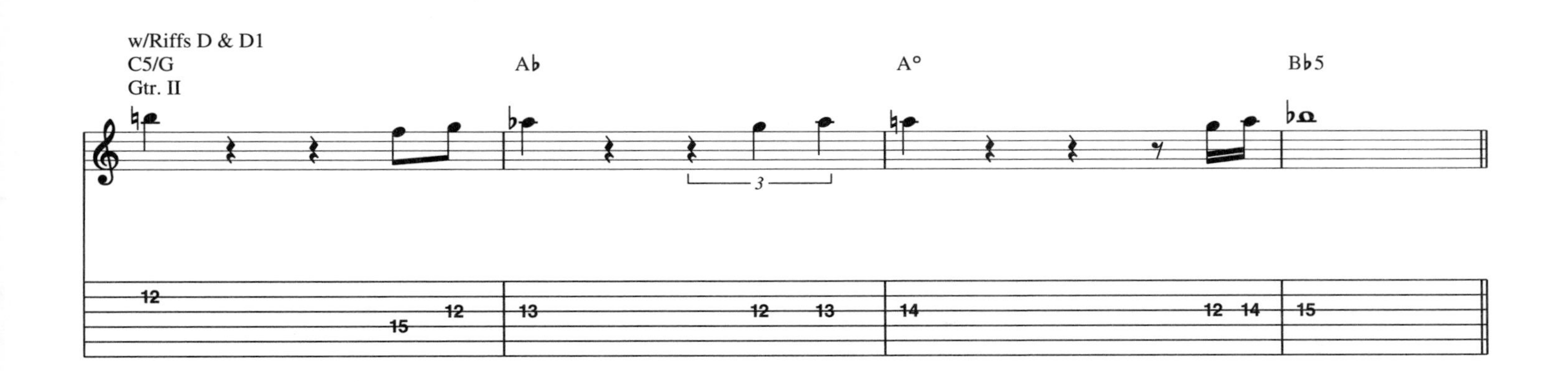
w/Riffs D & D1
C5/G
Gtr. II
A♭
A°
B♭5

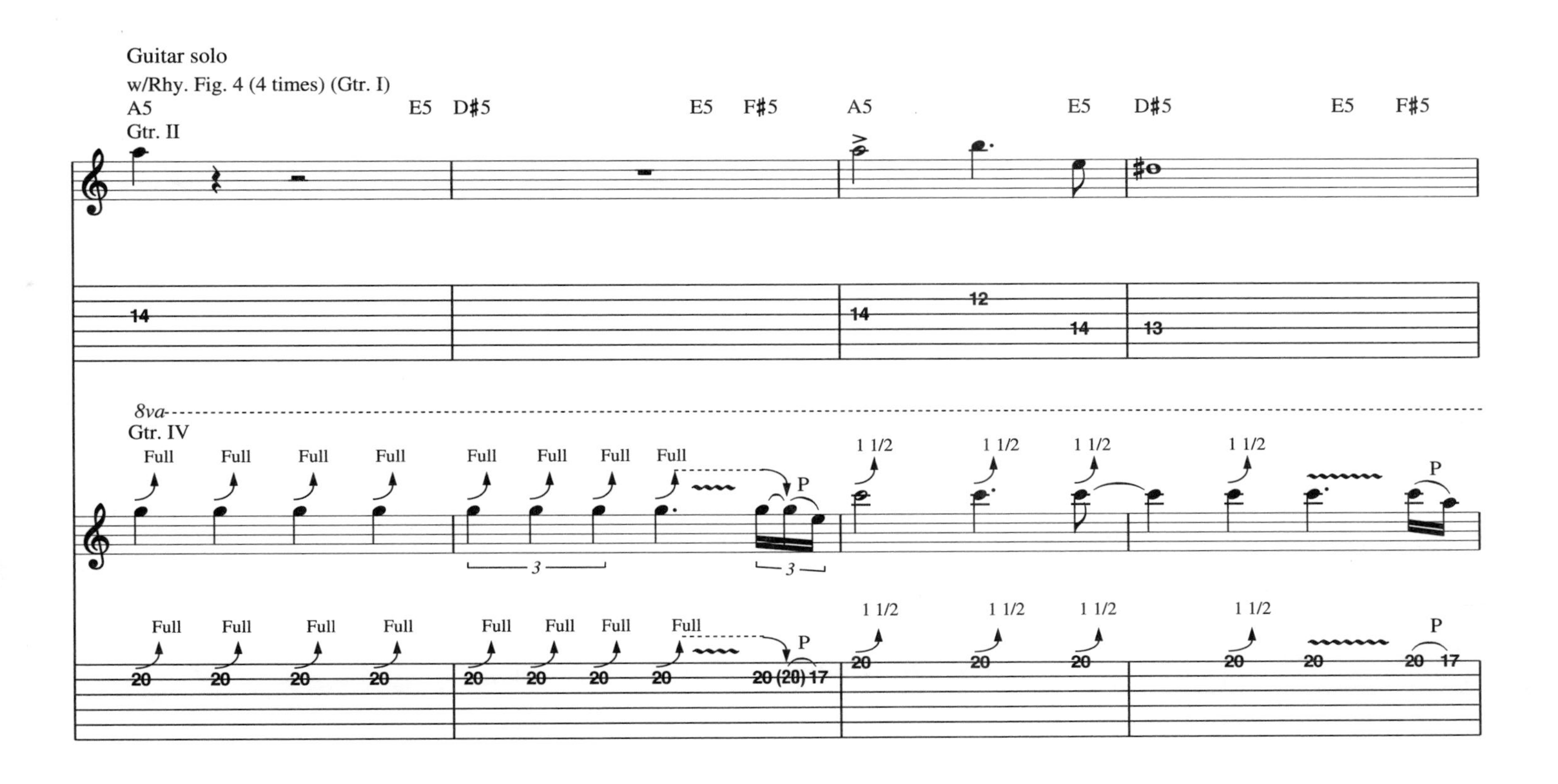
Guitar solo
w/Rhy. Fig. 4 (4 times) (Gtr. I)
A5
E5
D♯5
F♯5
Gtr. II
8va
Gtr. IV
Full
1 1/2
P

A5
E5
D♯5
F♯5
8va
Full
P

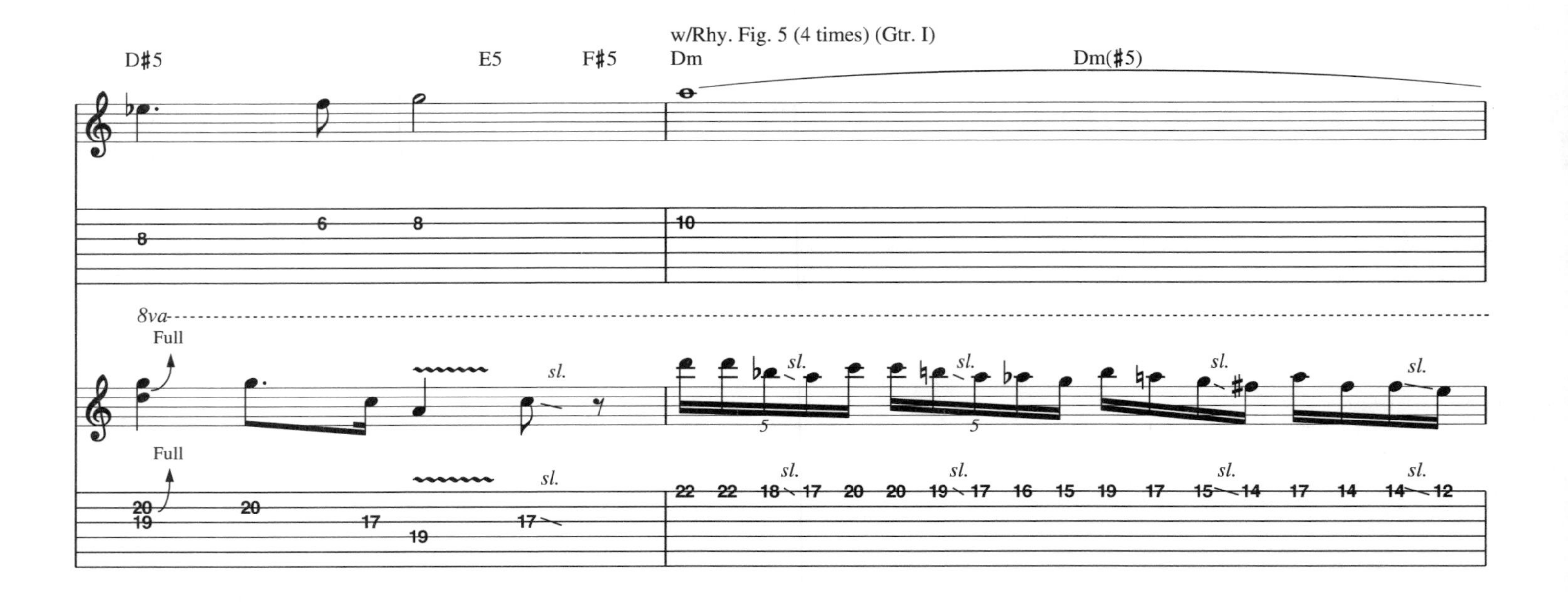
w/Rhy. Fig. 5 (4 times) (Gtr. I)
D♯5
E5
F♯5
Dm
Dm(♯5)
8va
Full
sl.

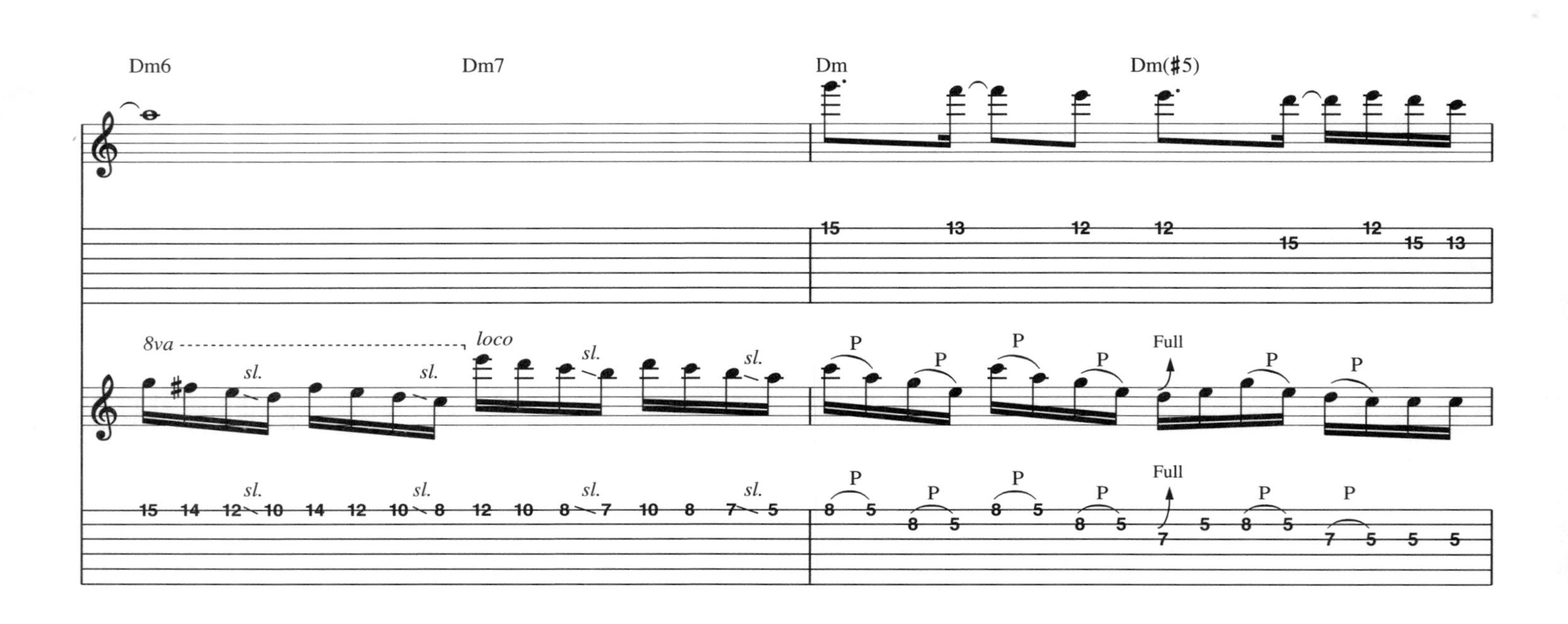
Dm6
Dm7
Dm
Dm(♯5)
8va
loco
sl.
P
Full

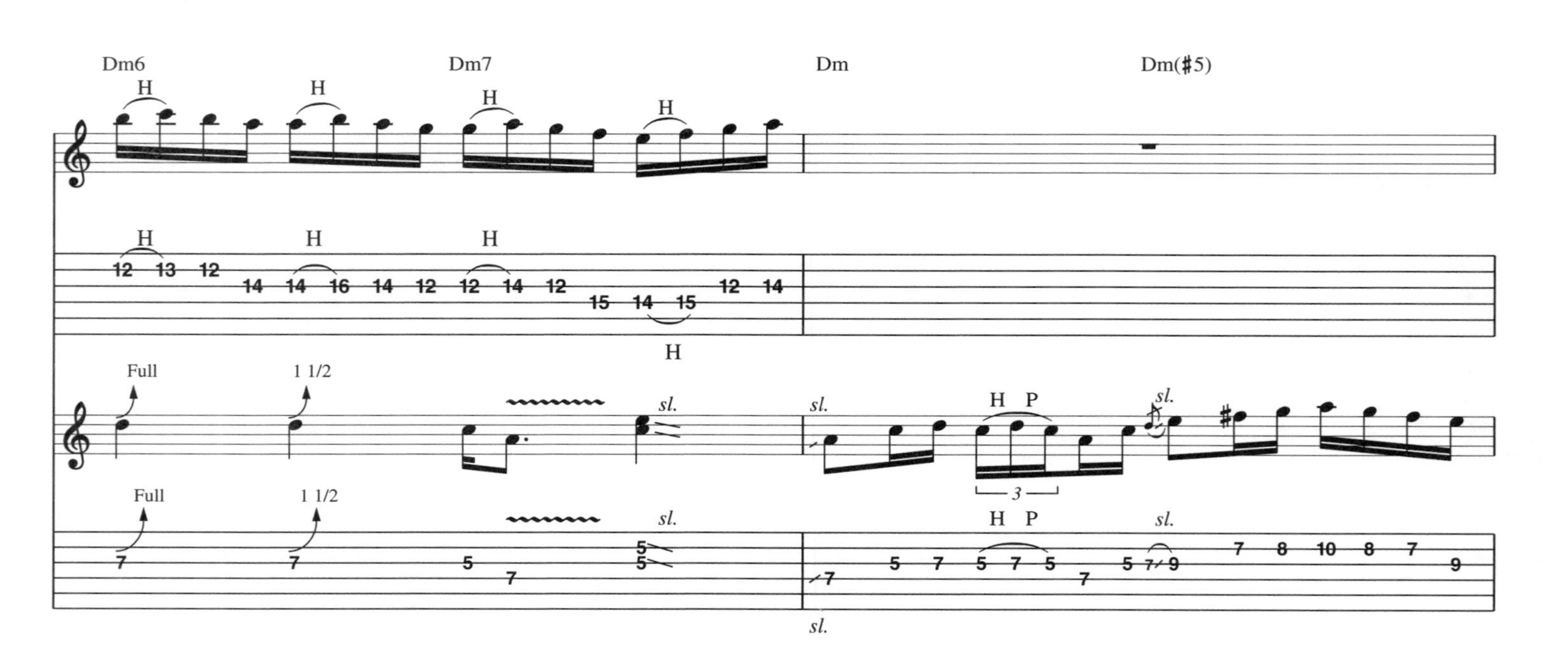
Dm6
Dm7
Dm
Dm(♯5)
H
P
Full
1 1/2
sl.

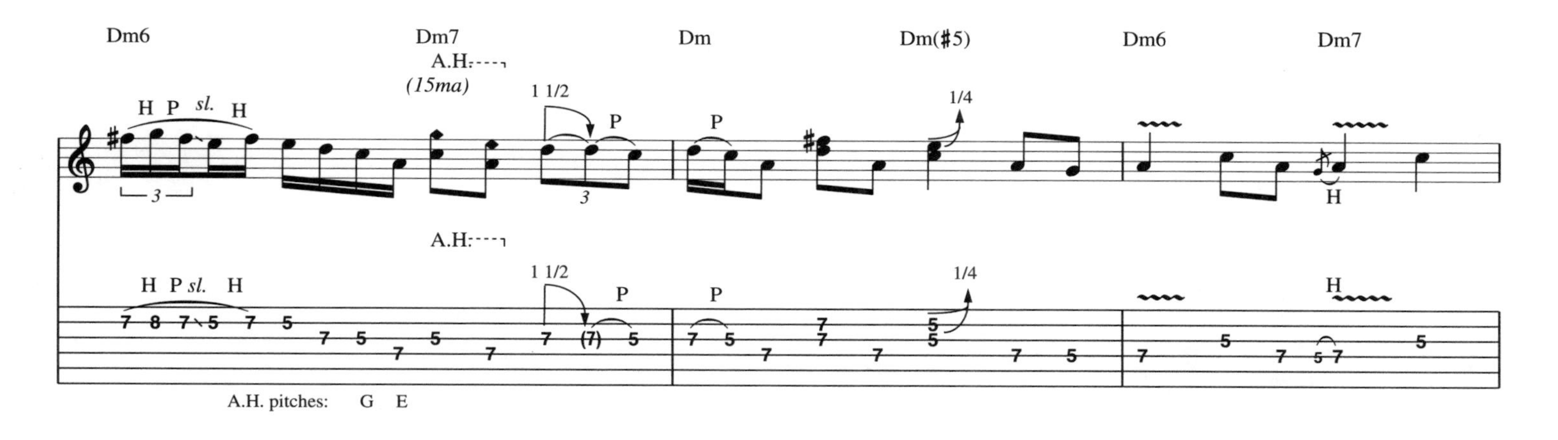

Dm6
Dm7
Dm
Dm(♯5)
Dm6
Dm7
A.H.
(15ma)
1 1/2
1/4
H P sl. H
P
H
A.H. pitches: G E

w/Rhy. Fig. 4 (4 times) (Gtr. I)
A5
E5
D♯5
E5
F♯5
(Gtr. III out)
Gtr. III
mp
Gtr. II
sl.
P

A5
Gtr. II
E5
D♯5
E5
F♯5
A5
E5
8va
1 1/2
sl.
P

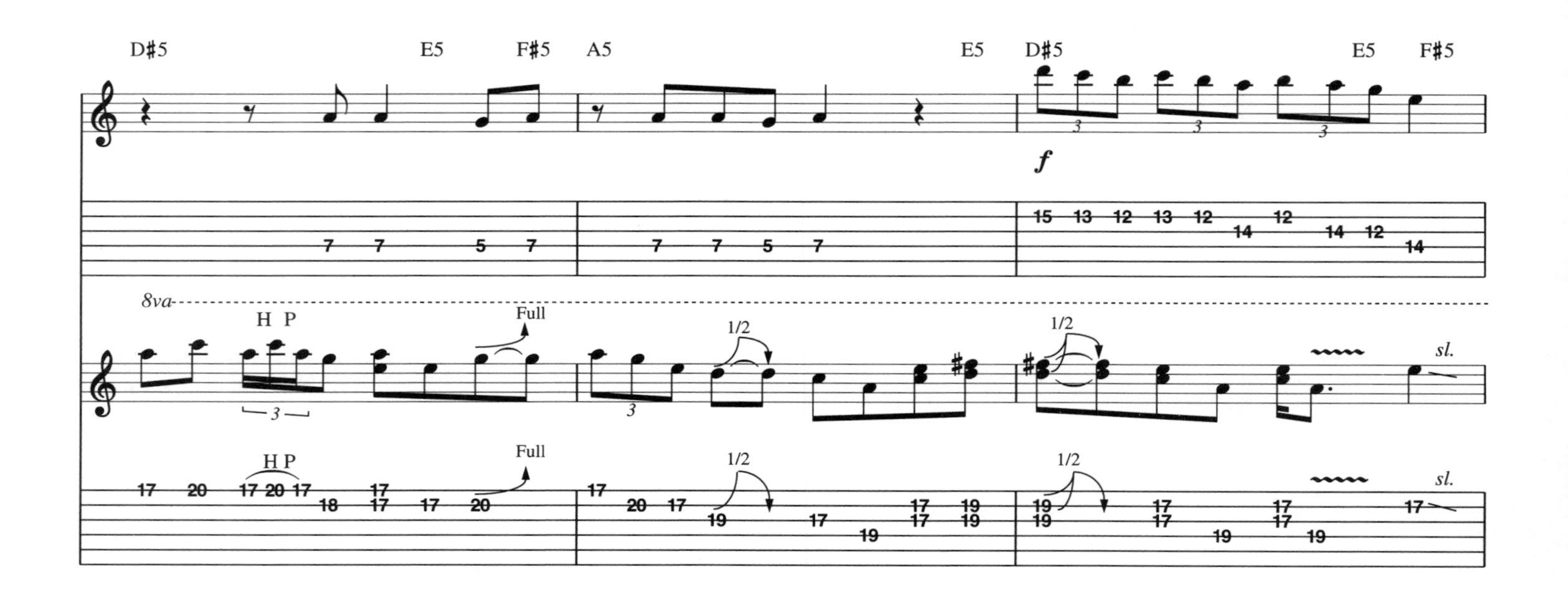
D#5
E5
F#5
A5
E5
D#5
E5
F#5
8va
H P
Full
1/2
1/2
sl.

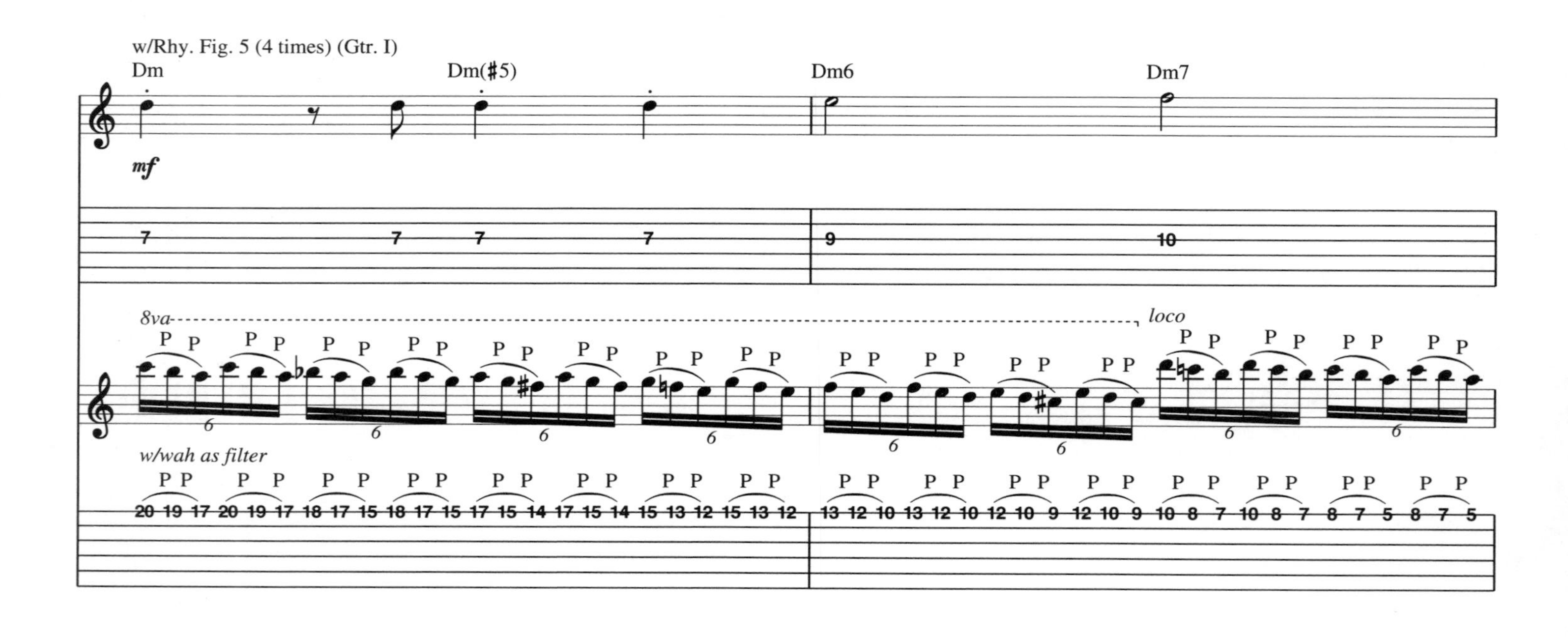
w/Rhy. Fig. 5 (4 times) (Gtr. I)
Dm
Dm(#5)
Dm6
Dm7
8va
loco
w/wah as filter

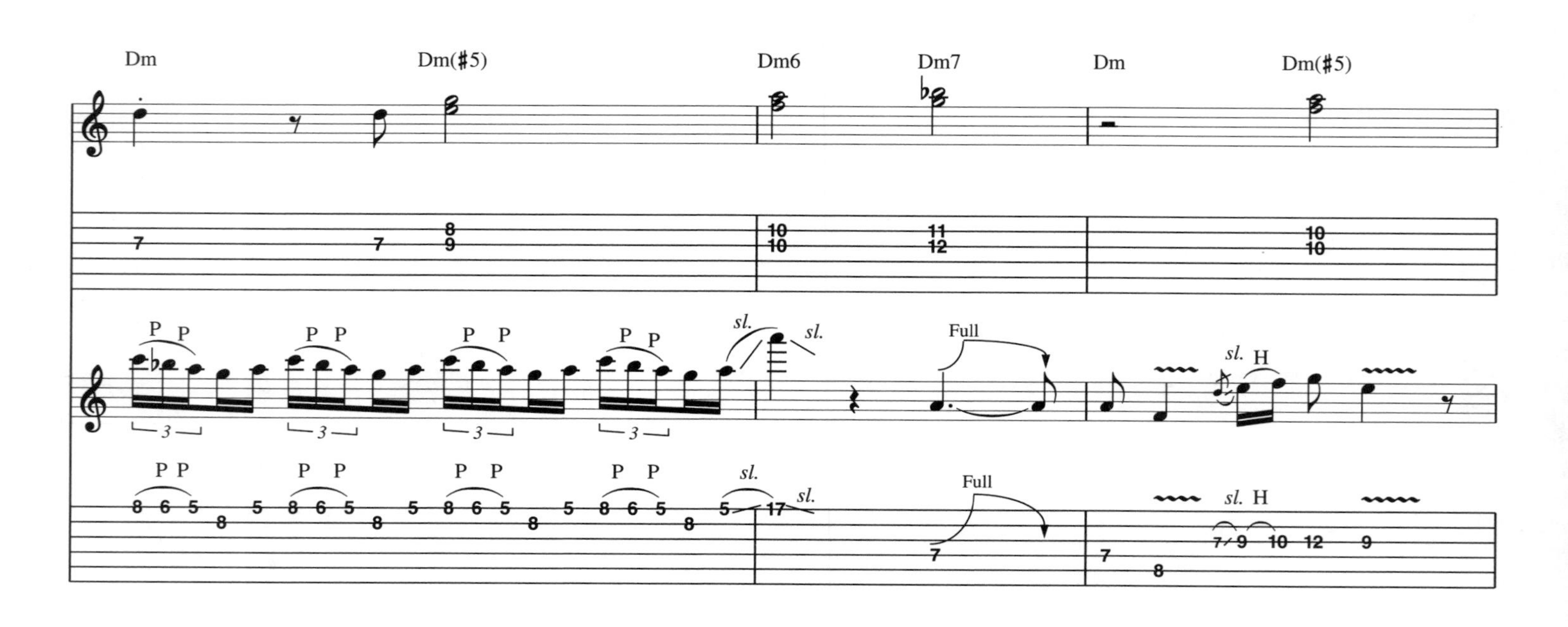
Dm
Dm(#5)
Dm6
Dm7
Dm
Dm(#5)
sl.
Full
sl. H

Dm6
Dm7
Dm
Dm(♯5)
1 1/2
P
sl.
8va
H P
(end half time feel)
A5
E5
D♯5
F♯5
Full
Rhy. Fig. 6 (Gtrs. I & IV)
loco
(end Rhy. Fig. 6)
(wah off)
P.M.
w/Rhy. Fig. 6 (3 times)
Gtr. II
w/Rhy. Fig. 5 (4 times) (Gtrs. I & IV)

w/Riff C (1st 2 bars only) (4 times)
Dm
Dm(#5)
Dm6
Dm7
A5/E
F
Play 4 times
Play 3 times
B5/F#
Gtr. II
G
C5/G
Ab
Gtrs. I & IV
P.M.
D5/A
Bb
(cont. in slashes)

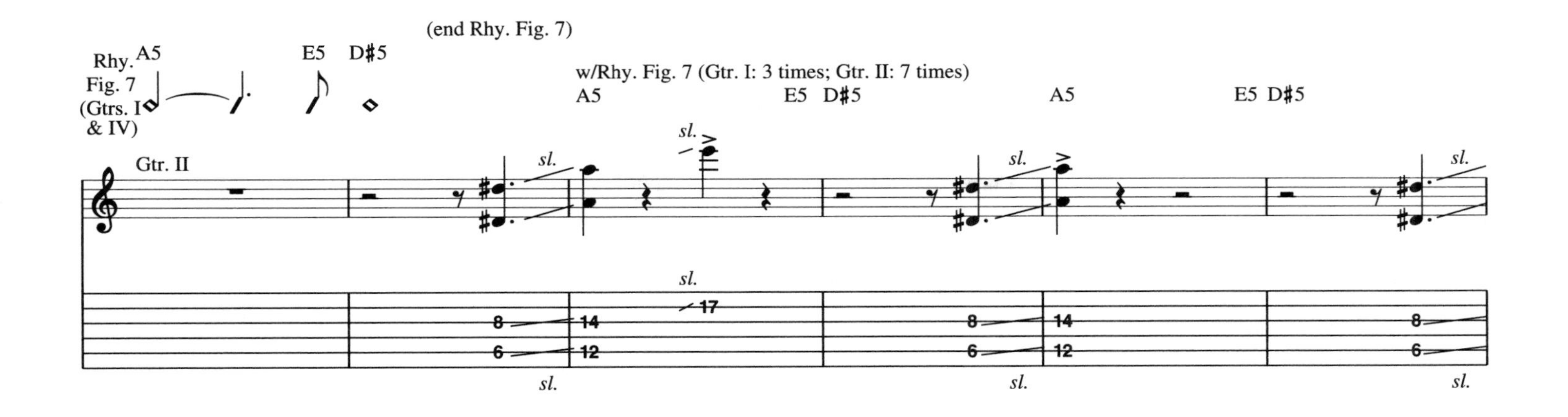
Rhy. Fig. 7 (Gtrs. I & IV)
A5 E5 D#5
(end Rhy. Fig. 7)
w/Rhy. Fig. 7 (Gtr. I: 3 times; Gtr. II: 7 times)
A5 E5 D#5 A5 E5 D#5
Gtr. II
sl.

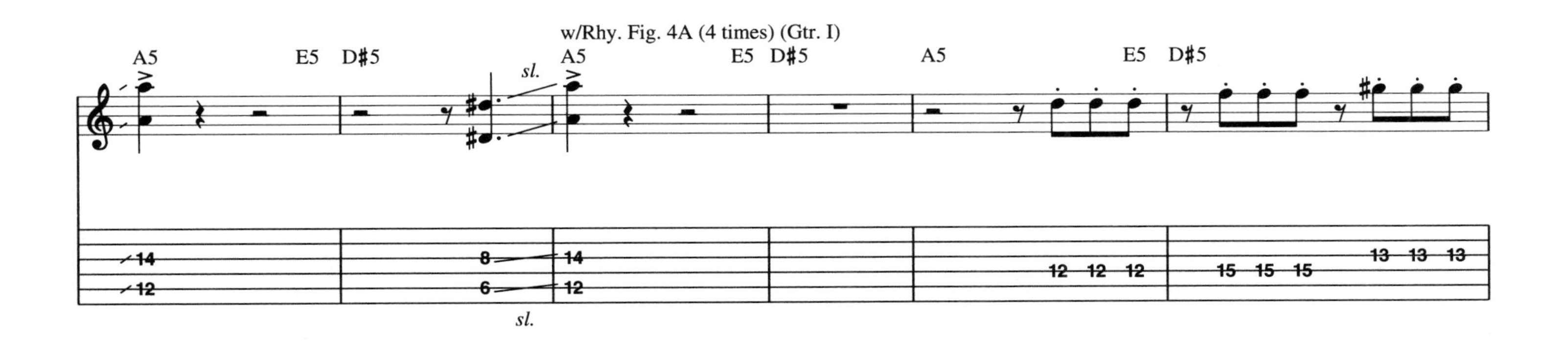
A5 E5 D#5
w/Rhy. Fig. 4A (4 times) (Gtr. I)
A5 E5 D#5 A5 E5 D#5
sl.

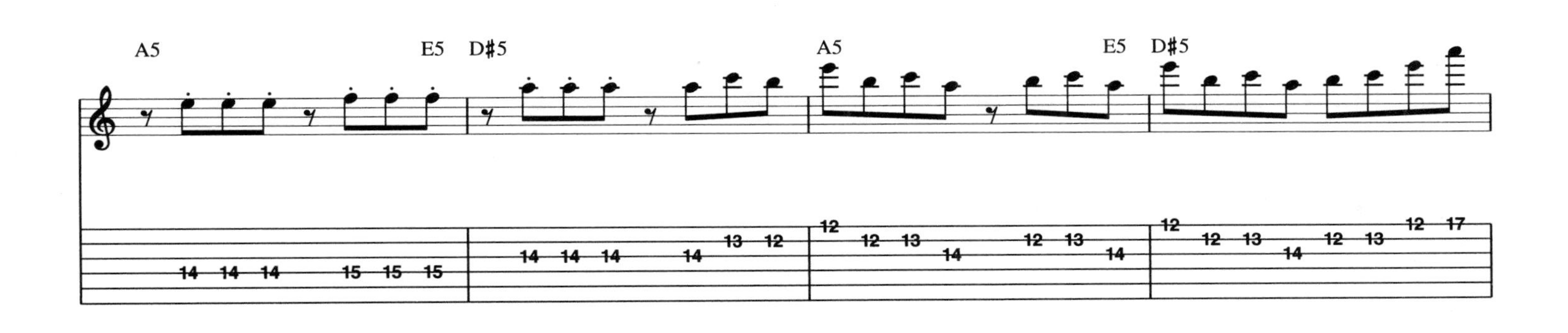
A5 E5 D#5 A5 E5 D#5

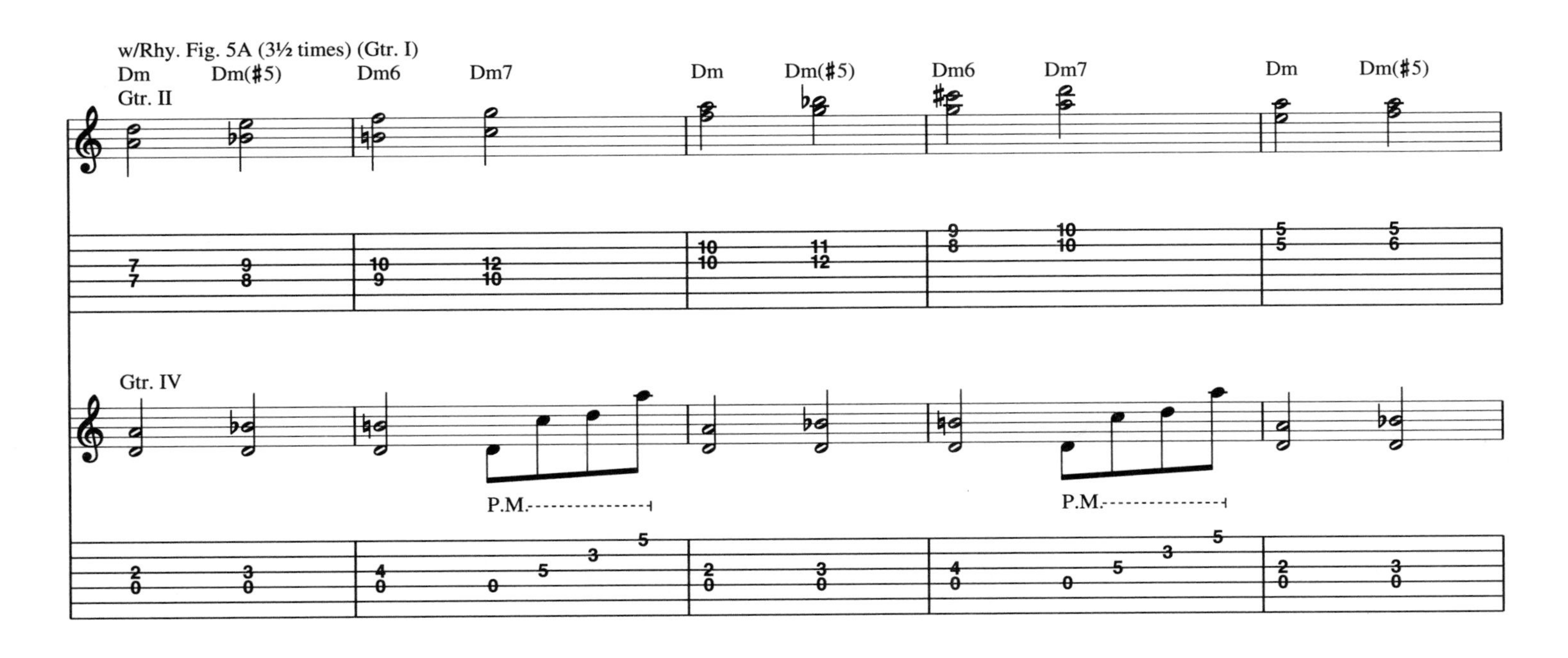
w/Rhy. Fig. 5A (3½ times) (Gtr. I)
Dm Dm(#5) Dm6 Dm7 Dm Dm(#5) Dm6 Dm7 Dm Dm(#5)
Gtr. II
Gtr. IV
P.M.

A little slower ♩ = 108
Dm6
Dm7
Dm
Dm(♯5)
w/Rhy. Fill 1
Dm6
Em
(Gtr. II out)
P.M.
Gtrs. I & IV
(Gtr. IV cont. on upper staff)
G5 F♯5
Rhy. Fig. 8A (Gtr. IV)
G5 E5
Full
(end Rhy. Fig. 8A)
Rhy. Fig. 8 (Gtr. I)
(end Rhy. Fig. 8)
sl.
w/Rhy. Figs. 8 & 8A (both 3 times)
Gtr. II
1.
2.
E5

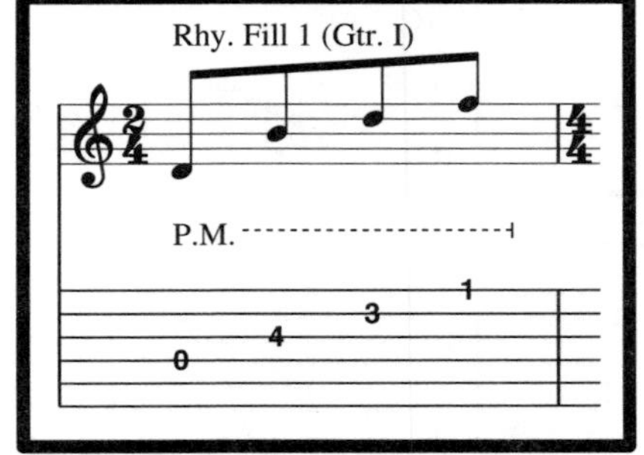
Rhy. Fill 1 (Gtr. I)
P.M.

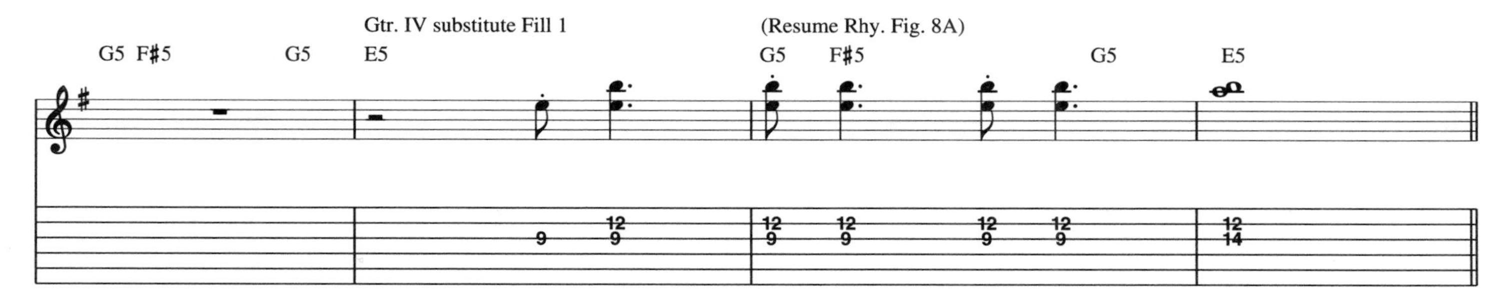

*Gtr. III to left of slash in TAB.

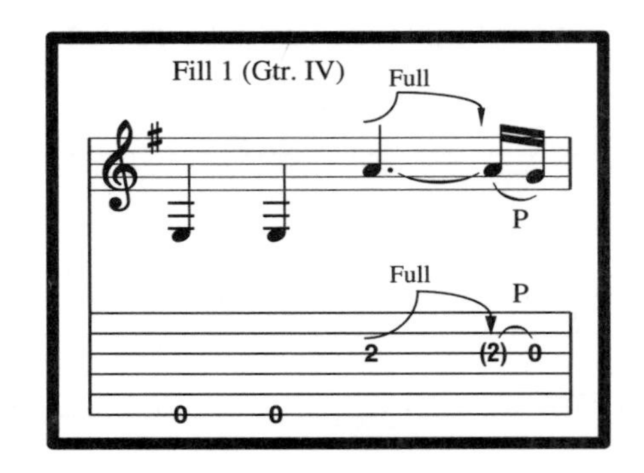

G5 F#5
Gtr. II
G5
E5
8va
loco
Gtr. IV
H P
sl.
D5
B5
Freely
(Gtr. IV cont. in slashes)
Gtr. I
*8va refers to Gtr. IV only.
(Gtr. IV out)
dim.

A tempo
w/Rhy. Fig. 1 (1½ times)
Dm
Gtr. II
B♭/D
C/D
H
mp
*Grad. vol. swell
Dm
*Gtr. IV
P
Gtr. II
H H
B♭/D
*Clean tone
**Gtr. II to left of slash in TAB.
C/D
(Gtr. IV)
(Gtr. II)
rit.
Dm
(Gtr. IV out)
Gtr. II
trem. pick
Gtr. I
(cont. in slashes)
Slower ♩ = 92
D5 C5 D5 B♭5 D5 F5 D5
Gtrs. I & IV
f dist. tone
Gtr. II
*Played by Gtr. IV only; Gtr. I tacet.
Free time
D5
sl.
p grad. cresc.
f
rit.
*While trem. picking, slowly slide up neck, past fretboard, reaching bridge pickup at last bar of song.

MASTER OF PUPPETS

Words and Music by James Hetfield,
Lars Ulrich, Kirk Hammett and Cliff Burton

D5
Db5
C5
N.C.
sl.
sl.
D5
Db5
C5
N.C.
(Gtr. IV out)
Rhy. Fig. 2A (Gtr. II)
E5
(end Rhy. Fig. 2A)
(cont. in notation)
N.C.
Gtr. III
sl.
steady gliss.
sl.
Rhy. Fig. 2 (Gtr. I)
Gtrs. I & II
(end Rhy. Fig. 2)
P.M.
sl.
sl.
sl.
sl.
sl.
sl.
w/Rhy. Figs. 2 & 2A
E5
N.C.
Oo,
yeah.
(Gtr. III)
sl.
steady gliss.
sl.

(Gtr. III)
B5
(Gtr. III out)
*
Rhy. Fig. 3 (Gtrs. I & II)
P.M.
*Vol. swell.
(Gtrs. I & II)
Gtrs. I, II & IV
(end Rhy. Fig. 3)
P.M.
sl.
w/Rhy. Fig. 3
E5
N.C.
Gtr. III
Gtr. III
(Gtr. IV out)
Rhy. Fill 1 (Gtr. IV)
B5
N.C.
w/last bar of Rhy. Fig. 3
P

w/Rhy. Fill 1 (Gtrs. I & IV)
E5
N.C.
Gtr. III
Gtr. I
(Gtr. III out)
Rhy. Fig. 4 (Gtr. I)
P.M.
sl.
Gtr. II
Rhy. Fig. 4A (Gtr. II)
*Omit note in parentheses when recalled unless otherwise indicated.
(E5)
(end Rhy. Fig. 4)
(end Rhy. Fig. 4A)
w/Rhy. Figs. 4 & 4A
pick slide
1st Verse
w/Rhy. Figs. 4 & 4A (both 4 times)
N.C. (E5)
End of pas - sion play,
crum - bl - ing a - way,

(E5)
N.C.
(E5)
N.C.
(Audience:) (I'm your source of self de - struc - tion.)
(E5)
N.C.
(E5)
N.C.
Veins that pump with fear, it was suck - ing dark - est clear,
Gtr. III
(E5)
N.C.
(E5)
N.C.
(Audience:)(lead - ing on your death's con - struc - tion.)
Oo.
F#5
N.C.
F#5
N.C.
Taste me, you will see more is all you need,
Gtr. III
Rhy. Fig. 5 (Gtr. I)
*P.M.
*P.M.
(end Rhy. Fig. 5)
H
sl.
Rhy. Fig. 5A (Gtr. II)
(end Rhy. Fig. 5A)
P.M.
P.M.
*P.M. applies to Gtr. I only.

(cont. in notation)
Rhy. Fill 2 (Gtr. II)
2fr.
B
w/Rhy. Figs. 5 & 5A
F#5
N.C.
F#5
N.C.
P.M.
ded - i - cat - ed to
how I'm kill-ing you.
Gtr. III
Gtr. III
Gtr. I
*P.M.
*P.M. applies to Gtr. I only.
**Gtr. III to left of slash.
Half time feel
Pre-chorus
E5 D5 E5 N.C. (B5) C5 B5 C5 D#5 B5
(Audience:) (Come crawl - ing
(Gtr. III)
Rhy. Fig. 6 (Gtr. I)
(end Rhy. Fig. 6)
*P.M.
*P.M.
*P.M.
Rhy. Fig. 6A (Gtr. II)
(end Rhy. Fig. 6A)
H
P.M.
P.M.
P.M.
P.M.
H
*P.M. appies to Gtr. I only.
w/Rhy. Figs. 6 & 6A (both 2¾ times)
E5 D5 E5 N.C. (B5) C5 B5 C5 D#5 B5
fast - er. O - bey your
Gtr. III

E5 D5 E5 N.C. (B5) C5 B5 C5 D#5 B5 E5 D5 E5 N.C.
mas - ter. Your life burns fast - er.)
H P
sl.
(B5) C5 B5 N.C. E5 F5 E5
Chorus
(end half time feel)
O - bey your master, (Audience:) (mas - ter). Mas - ter of Pup-pets,
(Gtr. III)
(Gtr. III out)
Gtr. IV
Rhy. Fill 3A (Gtr. II)
(end Rhy. Fill 3A)
Gtrs. I & II
Rhy. Fill 3 (Gtr. I)
P.M.
(end Rhy. Fill 3)
F#5 G5 C5
pull - ing your strings, yeah, twist - ing your mind and
P
P.M.

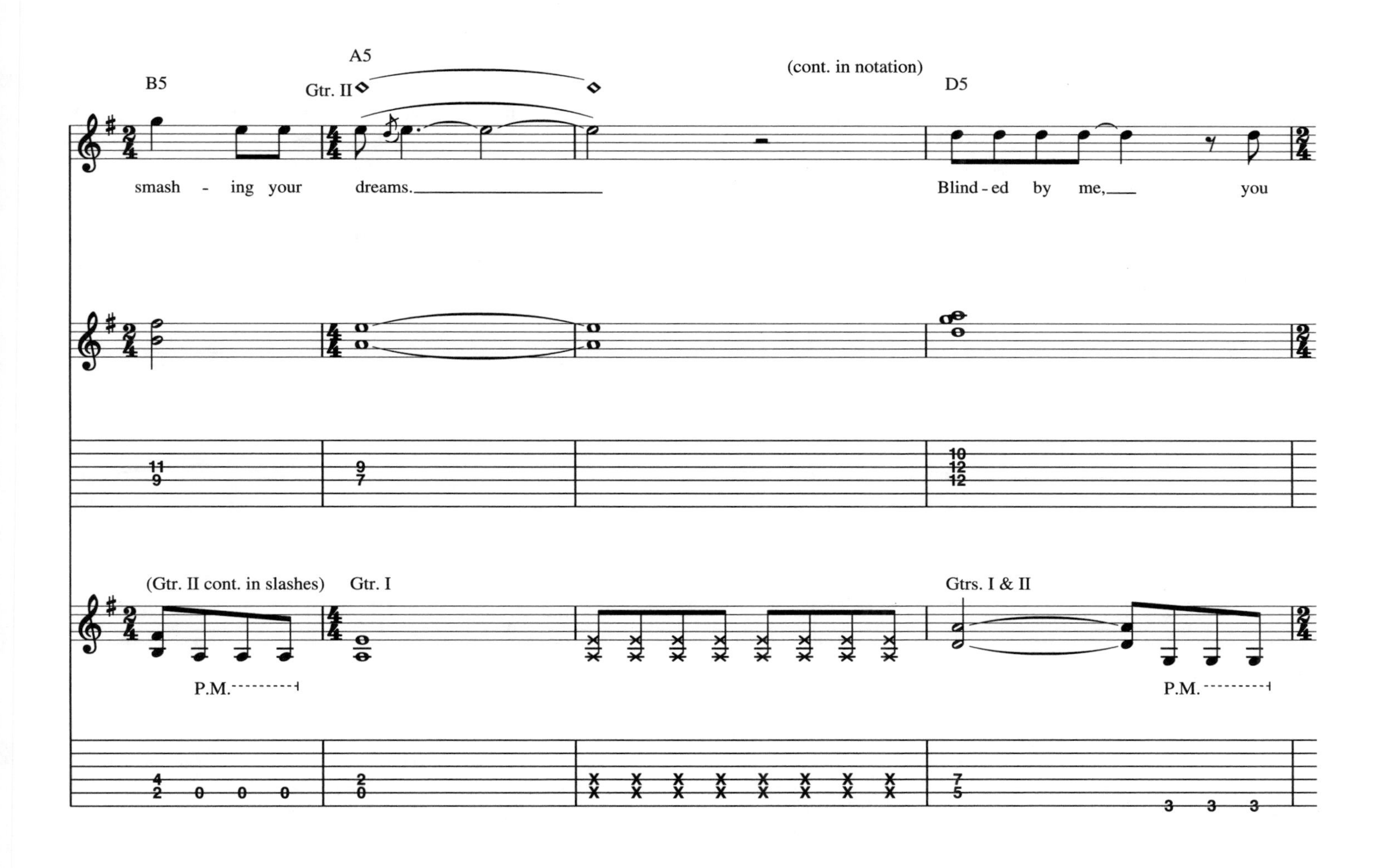
A5
(cont. in notation)
B5
Gtr. II
D5
smash - ing your dreams.
Blind - ed by me, you
(Gtr. II cont. in slashes)
Gtr. I
Gtrs. I & II
P.M.

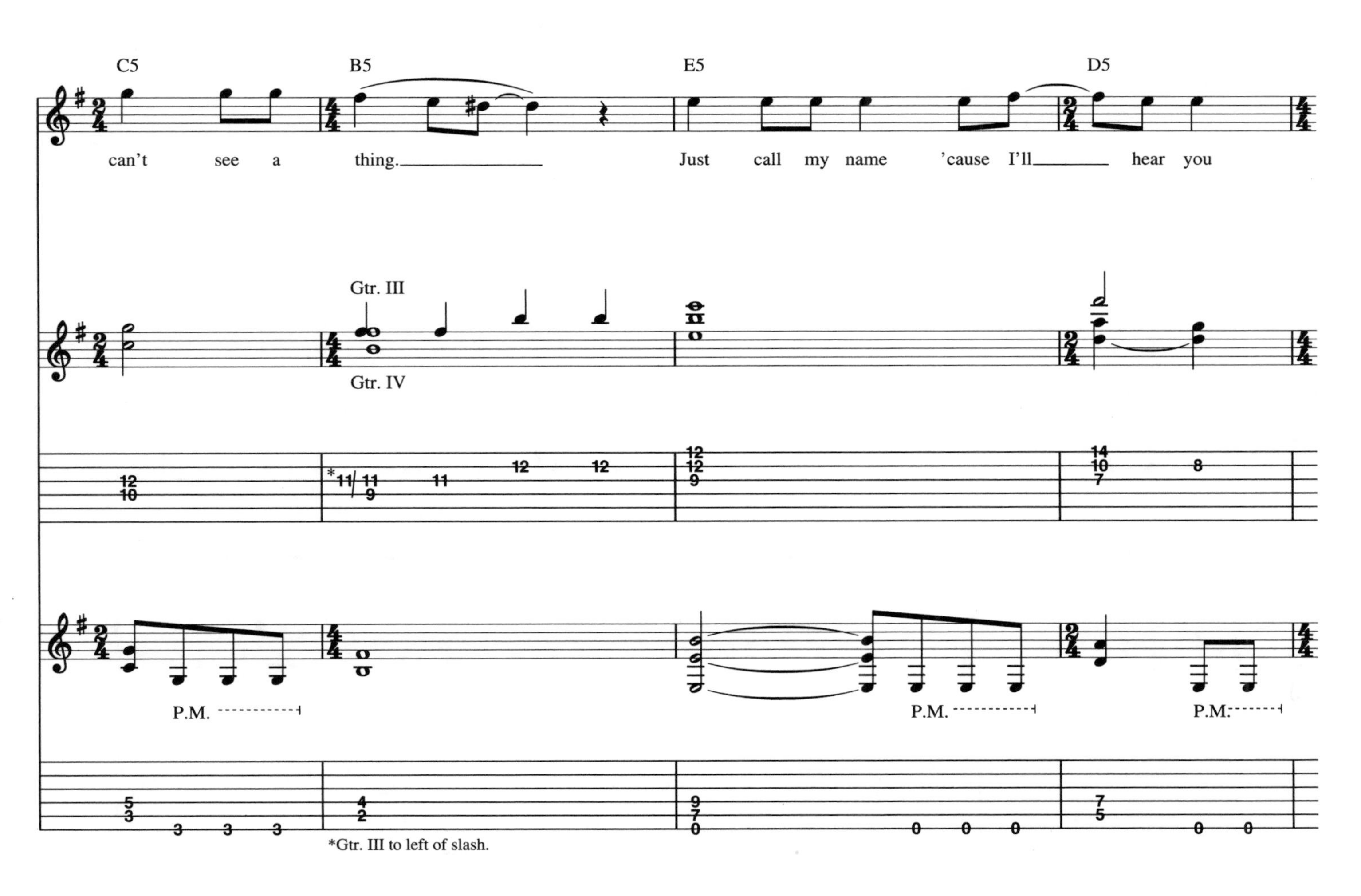
C5
B5
E5
D5
can't see a thing.
Just call my name 'cause I'll hear you
Gtr. III
Gtr. IV
P.M.
*Gtr. III to left of slash.

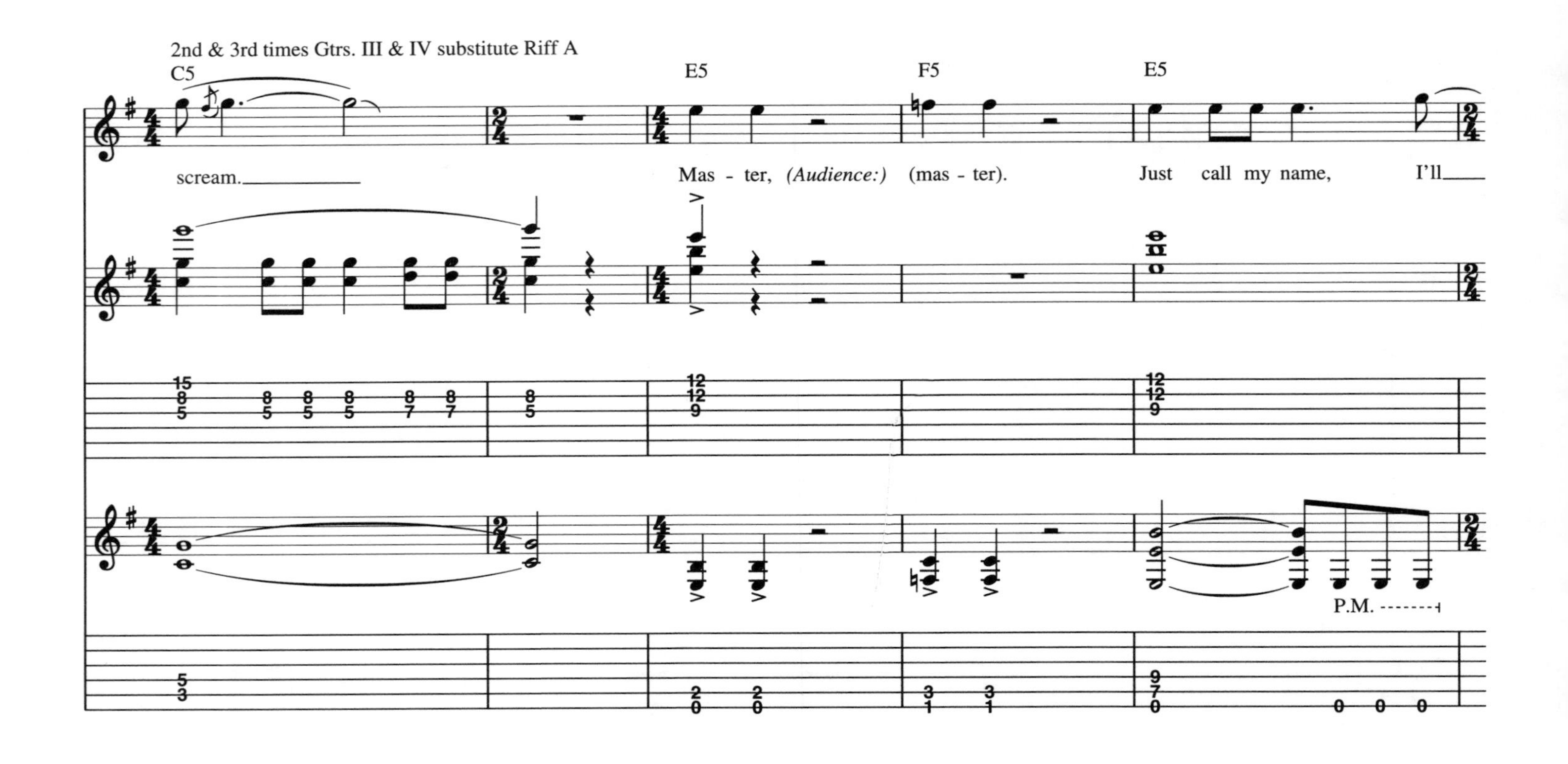
2nd & 3rd times Gtrs. III & IV substitute Riff A
C5
E5
F5
E5
scream.
Mas - ter, (Audience:) (mas - ter).
Just call my name, I'll
P.M.

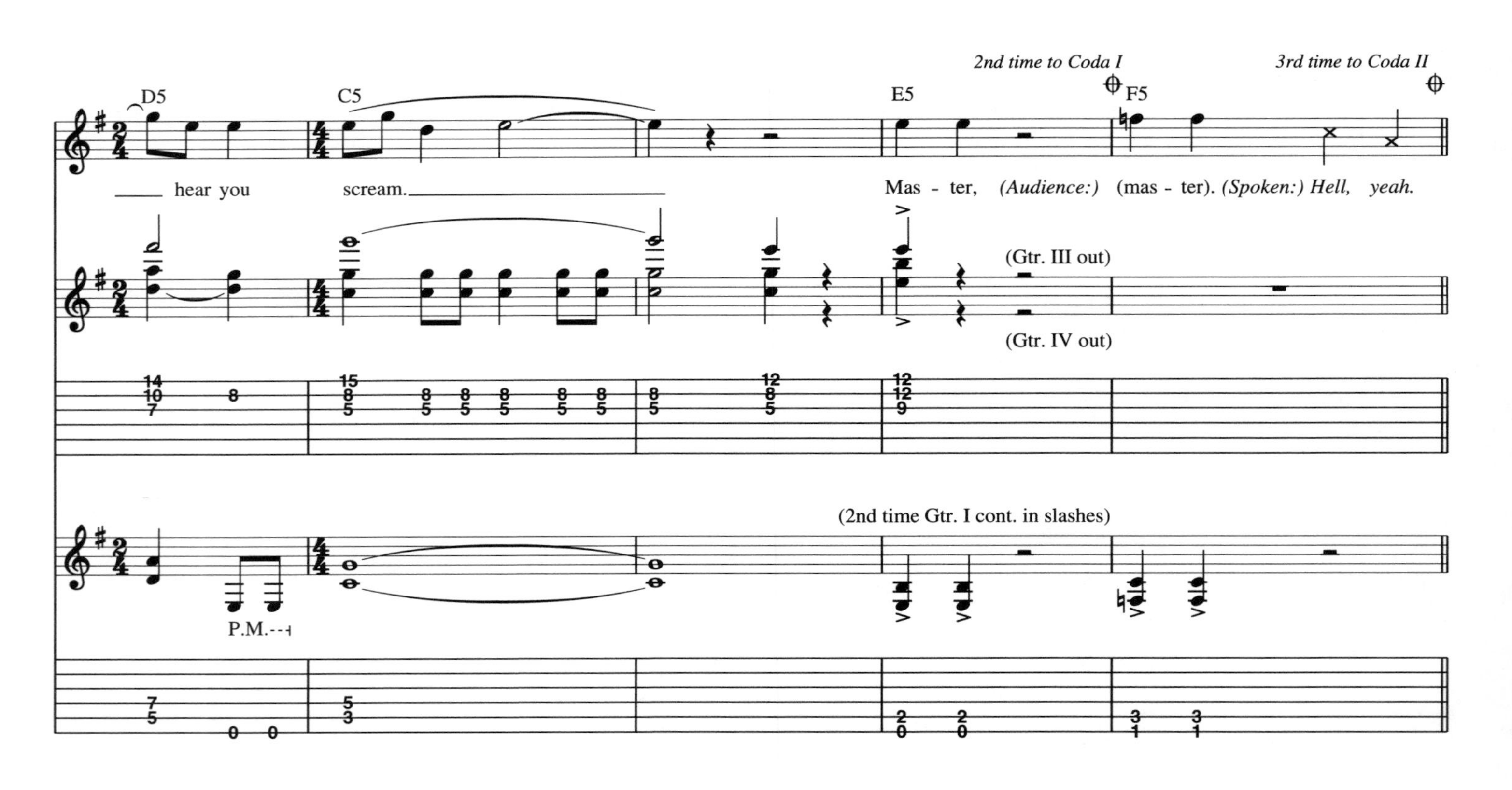
2nd time to Coda I
3rd time to Coda II
D5
C5
E5
F5
hear you scream.
Mas - ter, (Audience:) (mas - ter). (Spoken:) Hell, yeah.
(Gtr. III out)
(Gtr. IV out)
(2nd time Gtr. I cont. in slashes)
P.M.

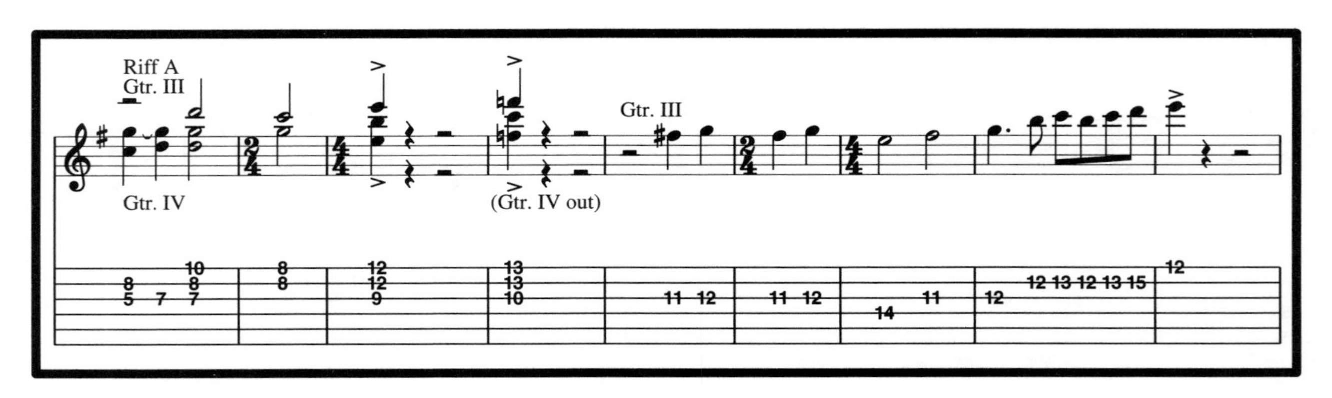
Riff A
Gtr. III
Gtr. IV
(Gtr. IV out)
Gtr. III

w/Rhy. Fig. 3
N.C.
Gtr. III
(Gtr. III out)
B5
N.C.
w/last bar of Rhy. Fig. 3
sl.
steady gliss.
2nd Verse
w/Rhy. Figs. 4 & 4A (both 4 times)
w/Rhy. Fill 1
E5
N.C.
(E5)
Nee - dle - work the way,
nev - er you be - tray,
(Audience:) (life of death be - com - ing clear - er).
Gtr. III
8va
Pain mo - nop - o - ly,
ri - ri - ri - ri - rit - ual mis - er - y,
loco
(Audience:)
(chop your break - fast on a mir - ror).
Oo, oo.
Gtr. IV
(Gtr. IV out)

w/Rhy. Figs. 5 & 5A (both 2 times)
F#5
N.C.
F#5
N.C.
Taste me, you will see
more, that's all you need,
w/Rhy. Fill 2
(Gtrs. I & II)
2fr.
F#5
N.C.
F#5
N.C.
B
ded - i - cat - ed to
how I'm fuck-ing you.
sl.
steady gliss.
sl.
Half time feel
Pre-chorus
w/Rhy. Figs. 6 & 6A (both 3¾ times)
E5 D5 E5 N.C.
(B5) C5 B5 C5 D#5 B5 E5 D5 E5 N.C. (B5) C5 B5
(Audience:) (Come crawl - ing fast - er. O -
8va
C5 D#5 B5 E5 D5 E5 N.C. (B5) C5 B5 C5 D#5 B5 E5 D5 E5
bey your mas - ter. Your life burns fast - er.)

D.S. al Coda I
(end half time feel)
w/Rhy. Fills 3 & 3A
N.C.
(B5)
C5
B5
E5
F5
O - bey your master, (Audience:) (mas - ter).
8va
Gtr. III
Gtr. IV
Coda I
Freely ♩ = ca. 96
Gtr. I
(Gtr. I out)
trem. pick
*mas - ter, uh.
Gtr. II
*w/processed echo repeats.
Moderately ♩ = 108
Interlude
Em
D
Cadd9
mp
Fdbk.
(8va)
(Gtr. II out)
Rhy. Fig. 7 (Gtr. I)
let ring
clean tone
H P
Fdbk. pitches: E G

*w/Rhy. Fig. 7
Amsus2
B7
B7/D#
Em
D
Cadd9
(end Rhy. Fig. 7)
Gtr. II
*Omit last note.
**Vol. knob swells.
N.C.(Em)
(D)
8va
*Riff B1 (Gtr. II)
*Riff B (Gtr. I)
mf
dist. tone
sl.
*Play with slight variations ad lib when recalled.
**Gtr. II to left of slash.
(Cadd9)
(Amsus2)
(B7)
(B7/D#)
(end Riff B1)
(end Riff B)
H P

w/Riffs B & B1
(Em)
Riff C (Gtr. III)
(D)
(Cadd9)
(Amsus2)
(B7)
*Omit note in parentheses when recalled.
(B7/D♯)
(end Riff C)
Guitar solo I
w/Riff C (2 times)
*w/Rhy. Fig. 7 (2 times) (Gtr. II)
Em
Gtr. I
D
w/echo
*Clean tone w/chorus, 2nd time omit last note.
Cadd9
Amsus2
B7
B7/D♯
loco
Full
Em
D
Cadd9
P.M.
Amsus2
B7
B7/D♯
*w/Riffs B & B1 (both 2 times)
N.C.(Em)
Gtr. III
(echo off)
*Resume dist. tone, Gtr. II chorus off.
(D)
(Cadd9)
(Amsus2)
(B7)
(B7/D♯)

(Em)
(D)
(Cadd9)
(Amsus2)
(B7)
(B7/D♯)
E5VII
D5
C5
A5
B5
D♯5
Gtr. II
Gtr. III
Riff D (Gtr. IV)
*P.M.
(end Riff D)
Gtr. I
H P
P.M.
1/2
*P.M. applies to Gtr. IV only.
w/Riff D
(cont. in slashes)

(cont. in notation)
E5
Gtrs. I & II
P.M.
F#5 G5 F#5 G5 F#5 G5 F#5 G5 C#5
(Gtr. III)
(Gtr. III out)
Rhy. Fig. 8 (Gtrs. I & II)
(end Rhy. Fig. 8)
P.M.
Gtr. IV
(Gtr. IV out)
*P.M.
*P.M. applies to downstem notes only.
w/Rhy. Fig. 8
F#5 G5 F#5 G5 F#5 G5 F#5 G5 C#5
w/Rhy. Fig. 8 (4 times)
F#5 G5 F#5 G5 F#5 G5 F#5 G5 C#5
(Mas-ter, mas-ter,) where's the dreams that I've __ been af - ter?
Gtr. III
8va
trem. pick
F#5 G5 F#5 G5 F#5 G5 F#5 G5 C#5 F#5 G5 F#5 G5
(Mas - ter, mas - ter,) prom-ised on - ly lies. ____ (Laugh-ter, laugh - ter,)
8va

F#5 G5 F#5 G5 C#5 F#5 G5 F#5 G5 F#5 G5 F#5 G5 C#5
all I hear or see is laugh - ter. (Laugh-ter, laugh - ter,) laugh - ing at my cries.
8va
sl.
steady gliss.
Double time ♩ = 116
(Gtr. I cont. in notation)
(cont. in notation)
G5
Gtrs. I & II
F#5
Gtr. II
(Ha, ha, ha.) Fix me.
loco
(Gtr. III out)
Gtr. I
Guitar solo II
w/Rhy. Fig. 4 (4 times)
N.C.(E5)
N.C.
(E5)
N.C.
(E5)
N.C.

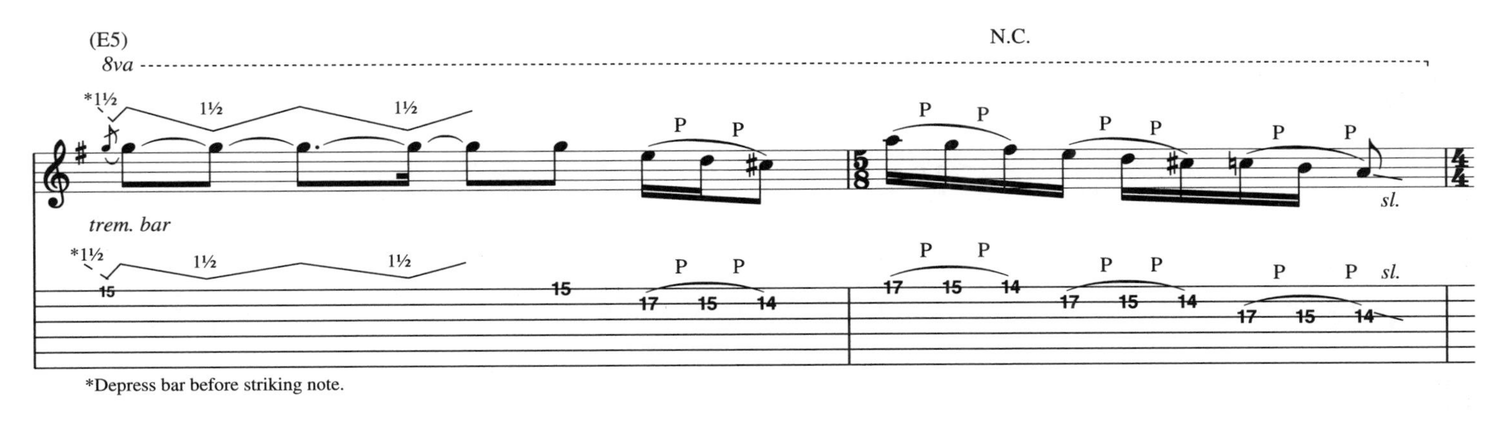
(E5)
8va
N.C.
trem. bar
sl.
*Depress bar before striking note.

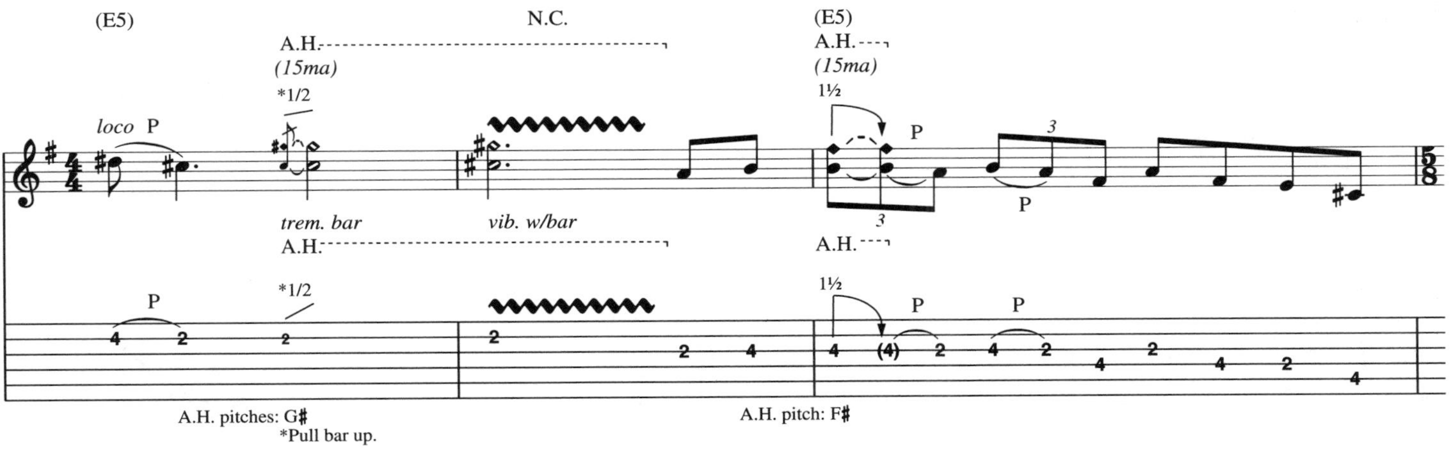
(E5)
N.C.
A.H.
(15ma)
loco
trem. bar
vib. w/bar
A.H. pitches: G♯
*Pull bar up.
A.H. pitch: F♯

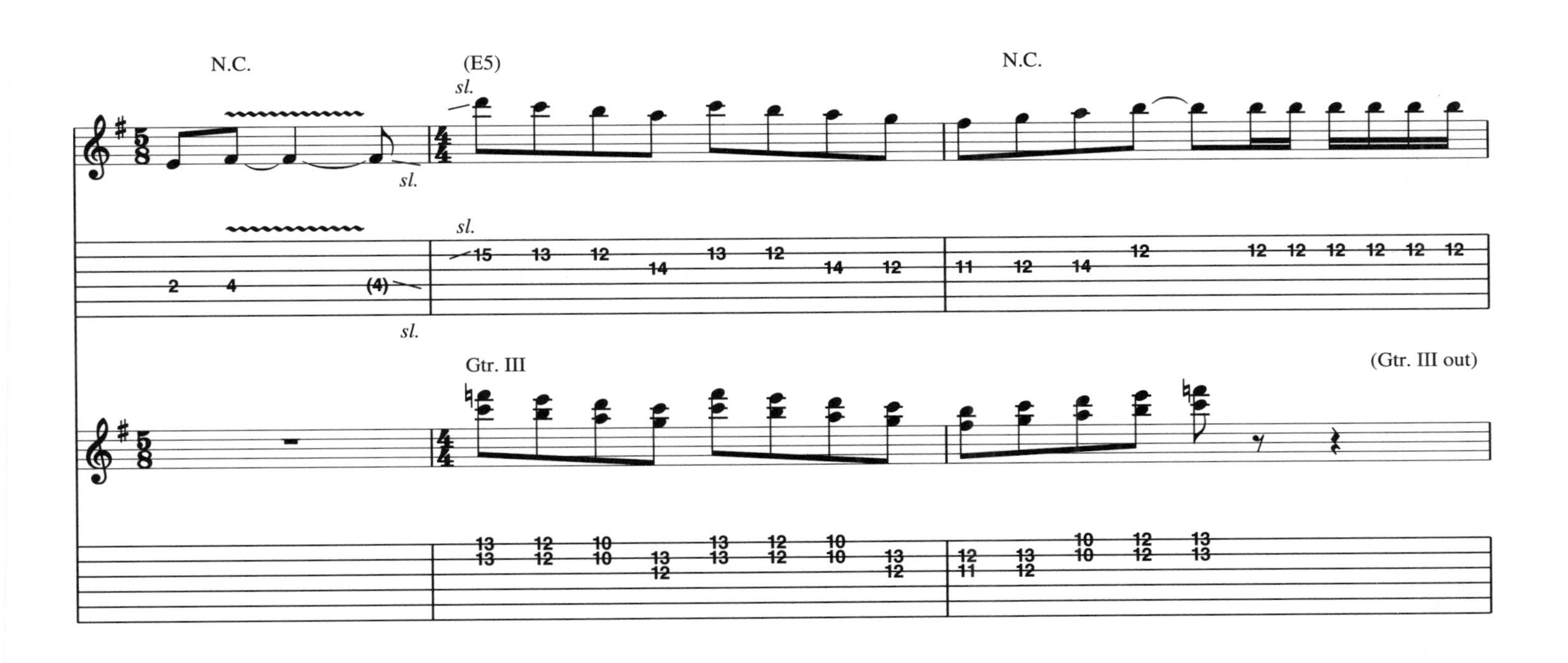
N.C.
(E5)
sl.
Gtr. III
(Gtr. III out)

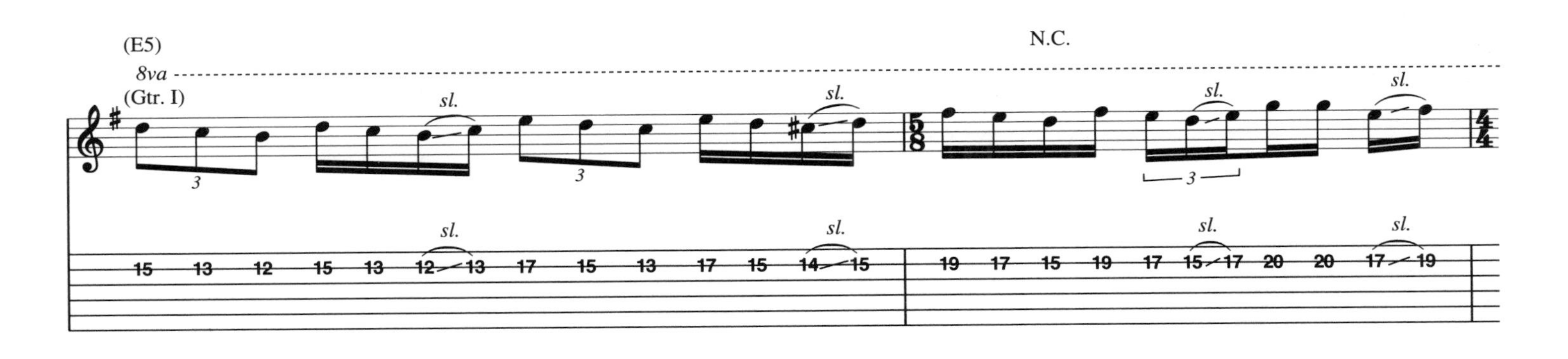
(E5)
8va
(Gtr. I)
N.C.
sl.

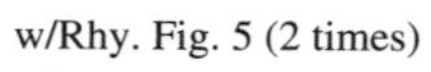
w/Rhy. Fig. 5 (2 times)

F#5
8va
N.C.
F#5
P
P
Full
Full
Full
sl.

N.C.
8va
F#5
N.C.
P
P
Full
sl.

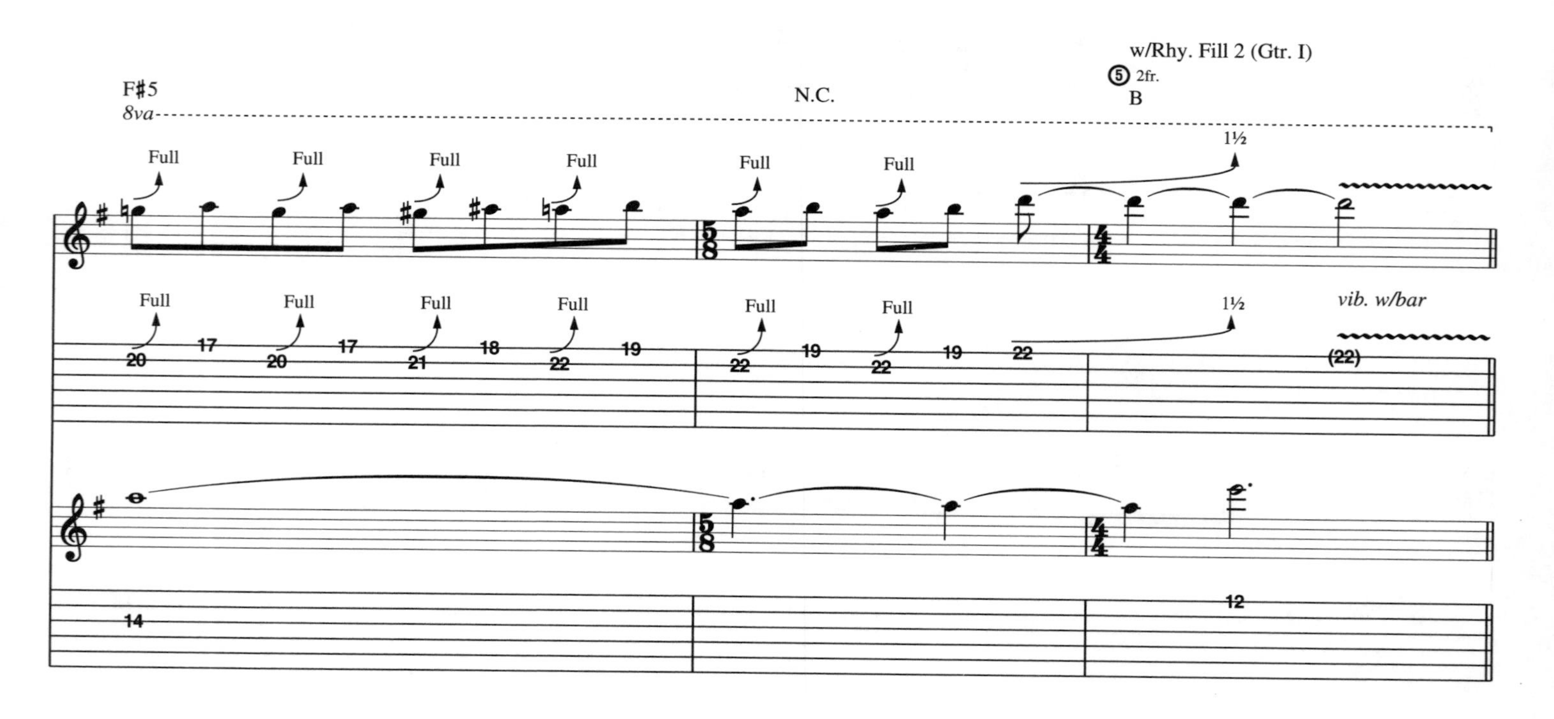
w/Rhy. Fill 2 (Gtr. I)
2fr.
B
F#5
8va
N.C.
Full
1½
vib. w/bar

Half time feel
N.C.
Gtr. III
Rhy. Fig. 9 (Gtrs. I & II)
*P.M.
*P.M.
*P.M. applies to Gtrs. I & II only.
B5
w/Rhy. Fig. 9
N.C.
Gtr. III
B5
(Gtr. III out)
(end Rhy. Fig. 9)
N.C.
(end half time feel)
Gtrs. I & II
Gtr. III
Riff E (Gtrs. I & II)
P.M.
*P.M.
*P.M.
*P.M. applies to Gtrs. I & II only.
w/Riff E (2 times)
Gtr. III
(end Riff E)

Gtr. III
E5
N.C.
P
Gtr. I
*P.M.
*P.M.
*P.M.
P
sl.
sl.
Gtr. II
P.M.
P.M.
P.M.
*P.M. applies to Gtr. I only.
w/Rhy. Figs. 2 & 2A
E5
Gtr. III
N.C.
Gtr. IV

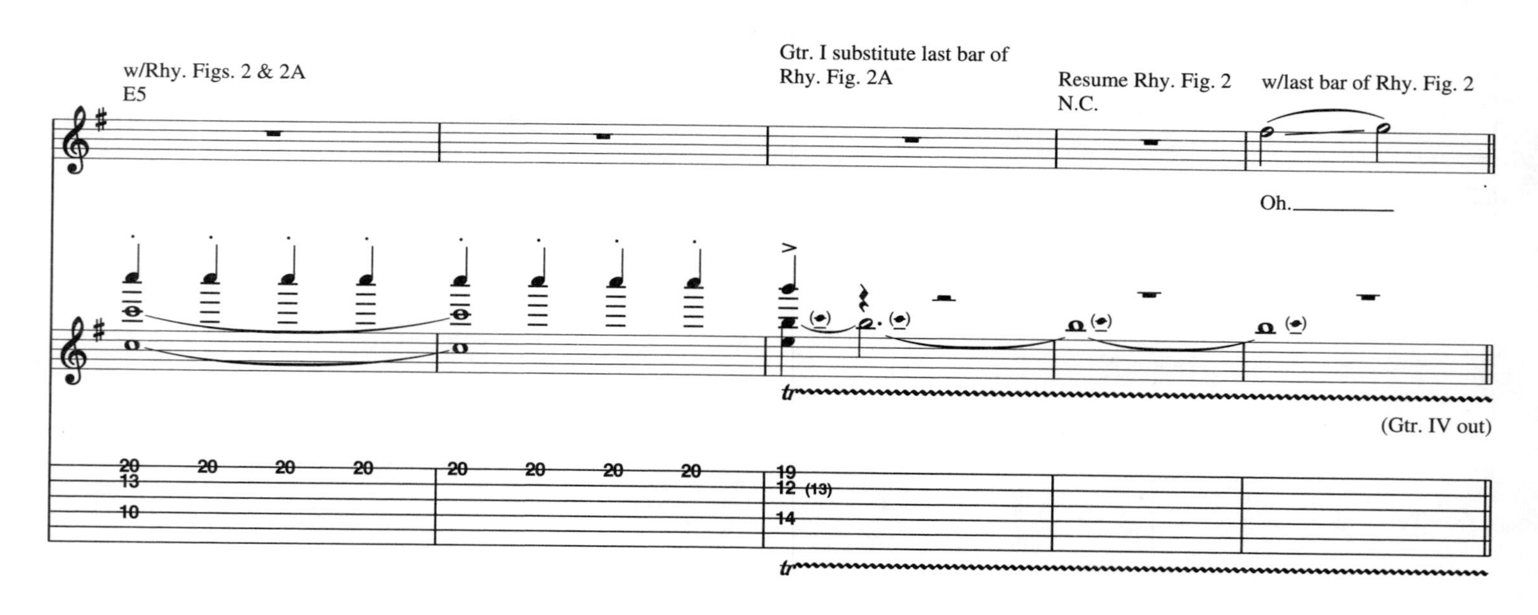
w/Rhy. Figs. 2 & 2A
E5
Gtr. I substitute last bar of
Rhy. Fig. 2A
Resume Rhy. Fig. 2
N.C.
w/last bar of Rhy. Fig. 2
Oh.
(Gtr. IV out)

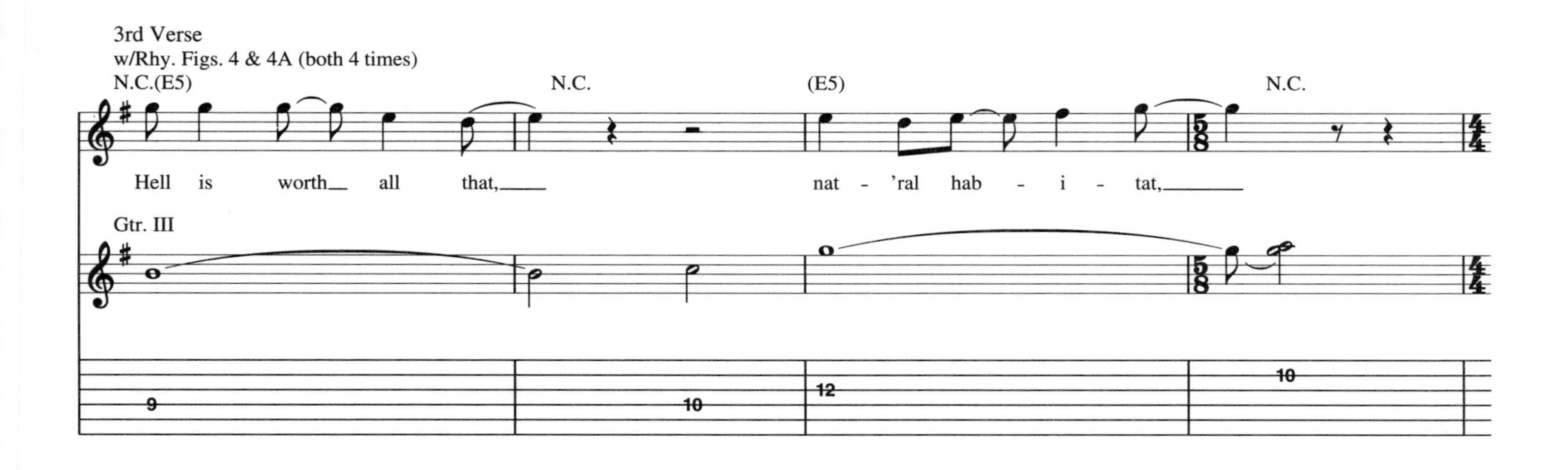
3rd Verse
w/Rhy. Figs. 4 & 4A (both 4 times)
N.C.(E5)
N.C.
(E5)
N.C.
Hell is worth all that, nat - 'ral hab - i - tat,
Gtr. III
9
10
12
10

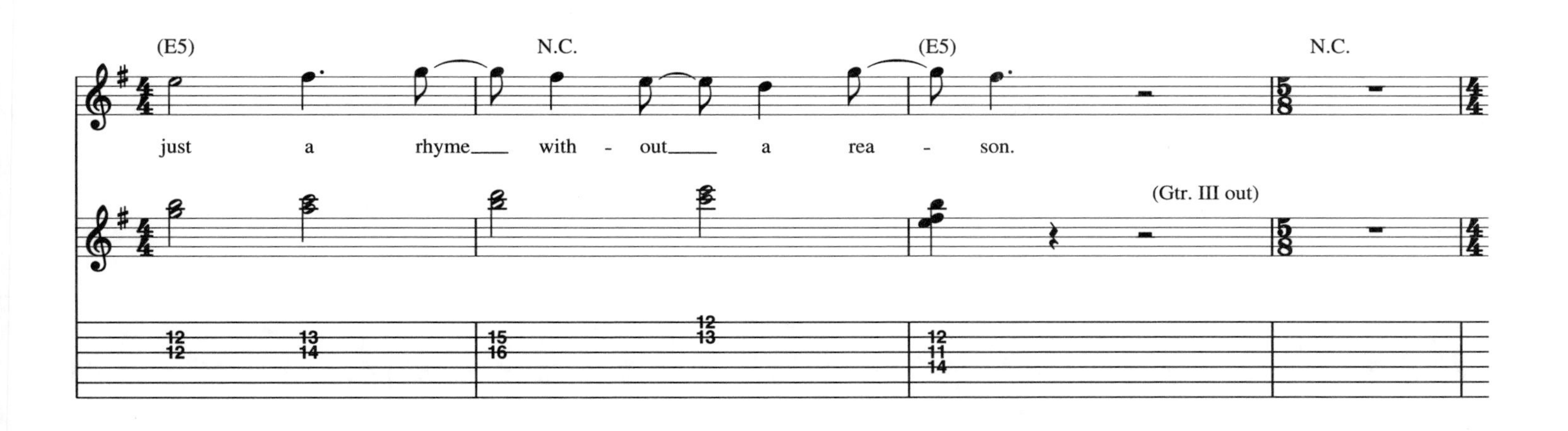
(E5)
N.C.
(E5)
N.C.
just a rhyme with - out a rea - son.
(Gtr. III out)
12 12
13 14
15 16
12 13
12 11 14

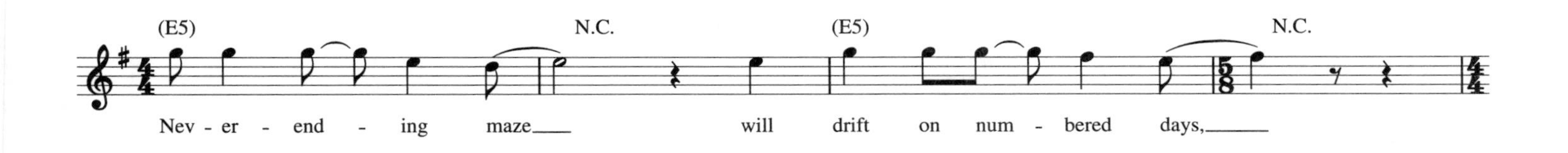
(E5)
N.C.
(E5)
N.C.
Nev - er - end - ing maze will drift on num - bered days,

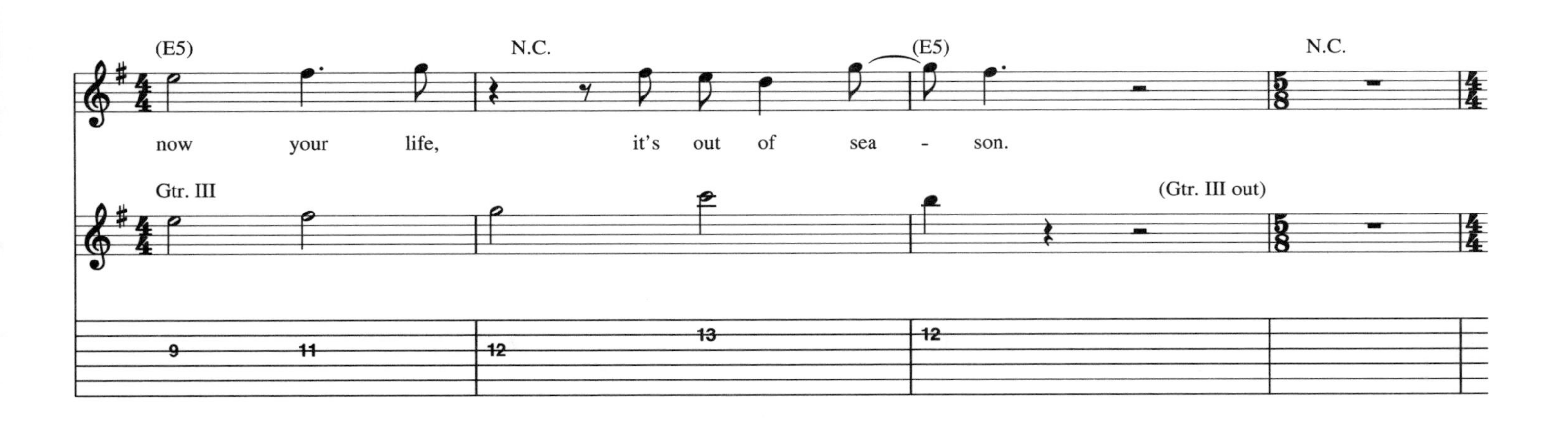
(E5)
N.C.
(E5)
N.C.
now your life, it's out of sea - son.
Gtr. III
(Gtr. III out)
9
11
12
13
12

w/Rhy. Figs. 5 & 5A (both 2 times)
F#5
N.C.
F#5
N.C.
I will oc - cu - py, I will help you die,

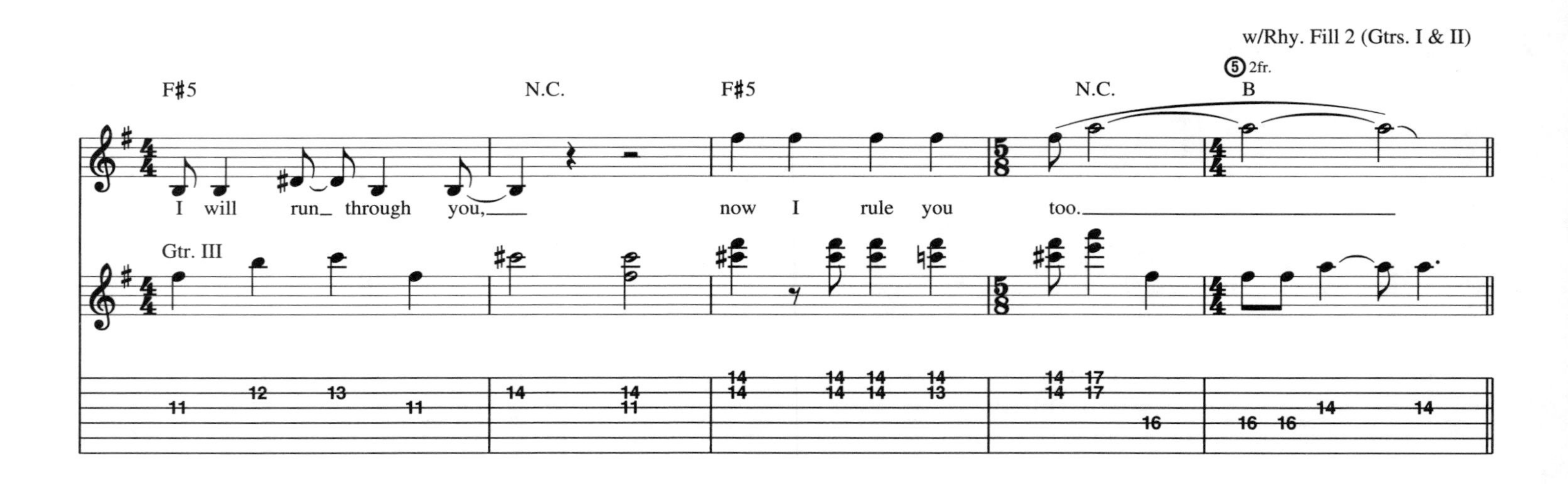
w/Rhy. Fill 2 (Gtrs. I & II)
F♯5 N.C. F♯5 N.C. B
I will run through you, now I rule you too.
Gtr. III

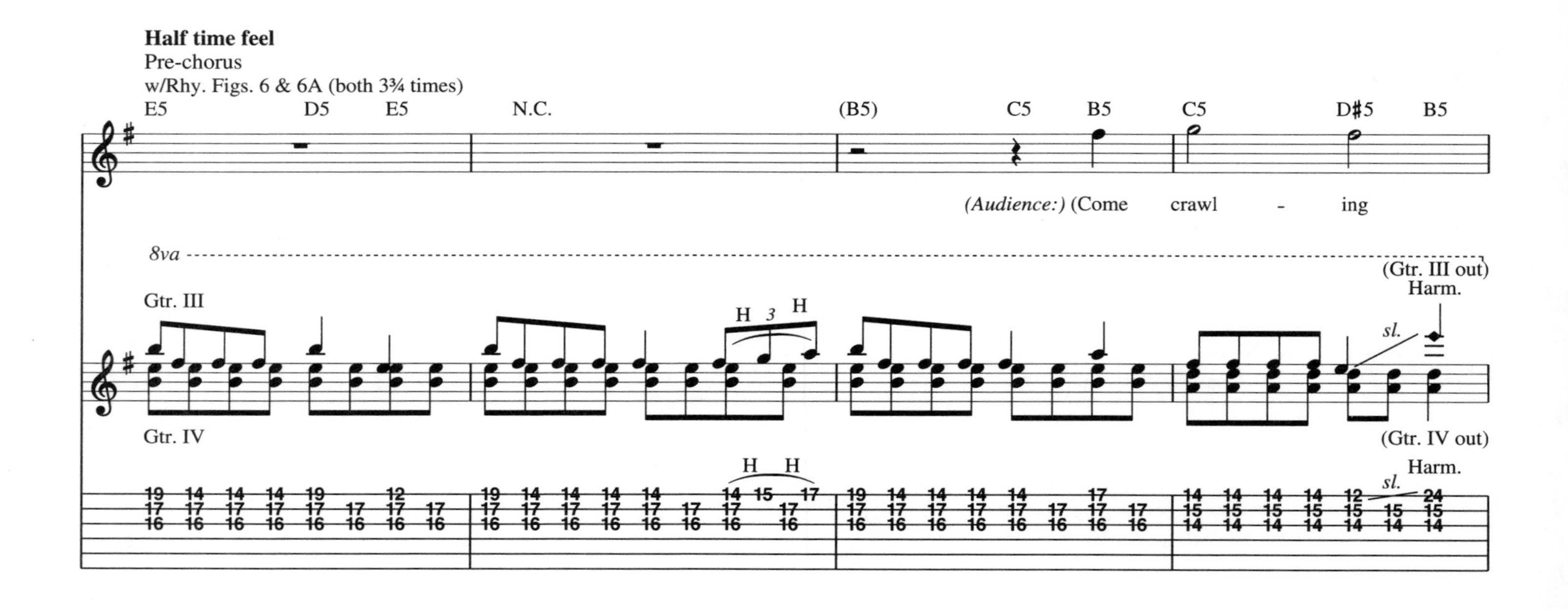
Half time feel
Pre-chorus
w/Rhy. Figs. 6 & 6A (both 3¾ times)
E5 D5 E5 N.C. (B5) C5 B5 C5 D♯5 B5
(Audience:) (Come crawl - ing
8va
Gtr. III
(Gtr. III out)
Harm.
Gtr. IV
(Gtr. IV out)
Harm.

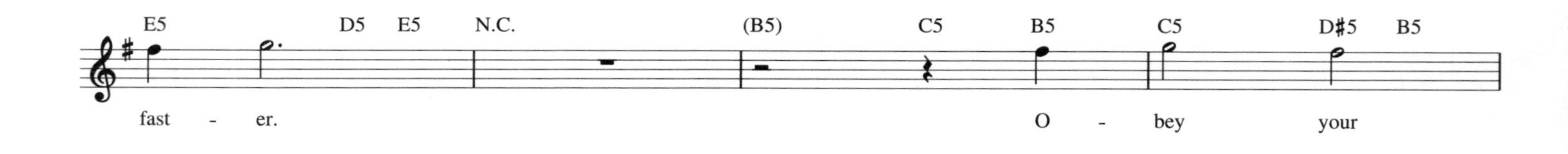
E5 D5 E5 N.C. (B5) C5 B5 C5 D♯5 B5
fast - er. O - bey your

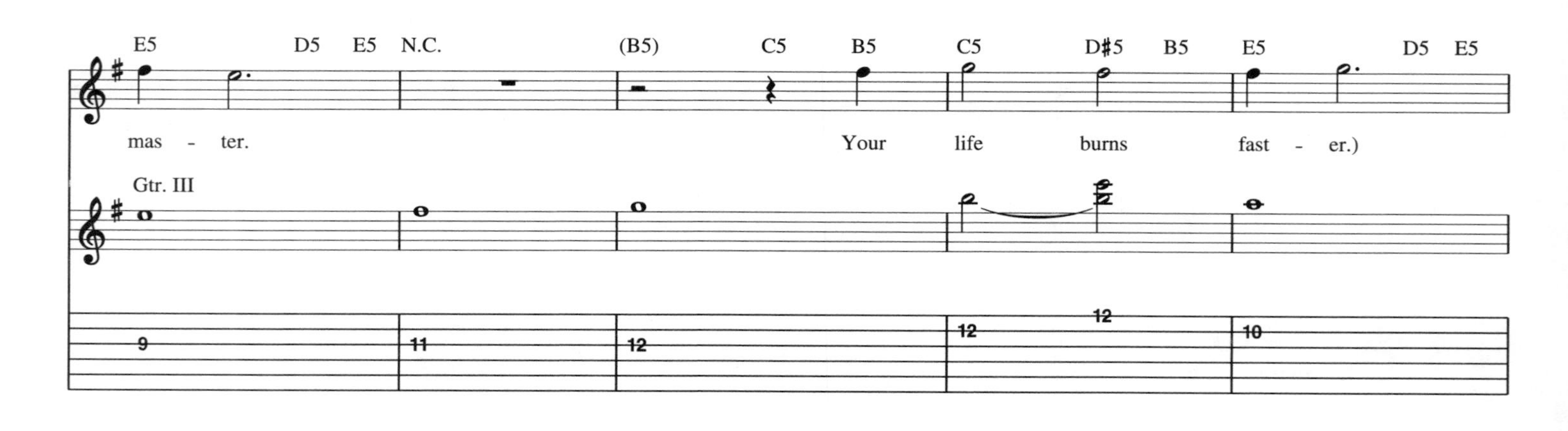
E5 D5 E5 N.C. (B5) C5 B5 C5 D♯5 B5 E5 D5 E5
mas - ter. Your life burns fast - er.)
Gtr. III

w/Rhy. Fills 3 & 3A
D.S. al Coda II
N.C.
(B5)
C5
B5
N.C.
E5
F5
(end half time feel)
O - bey your mas - ter, (Audience:) (mas - ter).
sl.
Outro
*w/Rhy. Figs. 4 & 4A (both 4 times)
E5
N.C.
(E5)
N.C.
Coda II Gtr. III
P
*1st time Gtr. I plays E5 on beat 1 of 1st bar.
Gtr. I substitute
Rhy. Fill 4
w/laughter ad lib

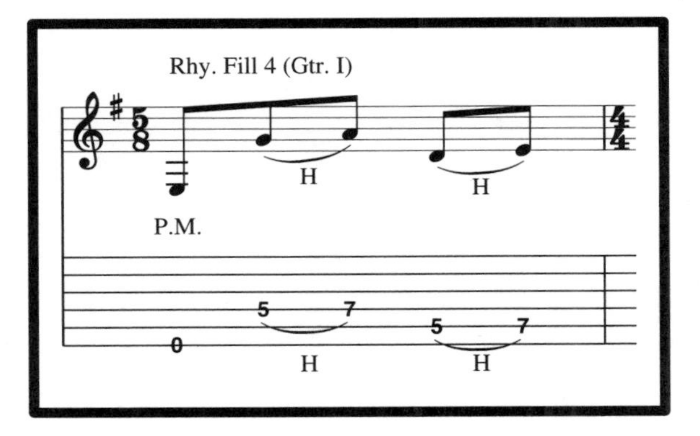
Rhy. Fill 4 (Gtr. I)
H
P.M.

N.C.
(E5)
N.C.
Gtrs. I & II
w/last bar of Rhy. Fig. 2
Ha, ha, ha, ha, ha.
Yeah.
8va
loco
Free time
E5 (type2)
Gtrs. I & II
(Gtr. II cont. in notation)
Yeah.
Woh,
yeah.
Thank you ver-y much.
Gtr. I
trem. pick
sl.
E5 VII
Gtr. III
sl.
trem. pick
sl.
Gtr. II
trem. pick
sl.
sl.

NO LEAF CLOVER

Words and Music by
James Hetfield and Lars Ulrich

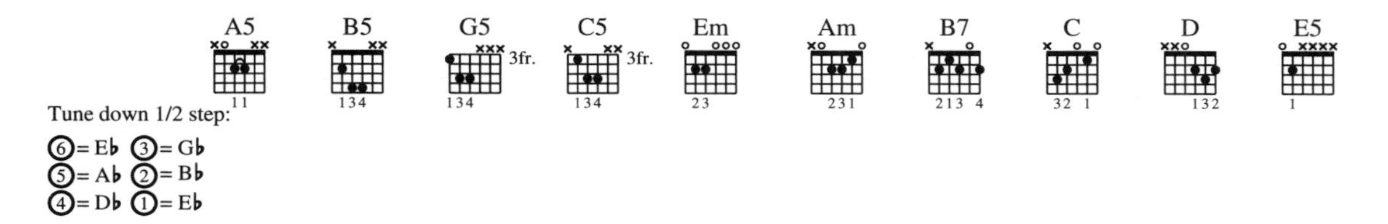

Tune down 1/2 step:
⑥=E♭ ③=G♭
⑤=A♭ ②=B♭
④=D♭ ①=E♭

*Orchestra arr. for gtr.

1st Verse
F♯5
N.C.
A5
B5
N.C.
1. And it feels right this time,
loco
(end Rhy. Fig. 2)
Rhy. Fig. 3
P.M.
P.M.
P.M.
P
P.M.
P.M.
P

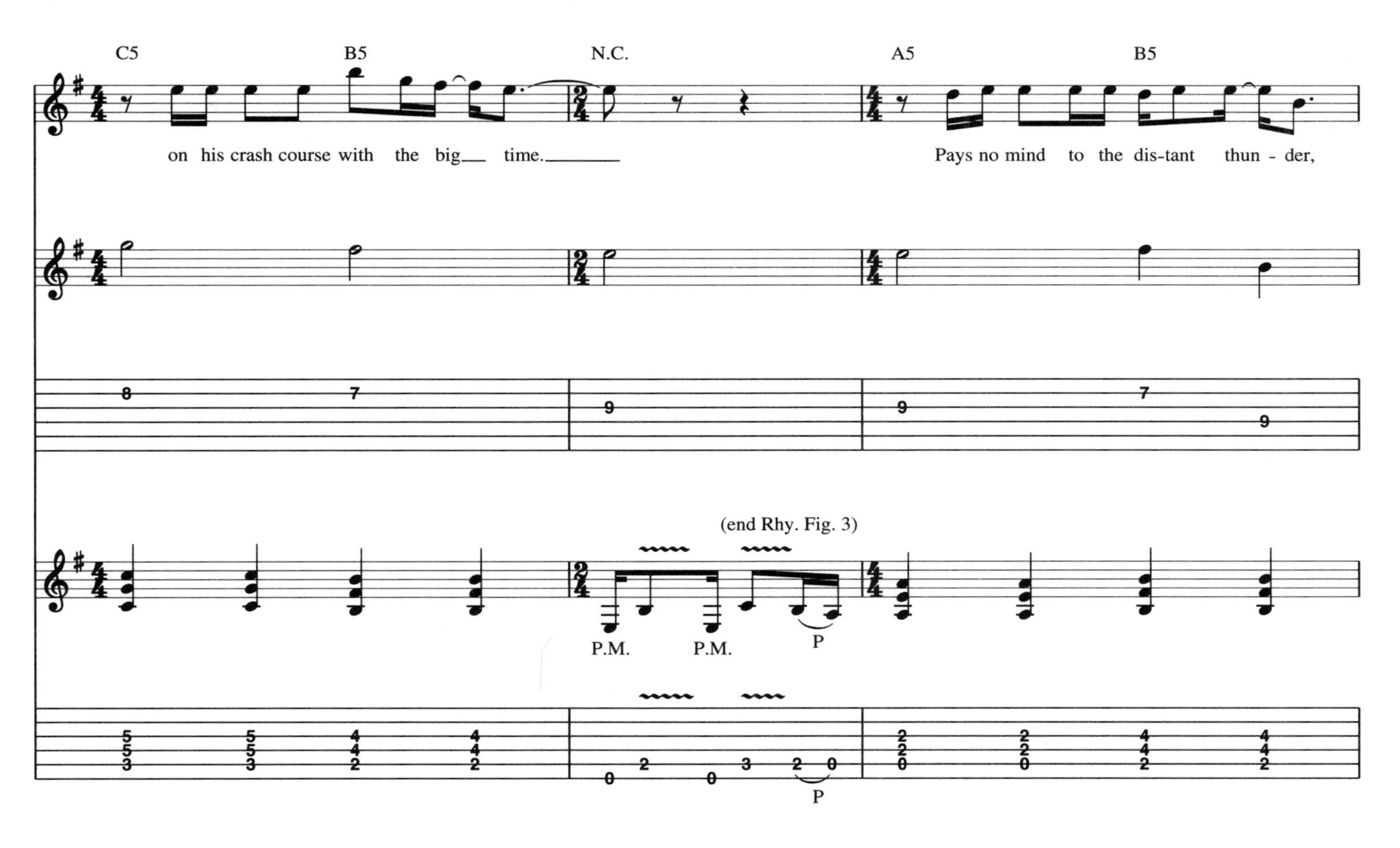
C5
B5
N.C.
A5
B5
on his crash course with the big time.
Pays no mind to the dis-tant thun - der,
(end Rhy. Fig. 3)
P.M.
P.M.
P

C5
*C5/B
B5
N.C.
new day fills his head with won - der... Boy.
H P
H P
*B played by bass only.
2nd, 3rd Verses
w/Rhy. Fig. 3
A5
B5
N.C.
C5
B5
N.C.
2. Says it feels right this time. Turned it 'round and found the right line.
3. Don't it feel right like this? All the piec - es fall to his wish.
Gtr. I
*Orchestra plays w/variations ad lib on repeat.
A5
B5
G5
C5
B5
(Gtr. IV out)
Gtrs. II & IV
P.M.
"Good day to be a - live, sir. Good day to be a - live," he says. Yeah.
"Suck-er for that quick re - ward, boy. Suck-er for that quick re-ward," they say. Yeah.

Chorus
w/Rhy. Fig. 1 (2 times)
Em
Am
B
Am
Then it comes to be that the sooth-ing light at the end of your tun - nel
Gtr. I
mp
Gtr. III
P
Em
Am
B
Am
was just a freight train com - in' your way, hey, yeah,
Gtr. I
(Gtr. III out)
Gtr. IV
*Orchestra arr. for gtr.
Em
Am
B7
Am
Gtr. II
yeah. Then it comes to be that the sooth-ing light at the end of your tun - nel
mf
1/2
sl.
Full
P

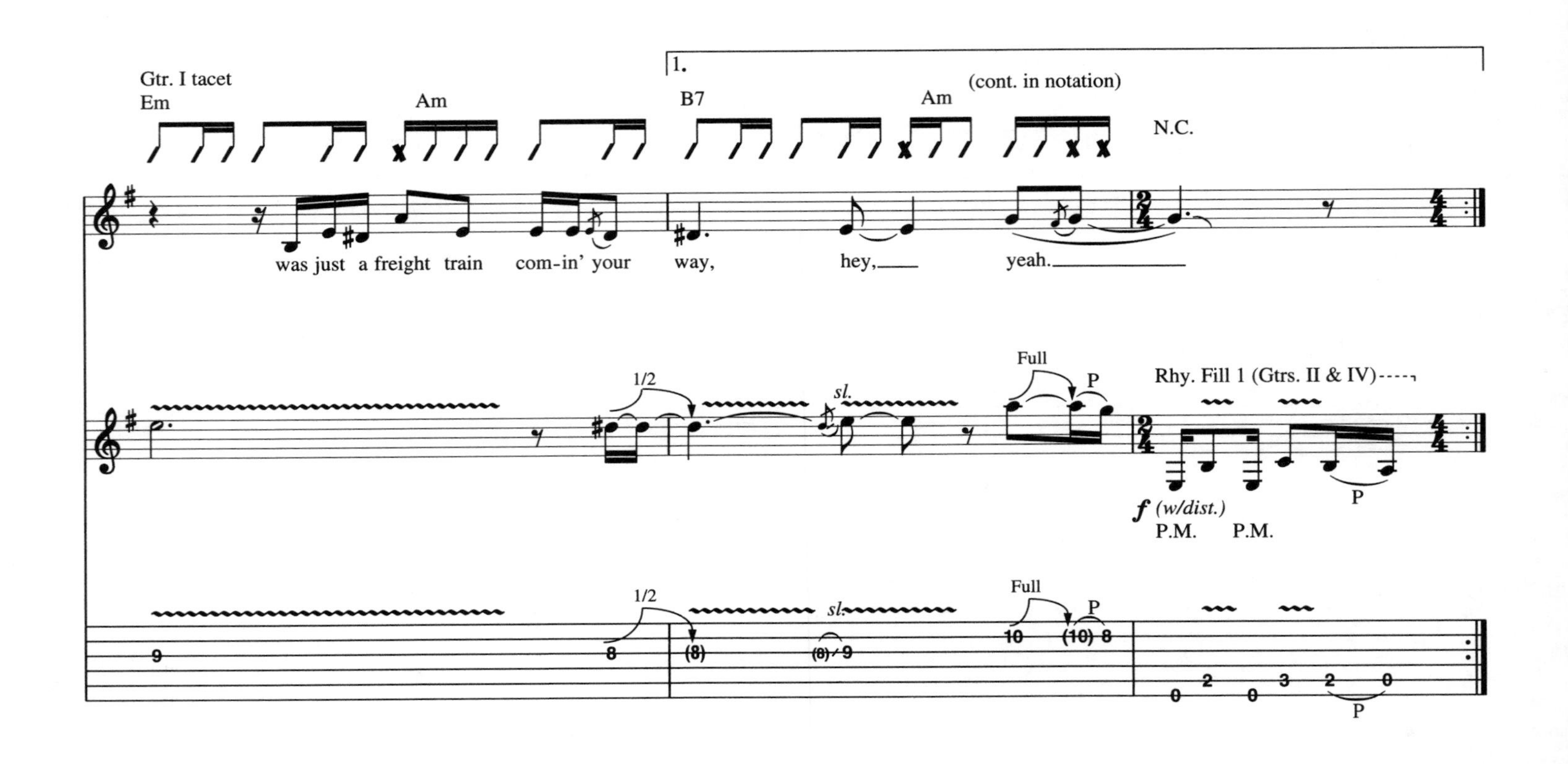
1.
Gtr. I tacet
Em
Am
B7
Am
(cont. in notation)
N.C.
was just a freight train com-in' your way, hey, yeah.
1/2
sl.
Full
P
Rhy. Fill 1 (Gtrs. II & IV)
f (w/dist.)
P.M. P.M.
P

2.
B7
Am
C
B7
way, hey, yeah.
It's com-in' your way.
Full
P
sl.

Em
B7
C
D
It's com-in' your way,
yeah.
Full
P
sl.
B5 C5 B5 C5 B5 C5 B5
w/Rhy. Fill 1 (Gtr. II)
N.C.
Guitar solo
w/Rhy. Fig. 2 (2 times) (Gtr. II)
E5
Oh,
yeah.
Here it comes...
1/2
w/wah as filter

F#5
N.C.
E5
8va
loco
trem. pick
Full
1 1/2
sl.
P
H P

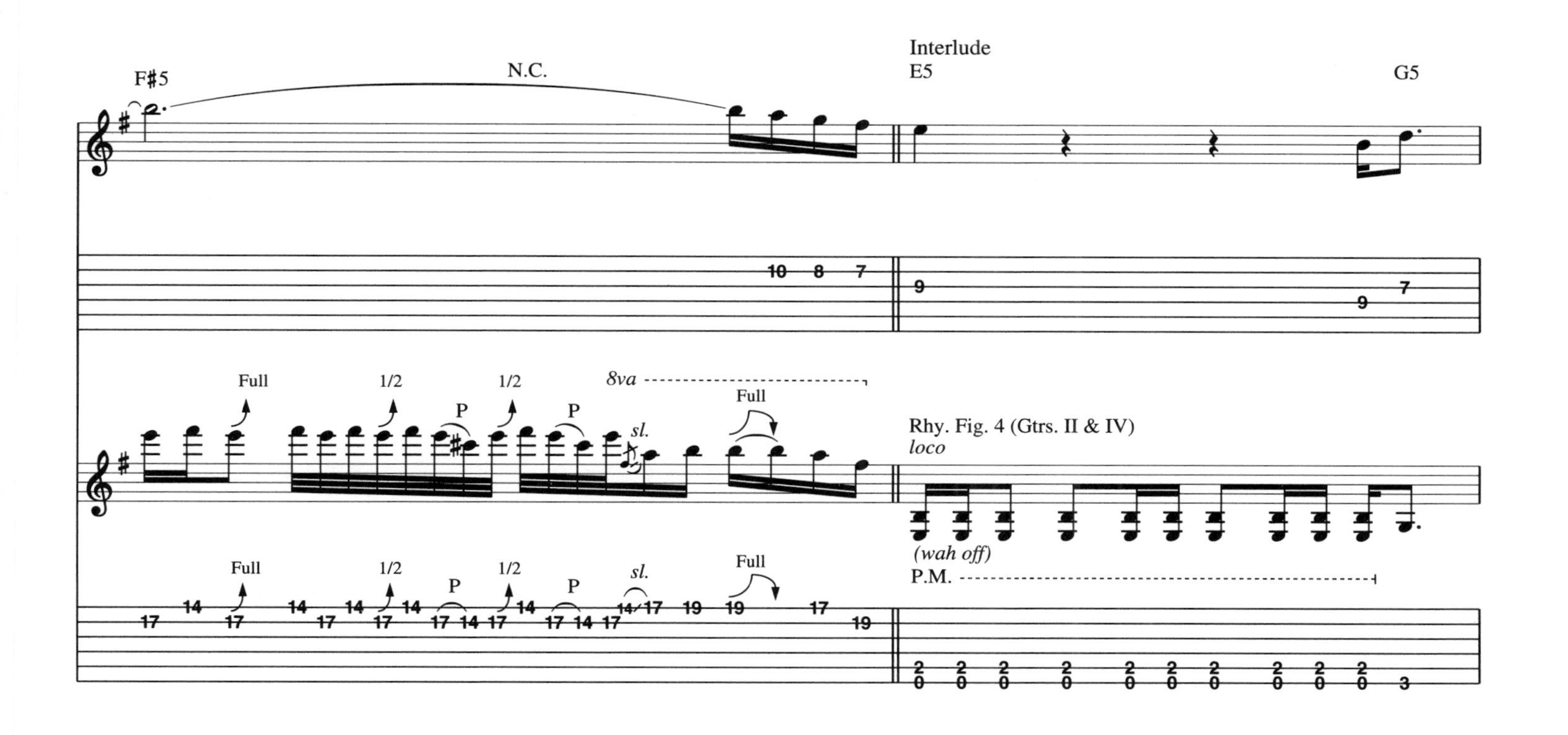

F♯5
N.C.
Interlude
E5
G5
Full
1/2
1/2
P
P
8va
sl.
Full
Rhy. Fig. 4 (Gtrs. II & IV)
loco
(wah off)
P.M.

E5
B♭5
E5
F5
N.C. F5
N.C. F5
(end Rhy. Fig. 4)
P.M.
P.M.
P.M.
P.M.
w/Rhy. Fig. 4 (Gtrs. II & IV)
E5
G5
E5
B♭5
E5
F5
N.C. F5
N.C. F5
Gtr. I

w/Rhy. Fig. 4 (Gtr. II)
E5 G5 E5 B♭5 E5 F5 N.C. F5 N.C. F5
Gtr. I
(Gtr. I out)
Gtr. IV
H
P.M. P.M.
E5 A5 B5
⑤ open
A B5 A5 B5 E5 A5 B5 A B5 A B5
Gtr. II
P.M.
Riff A (Gtr. III)
(end Riff A)
sl.
(cont. in slashes)
Chorus
w/Riff A (2 times)
E5 A5 B5 A5
Gtrs. II & IV
Yeah, then it comes to be that the sooth-ing light at the end of your tun - nel
Gtr. I

(Gtr. III out)
E5
A5
B5
A5
was just a freight train com-in' your way, hey, yeah.
(end Rhy. Fig. 5)
E5
B5
C5
B5
Rhy. Fig. 5
Then it comes to be, yeah, yeah. Then it comes to be, yeah, yeah.
w/Rhy. Fig. 5 (Gtrs. II & IV)
E5
B5
C5
B5
Then it comes to be, yeah, yeah. Then it comes to be, yeah.

w/Rhy. Fig. 5 (2 times) (Gtr. II)
E5
B5
C5
B5
Then it comes to be, yeah, yeah.
Then it comes to be, yeah.
Gtr. I
Gtr. IV
E5
B5
C5
B5
Outro
E5
G5
Then it comes to be, yeah, yeah.
Then it comes to be,
yeah.
P.M.
Gtrs. II & IV
P.M.
E5
F5
N.C.
F5
N.C.
F5
E5
P.M.
P.M.
P.M.
P.M.
P.M.
P.M.

HERO OF THE DAY

Words and Music by James Hetfield,
Lars Ulrich and Kirk Hammett

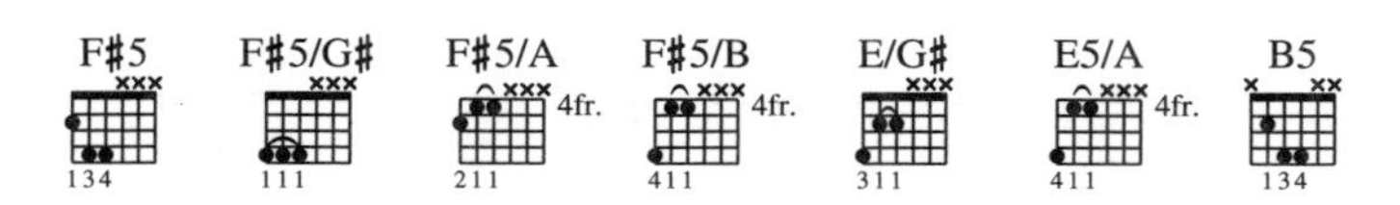

Tune down 1/2 step:
⑥= E♭ ③= G♭
⑤= A♭ ②= B♭
④= D♭ ①= E♭

*Orchestra arr. for gtr.

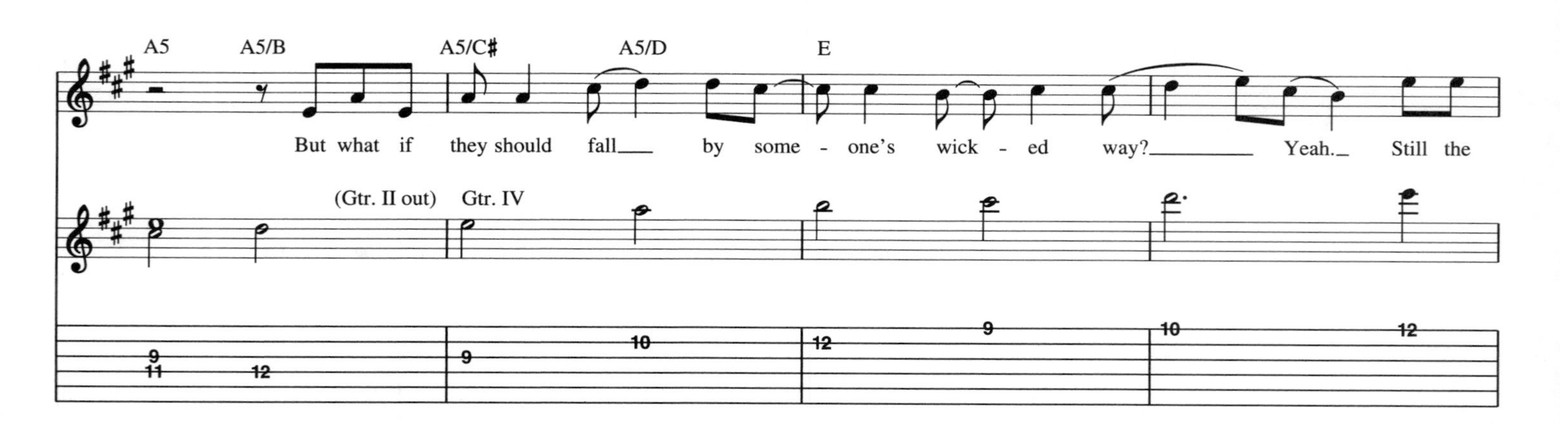

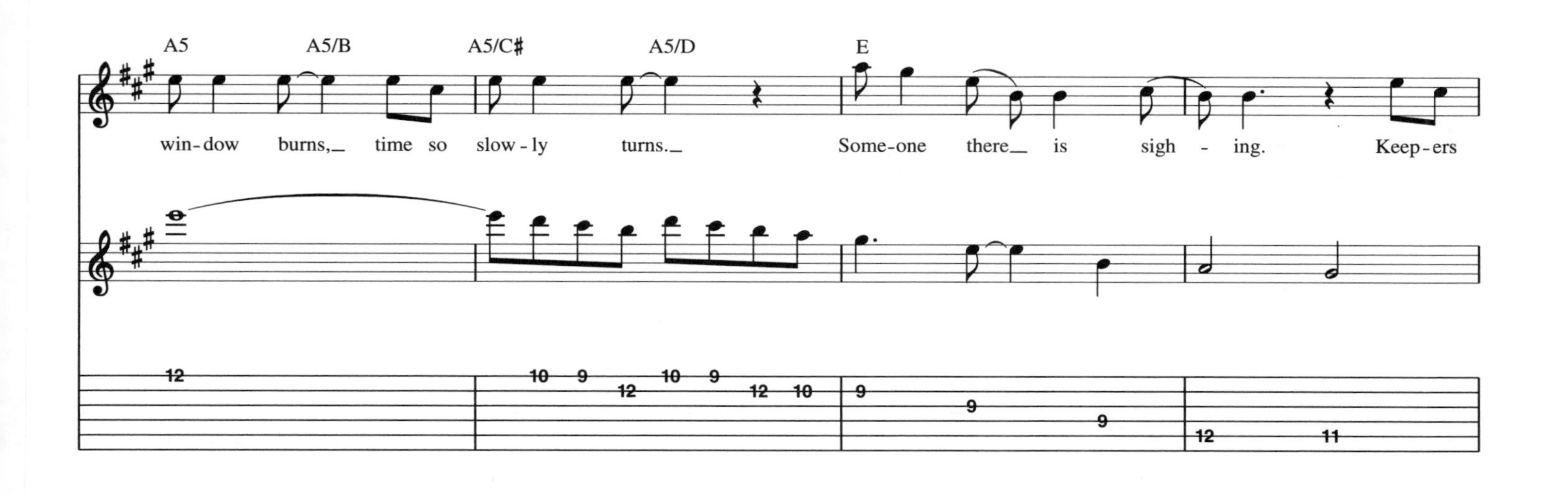
A5
A5/B
A5/C♯
A5/D
E
win-dow burns,_ time so slow-ly turns._ Some-one there_ is sigh - ing. Keep-ers
12
10 9 12 10 9 12 10
9 9 9
12 11

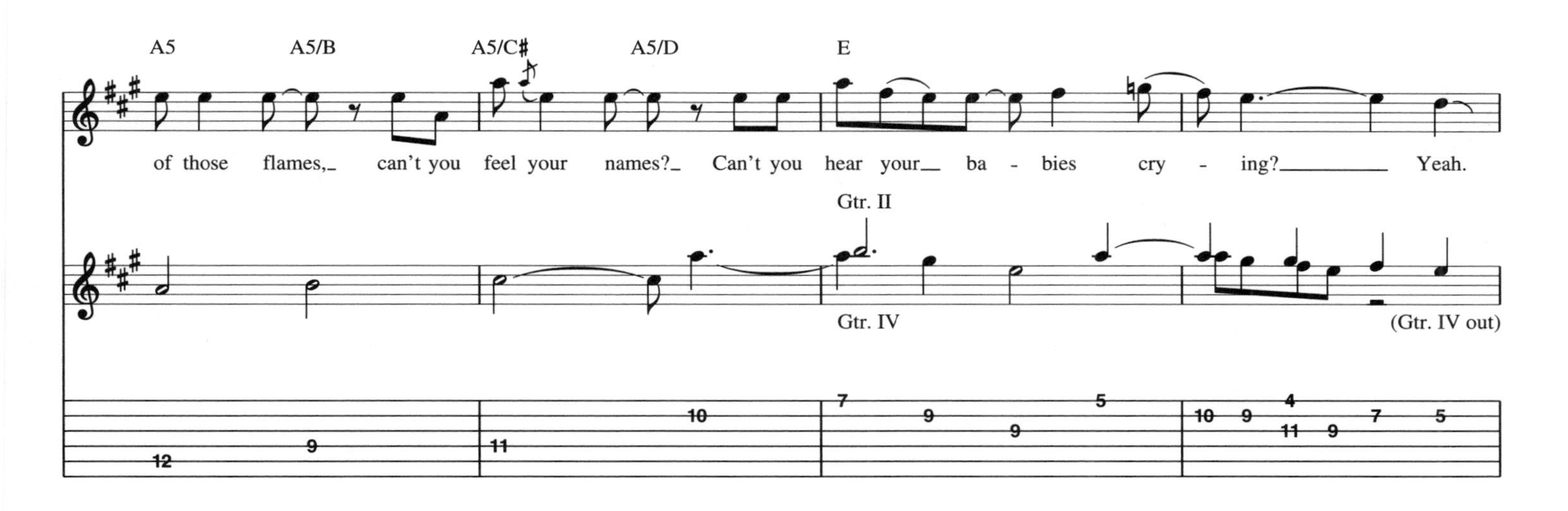
A5
A5/B
A5/C♯
A5/D
E
of those flames,_ can't you feel your names?_ Can't you hear your_ ba - bies cry - ing?_ Yeah.
Gtr. II
Gtr. IV
(Gtr. IV out)

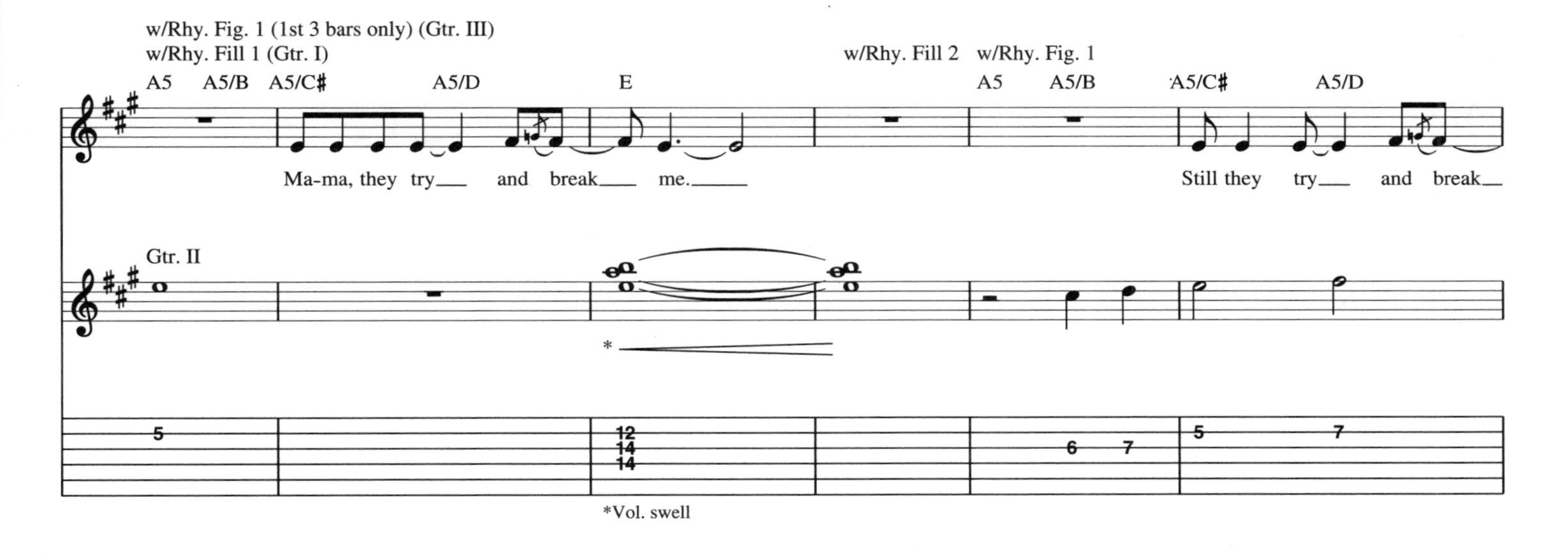
w/Rhy. Fig. 1 (1st 3 bars only) (Gtr. III)
w/Rhy. Fill 1 (Gtr. I)
w/Rhy. Fill 2
w/Rhy. Fig. 1
A5
A5/B
A5/C♯
A5/D
E
Ma-ma, they try_ and break_ me._
Still they try_ and break_
Gtr. II
*Vol. swell

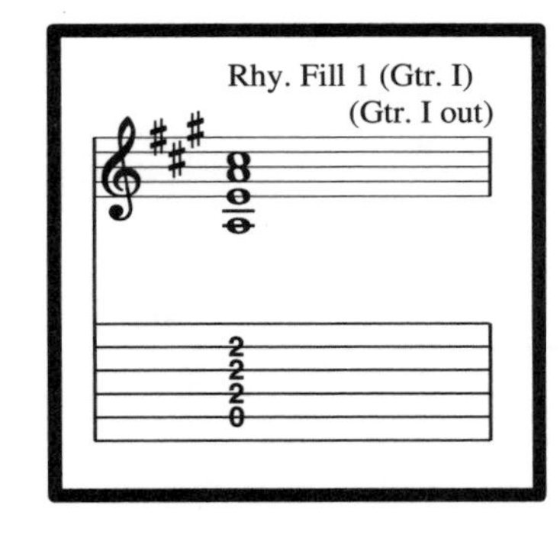
Rhy. Fill 1 (Gtr. I)
(Gtr. I out)

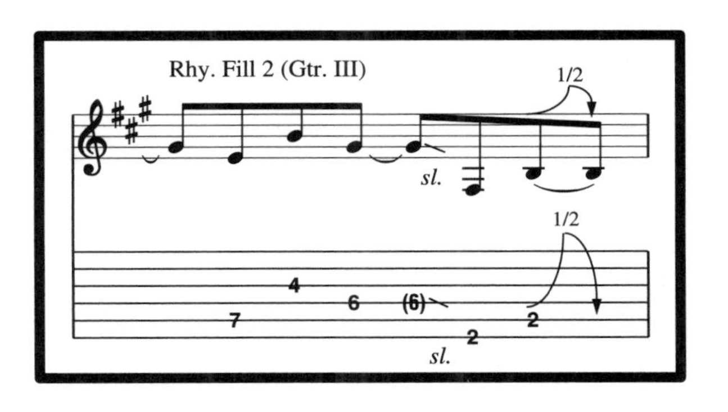
Rhy. Fill 2 (Gtr. III)
1/2
sl.

Half time feel
2nd Verse
w/Rhy. Fig. 1 (6 times) (Gtr. III)
E
A5
A5/B
A5/C#
A5/D
E
me.
Yeah.
Ex - cuse me while I tend to how I feel.

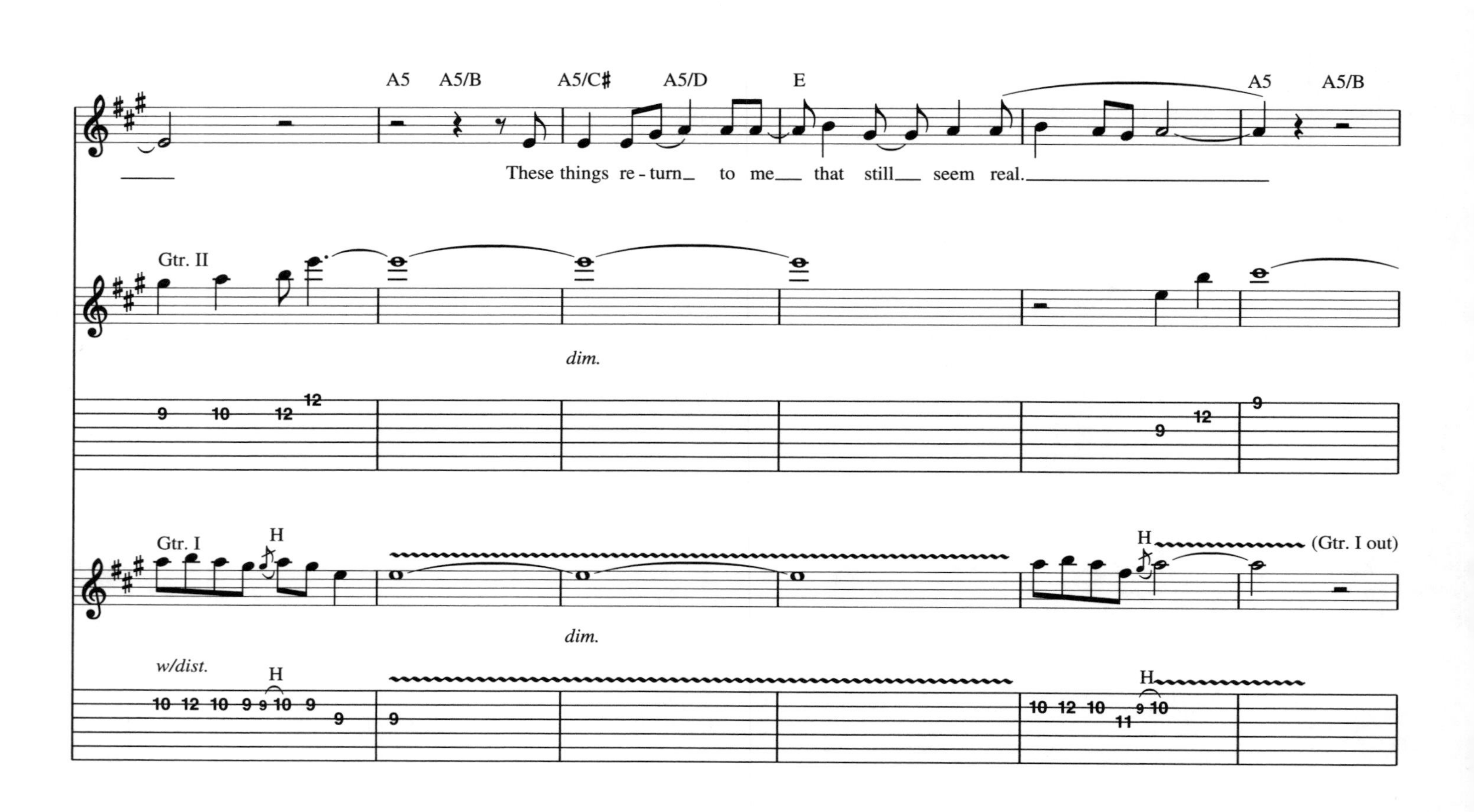
A5 A5/B A5/C# A5/D E A5 A5/B
These things re - turn to me that still seem real.
Gtr. II
dim.
Gtr. I
H
(Gtr. I out)
dim.
w/dist.

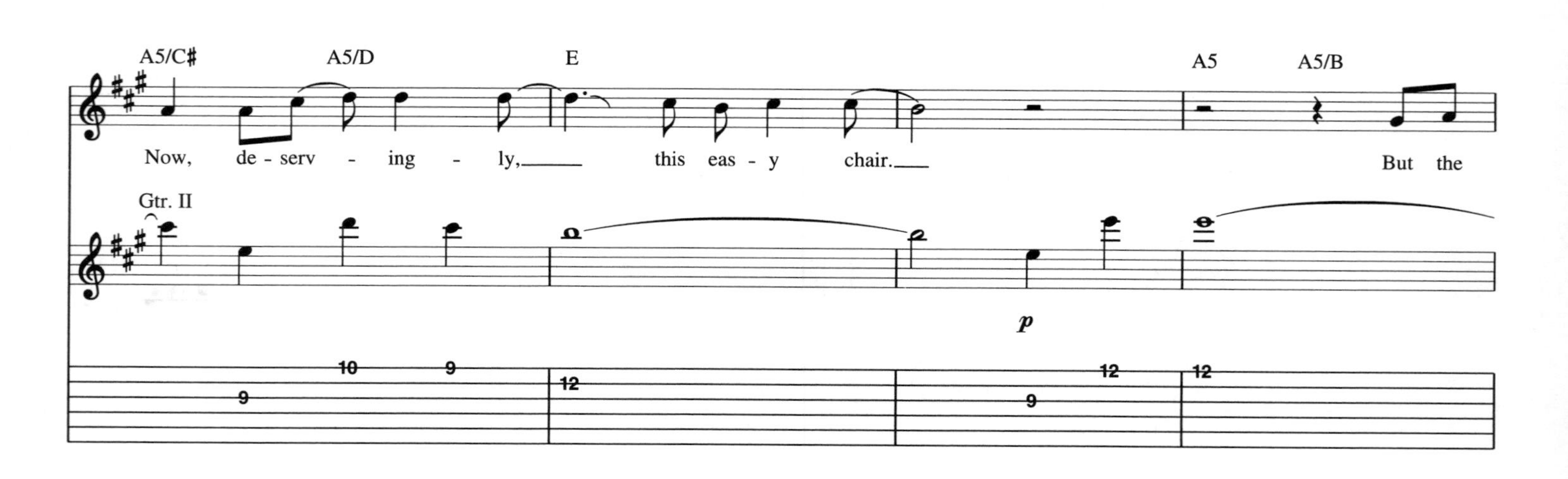
A5/C#
A5/D
E
A5
A5/B
Now, de - serv - ing - ly, this eas - y chair.
But the
Gtr. II
p

A5/C♯ A5/D E (end half time feel) A5 A5/B
rock-ing stopped_ by wheels_ of_ de - spair._ Don't want your aid,_ but the
A5/C♯ A5/D E A5 A5/B
fist I've made_ for years_ won't hold off fear._ No, I'm not all me,_ so
8va
A5/C♯ A5/D E
please ex - cuse_ me while I tend_ to how_ I feel._ Ah.
Chorus
F♯5 N.C. F♯5 N.C.
But now the dreams_ and wak - ing screams_ that ev -
(But now the dreams_ that ev -
Gtr. II
Rhy. Fig. 2 (Gtrs. I & III) (end Rhy. Fig. 2) Rhy. Fig. 2A (end Rhy. Fig. 2A)
f w/dist.

w/Rhy. Fig. 2A (3½ times)
F#5
N.C.
F#5
N.C.
er last the night.
er last the night.
So build the wall be - hind it, crawl and hide
So build the wall and hide
Gtr. II
8va
F#5
N.C.
F#5
un - til it's light.
un - til it's light.)
Can't you hear your ba -
bies cry - in' now?
Guitar solo
A5
A5/B
8va
Gtr. II
loco
Gtr. I
Fill 1
sl.
Gtr. III
Rhy. Fig. 3
let ring
sl.

A5/C#
A5/D
E
I can't hear you!
sl.
sl.
(end Rhy. Fig. 3)

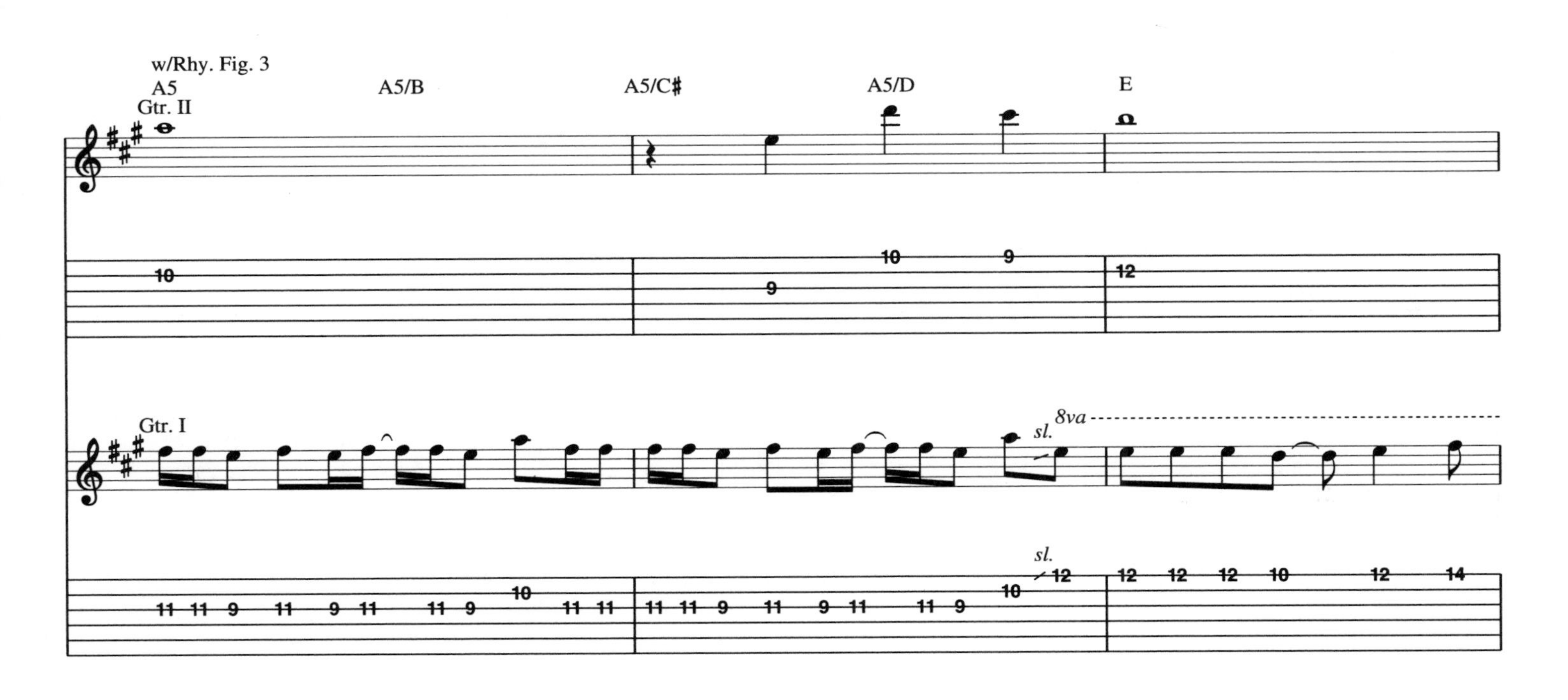
w/Rhy. Fig. 3
A5
A5/B
A5/C#
A5/D
E
Gtr. II
Gtr. I
sl.
8va
sl.

3rd Verse
w/Rhy. Fig. 3 (1¾ times)
A5
A5/B
A5/C♯
A5/D
Still the win - dow burns, time so slow - ly turns. And
(The win - dow burns.
sl.

E
A5
A5/B
some - one there is sigh - ing. Keep - ers of the flames, can't you
Some - one there is sigh - ing. Can't you
8va
loco
sl.

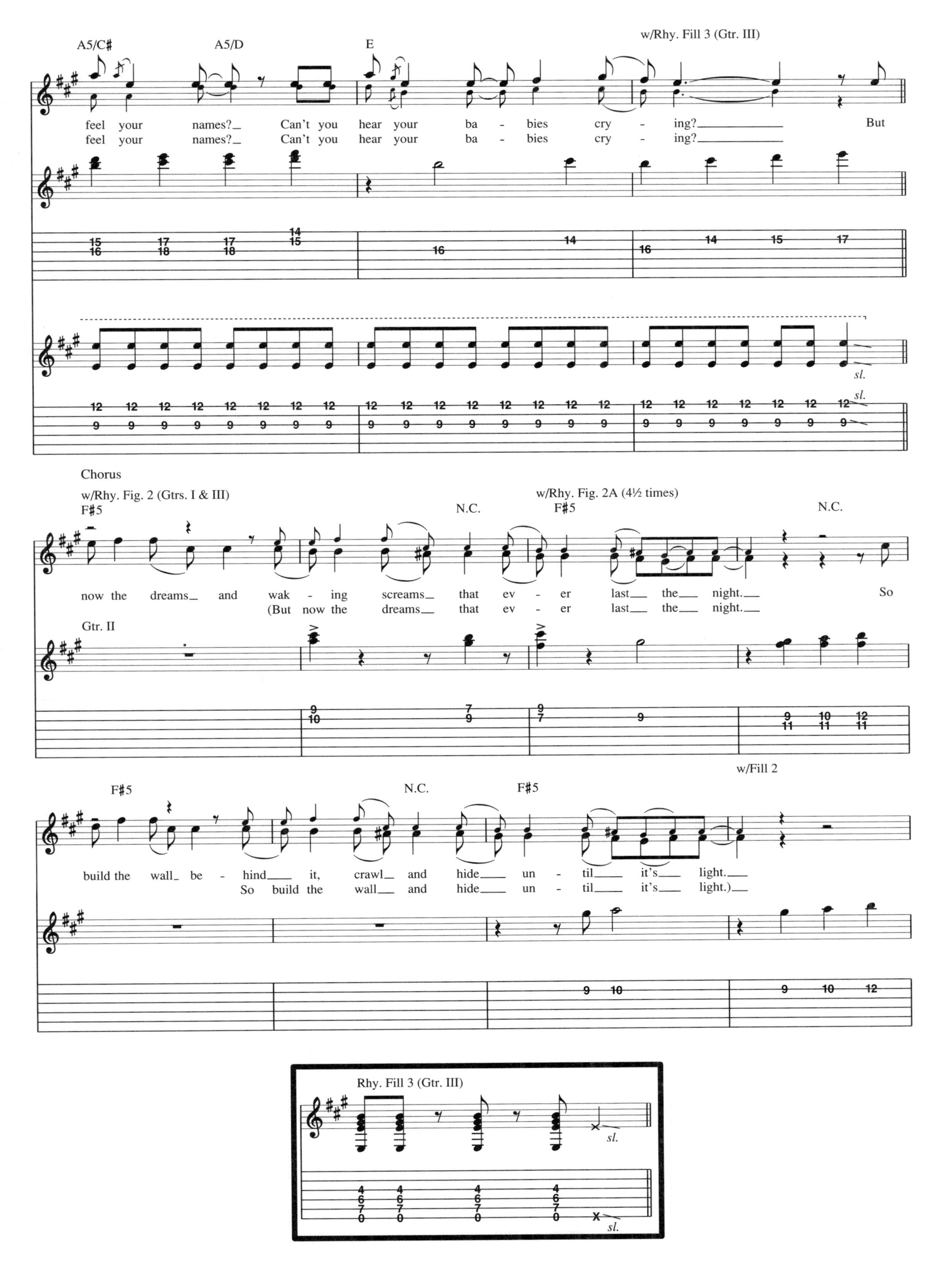
A5/C♯
A5/D
E
w/Rhy. Fill 3 (Gtr. III)
feel your names? Can't you hear your ba - bies cry - ing? But
feel your names? Can't you hear your ba - bies cry - ing?
sl.
Chorus
w/Rhy. Fig. 2 (Gtrs. I & III)
F♯5
N.C.
w/Rhy. Fig. 2A (4½ times)
F♯5
N.C.
now the dreams and wak - ing screams that ev - er last the night. So
(But now the dreams that ev - er last the night.
Gtr. II
F♯5
N.C.
F♯5
w/Fill 2
build the wall be - hind it, crawl and hide un - til it's light.
So build the wall and hide un - til it's light.)
Rhy. Fill 3 (Gtr. III)
sl.

F#5
N.C.
F#5
Can't you hear your ba - bies cry - in' now?
Outro
F#5
F#5/G#
Gtr. I
Ma - ma, they try and break me.
Gtr. II
Gtrs. I & III
(Gtr. I cont. in slashes)
Rhy. Fig. 4 (Gtr. III)
sl.
let ring

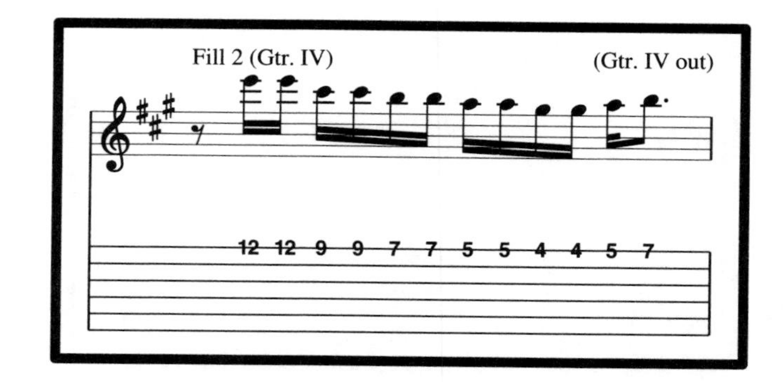

Fill 2 (Gtr. IV)
(Gtr. IV out)

F♯5/A
F♯5/B
F♯5
Ma - ma, they try___ and break___ me.
Ma - ma, they try___ and break_
H
H

E/G♯
E5/A
B5
___ me.
Ma - ma, they try,___
Ma - ma, they try.___ Hey!
(end Rhy. Fig. 4)

w/Rhy. Fig. 4
w/Fill 1 (8 times) (Gtr. I)
F#5
F#5/G#
F#5/A
F#5/B
Ma-ma, they try___ and break___ me.
(Ma-ma, they try___ and break___ me.
Ma-ma, they try___ and break___ me.
Ma-ma, they try___ and break___
Gtr. II
sl.
F#5
E/G#
E5/A
B5
Ma-ma, they try___ and break___ me.
___ me.
Ma-ma, they try___ and break___ me.)
Ma-ma, they try,___
Ma-ma, they try,___
Freely
N.C.
F#5
rit.
yeah.___
Ma-ma...
Gtr. II
Full
Gtr. I
Gtr. III

BLEEDING ME

Words and Music by James Hetfield,
Lars Ulrich and Kirk Hammett

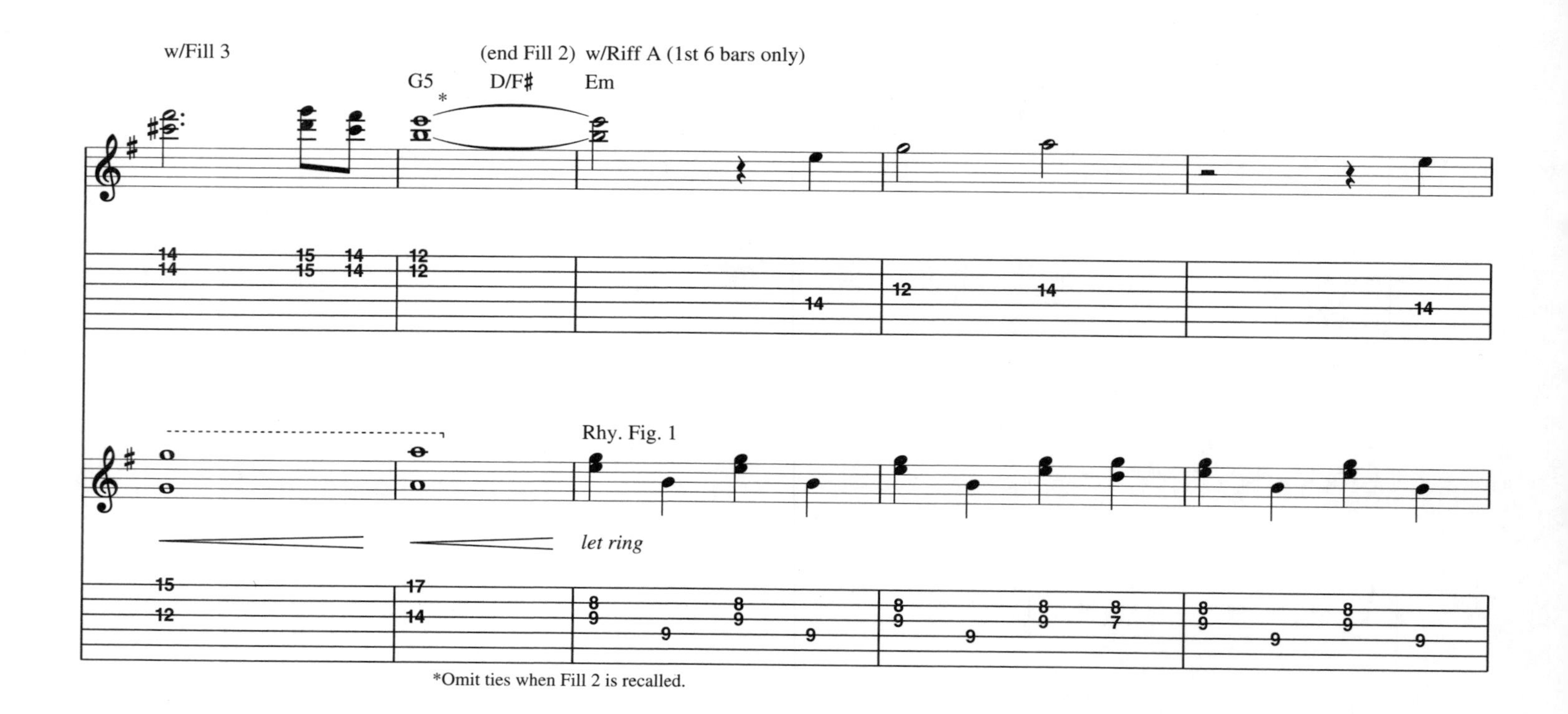

*Omit ties when Fill 2 is recalled.

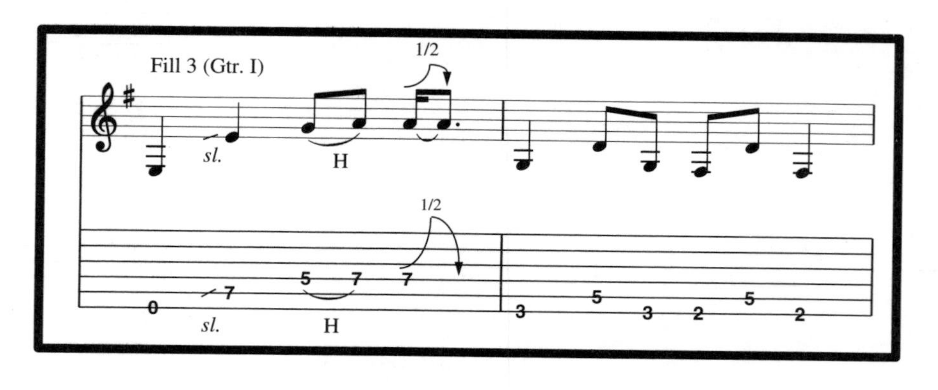

1st, 2nd Verses
w/Riff A (1st 7 bars only)
2nd time Gtr. II substitute Fill 5
Em
1. I'm dig - gin' my way. Yes, I'm dig - gin' my way to some - thin'.
2. I'm sow - in' the seeds. Yes, I'm sow - in' the seeds I've tak - en.
Riff B
sl.
P
let ring
Esus2
Em
w/Fill 4
G5
D/F#
I'm dig - gin' my way to some - thin' bet - ter.
I'm sow - in' the seeds I take for grant - ed.
(end Riff B)
Fill 4 (Gtr. I)
Fill 5 (Gtr. II)

w/Riff A
w/Riff B (1st 7 bars only)
2nd time Gtr. II substitute Fill 1
Em
I'm push - in' to stay.
This thorn in my side,
Yes, I'm push - in' to stay with some - thin'.
Yes, this thorn in my side is from the tree.
Gtr. II
12 14 14 14 12 15

I'm push - in' to stay with some - thin' bet - ter.
This thorn in my side is from the tree I've plant - ed. Ooh, it
12 14 12 14 14

(end half time feel)
G5 D/F# E5 D5
Rhy. Fig. 3 (Gtr. I)
f w/dist.
Woh, yeah.
tears me and I bleed, yeah.
Gtr. II
*
10 12 14 12 14
Gtr. III
Full Riff C
sl.
Full
sl. sl.
f w/dist.
9 7 8 (8) 9 7 7 (7) (7) 7 5 7
*w/variations ad lib on repeat

E5
Woh, woh, yeah.
And I bleed, woh,
Full
sl. sl.
sl.
P
H

1.
(end Rhy. Fig. 3)
⑥ open 3fr.
D5
A5
E G
(dist. off)
woh.
Oh, yeah.
(end Riff C)
Full
sl. sl.
P
H

Half time feel
w/Riff A (1st 6 bars only)
w/Rhy. Fig. 1
Em
Gtr. II
w/Fill 3
G5
D/F#
2.
(cont. in notation)
6 open 3fr.
A5
E
G
Hey.
Full
Full
P
H
Half time feel
Chorus
E5
D5
A5
N.C.
1.3. Caught un - der wheel's roll.
2. I'm caught un - der wheel's roll.
1. I take the leech, I'm bleed-ing me.
2.3. I take the leech, hey, I'm bleed-ing me.
Rhy. Fig. 4 (Gtrs. I & III)
(end Rhy. Fig. 4)
sl.

w/Rhy. Fig. 4 (2 times)
3rd time Gtr. III substitute Rhy. Fill 3
E5
D5
A5
N.C.
Can't stop to save my soul.
I can't stop to save my soul.
I take the leash that's lead-ing me.
Gtr. II
1st & 2nd times Gtr. III substitute Rhy. Fill 2
(Gtr. III resume Rhy. Fig. 4)
To Coda II
I'm bleed-ing me.
Ooh, woh.
Ooh, I can't take it.
(Gtr. II out)
1st time w/Rhy. Fig. 4
2nd time w/Rhy. Fig. 4 (1st 3 bars only)
To Coda I
Gtr. III substitute Rhy. Fill 1
Caught un - der wheel's roll.
Woh.
Oh, the bleed - ing of me.

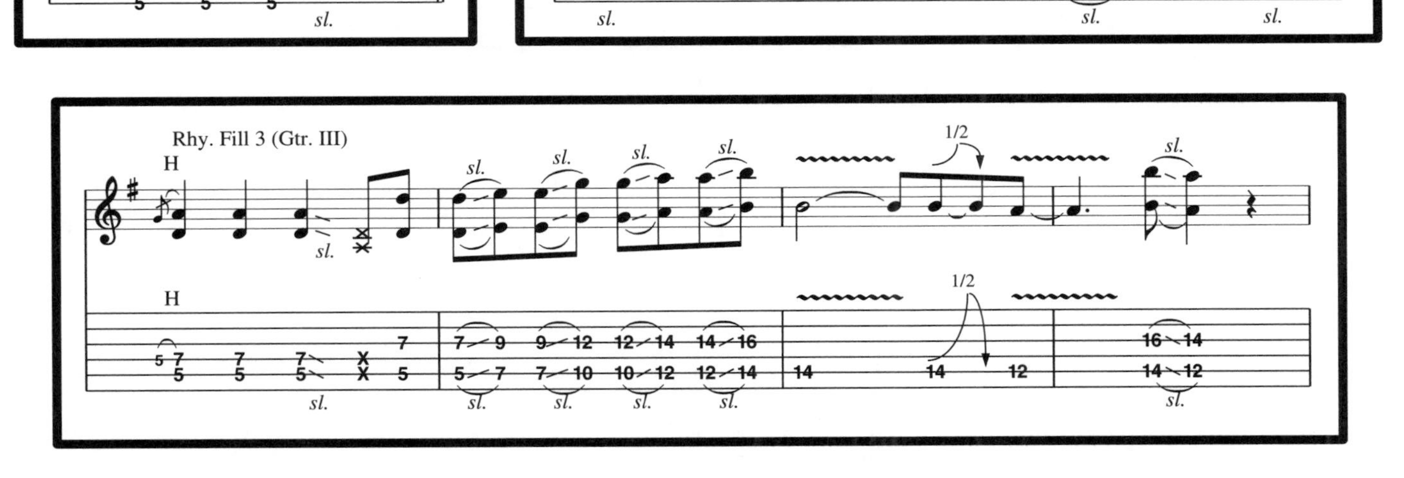
Rhy. Fill 1 (Gtr. III)
Full
Rhy. Fill 2
1/2
Rhy. Fill 3 (Gtr. III)
sl.

w/Rhy. Fig. 3 and Riff C
E5
D5
E5
Ooh, yeah.
Yes, of me.
Gtr. II
D5
A5
N.C.
Woh, oh.
Oh, the bleed - ing of me.
Interlude
w/Riff A (1st 6 bars only)
N.C.(Em)
Gtr. II
Gtr. III
mf
w/light dist. & slide
sl.
*Fill 6 (Gtr. I)
Harm.
sl.
f w/dist.
Harm.
sl.
*While lightly resting L.H. finger on string, slide up neck while picking in eighth note rhythm, thereby sounding random harmonics.

w/Fill 3
G5
D/F♯
w/Riff A (1st 7 bars only)
N.C.(Em)
8va
w/Fill 6
(G5)
(D/F♯)
D.S. al Coda I
Hey!

*Orchestra arr. for gtr.

N.C.(B5)
(C5)
E5
P.M.
A tempo
Gtr. II
Gtr. IV
Rhy. Fig. 5 (Gtr. I)
(end Rhy. Fig. 5)
Rhy. Fig. 5A
(end Rhy. Fig. 5A)
H
P

w/Rhy. Fig. 5A (2 times)
Gtr. III
Huh, huh.
Gtr. II
Gtr. IV
Half time feel
w/Rhy. Fig. 5A (4 times) (Gtrs. I & III)
w/Fill 2
E5
N.C.
E5
N.C.
Gtr. IV
P.M.
E5
N.C.
E5
N.C.
Hey.
Bridge
w/Rhy. Fig. 5A (4 times) and Fill 1
E5
N.C.
E5
N.C.
I am the beast that feeds the beast. I am the blood, I am re - lease.
D.S. al Coda II
E5
N.C.
E5
N.C.
Come make me pure, bleed me a cure. I'm caught, caught, I'm caught un - der.

Coda II w/Rhy. Fig. 4 (Gtr. I)
E5 D5 A5 N.C.
I can't take it. I can't take it. No, oh, the bleed - ing of me.
Gtr. III
w/wah as filter
Full
sl.
Guitar solo
w/Rhy. Fig. 5 and Fill 1
E5 N.C.
w/Rhy. Fig. 5A (3 times)
E5 N.C.
Come on. Feel it, man.
P
E5 N.C. E5 N.C. (Gtr. II out)
1/2
B5 C5 A5 C5 A
⑤ open
Gtr. I
Gtr. II
Gtr. III

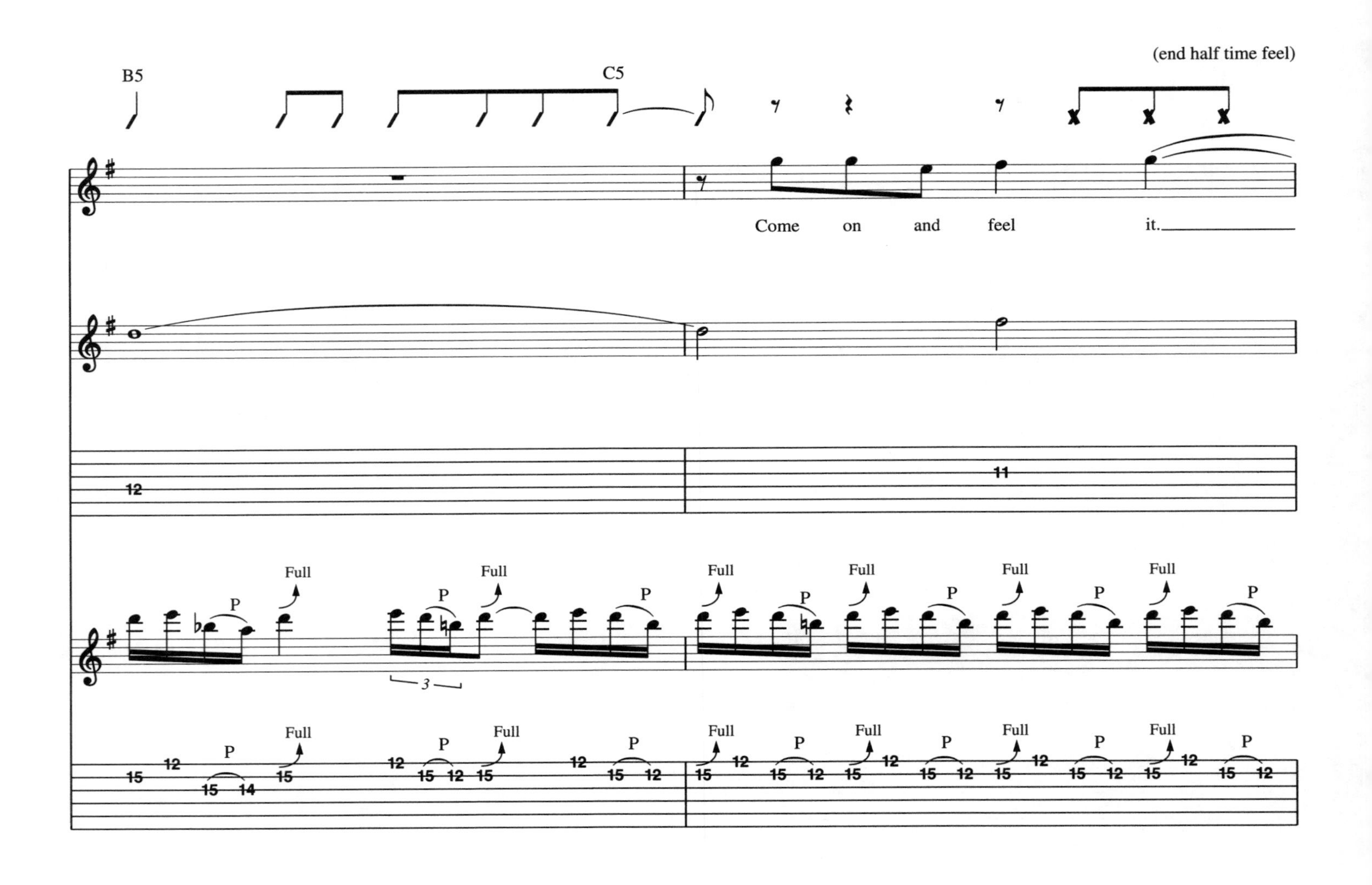
(end half time feel)
B5
C5
Come on and feel it.
Full
P
Full
P
Full
P
Full
P
Full
P
Full
P

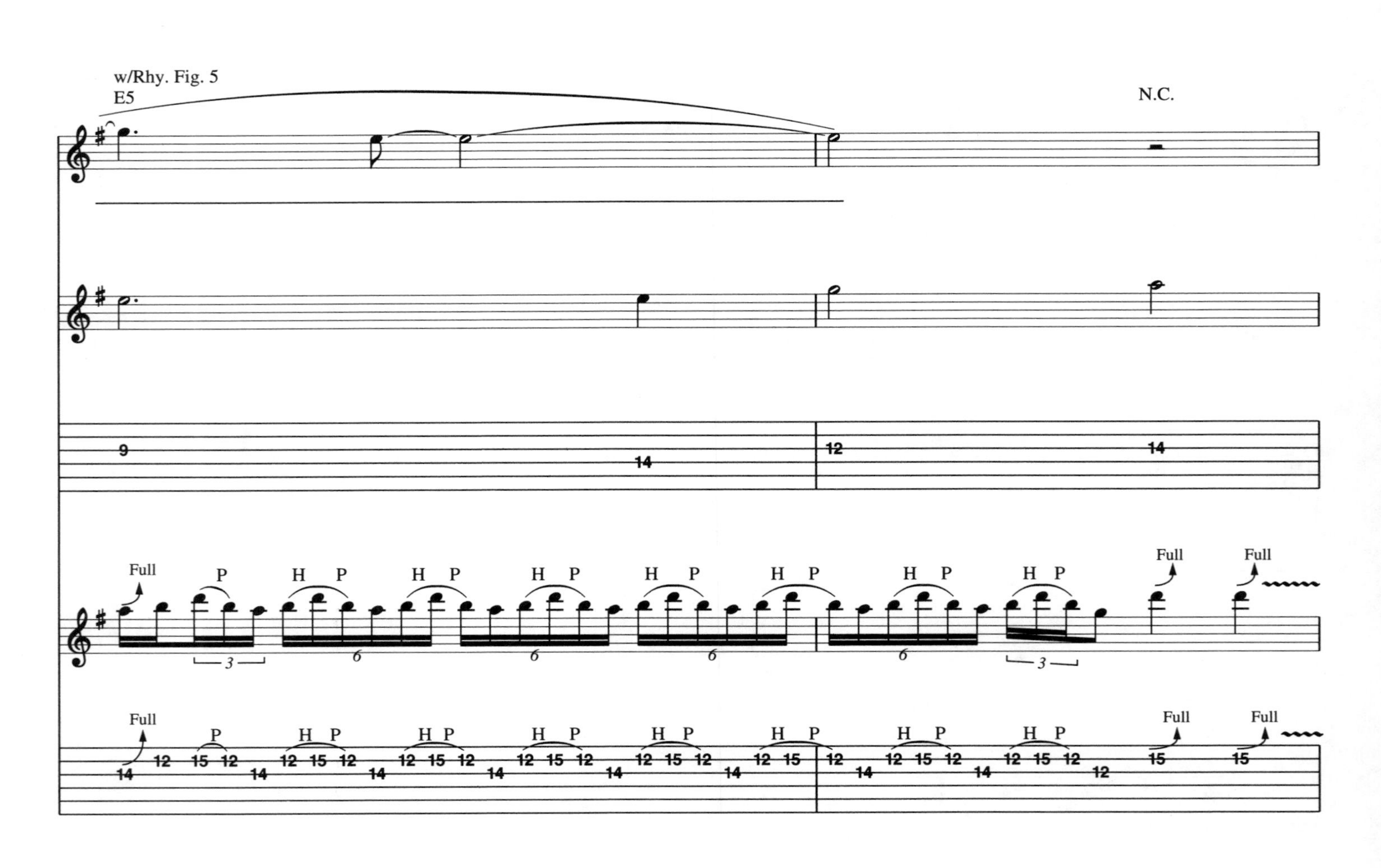
w/Rhy. Fig. 5
E5
N.C.
Full
P
H P
Full
Full

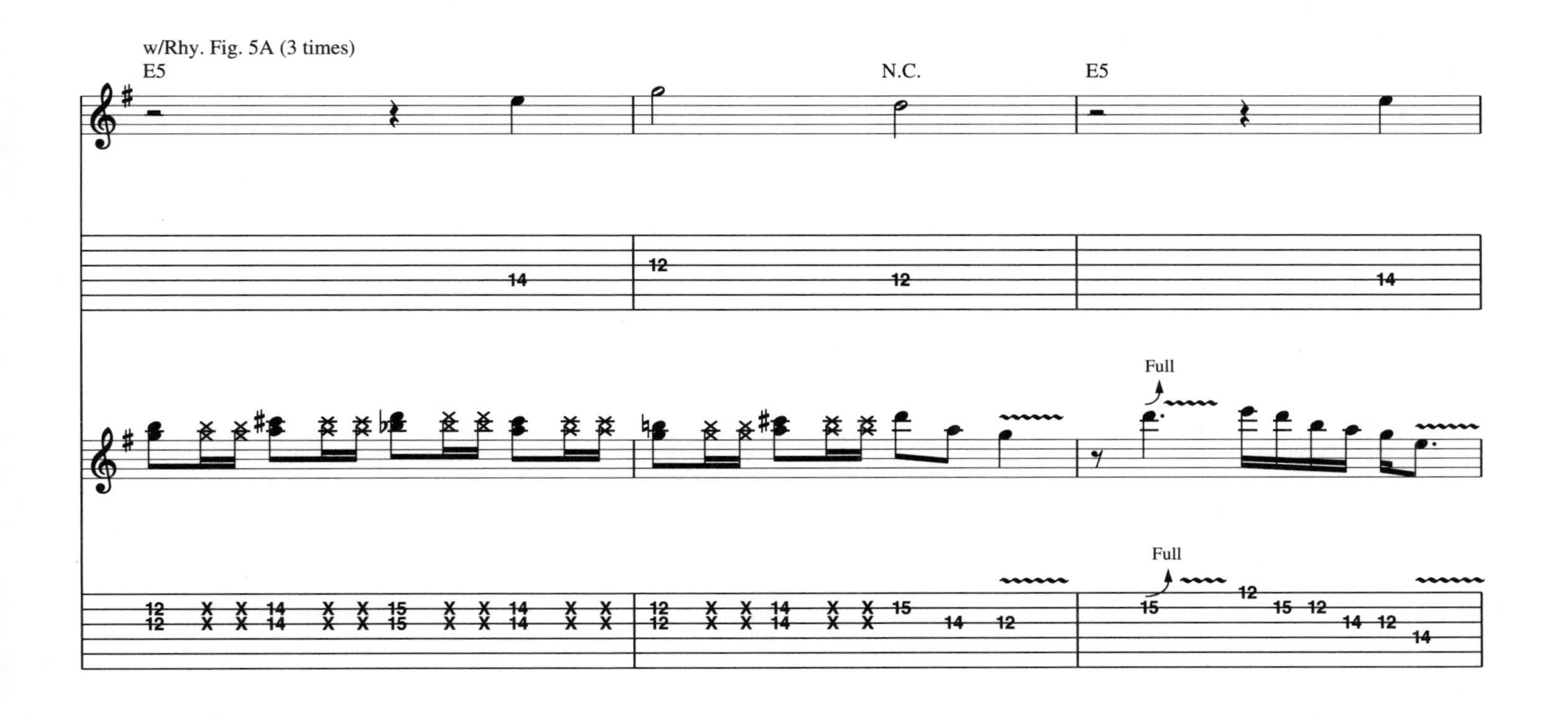
w/Rhy. Fig. 5A (3 times)
E5
N.C.
E5
Full
Full

N.C.
E5
N.C.
(Gtr. II out)
Full
Full
Full
Full
Full
1½
sl.

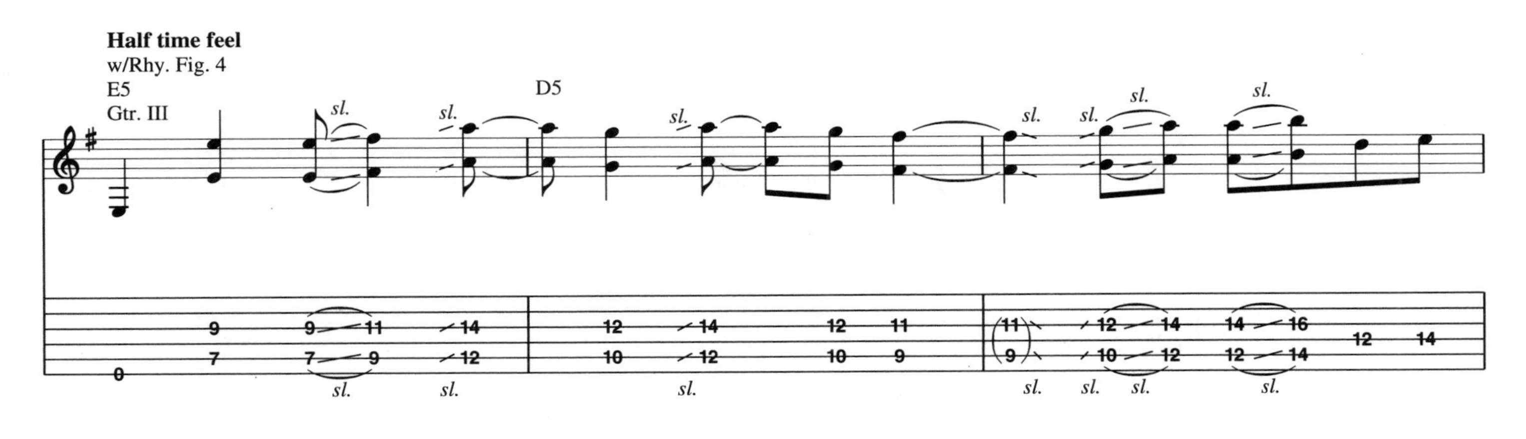
Half time feel
w/Rhy. Fig. 4
E5
Gtr. III
D5
sl.

w/Rhy. Fill 2 (Gtr. I)
A5
N.C.
E5
D5
sl.
w/Rhy. Fig. 4 (last 2 bars only)
A5
N.C.
*w/Riff A (Gtrs. I & III)
N.C.(Em)
Hey! Hey!
1/2
P
(wah off)
*w/dist.
Hey! Hey! Hey! Hey! Hey! Hey! Hey! Hey! Hey! Hey!
Gtr. II
f
Gtr. I substitute Fill 3
G5
D/F♯
(Gtr. III out)
**w/Riff A (1st 3 bars only) (Gtr. I)
N.C.(Em)
Hey!
mp
**Clean tone

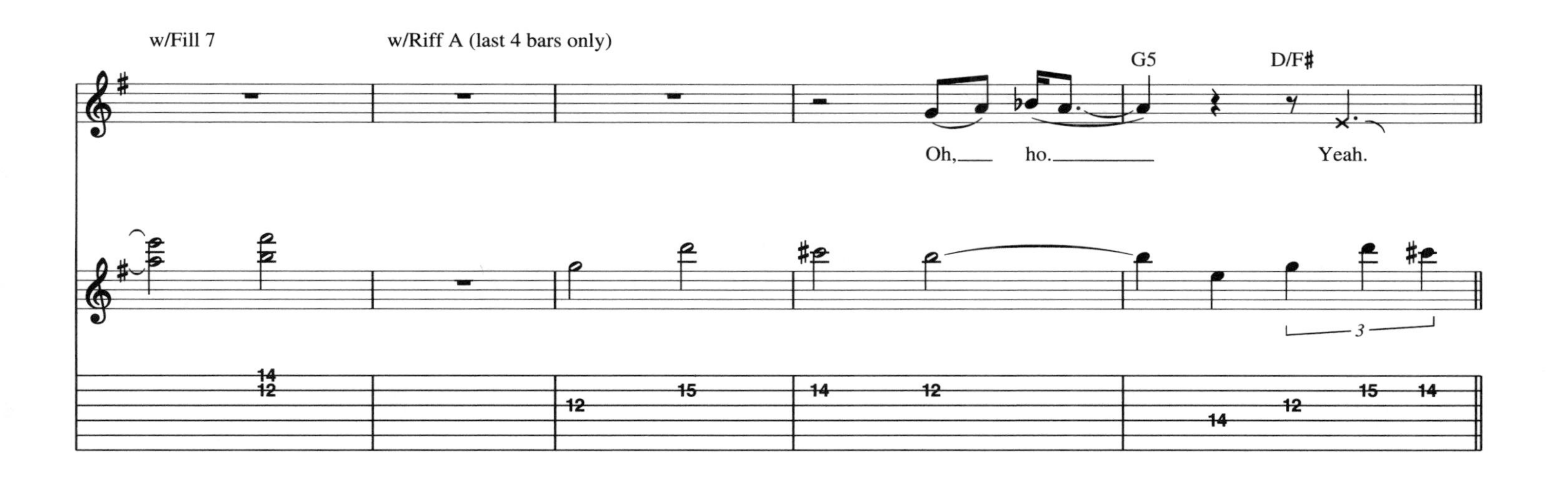
w/Fill 7
w/Riff A (last 4 bars only)
G5
D/F♯
Oh, ho. Yeah.

3rd Verse
w/Riff A (1st 7 bars only)
w/Riff B (2 times)
Em
3. I'm dig - gin' my way. Yes, I'm dig - gin' my way to some - thin'.

w/Fill 8
G5
D/F♯
I'm dig - gin' my way to some - thin' bet - ter, yeah.

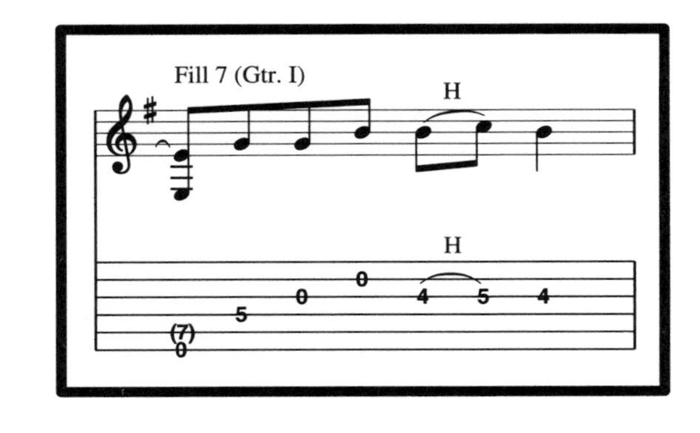
Fill 7 (Gtr. I)
H
H

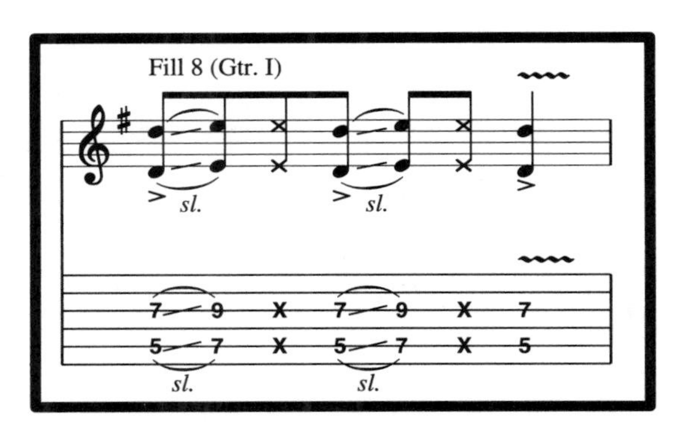
Fill 8 (Gtr. I)
sl.
sl.
sl.
sl.

w/Riff A
Em
I'm push - in' to stay.
Yes, I'm push - in' to stay with some - thin'.

(end half time feel)
G5
D/F#
I'm push - in' to stay with some - thin' bet - ter, yeah, with some - thin' bet -
grad. rit.

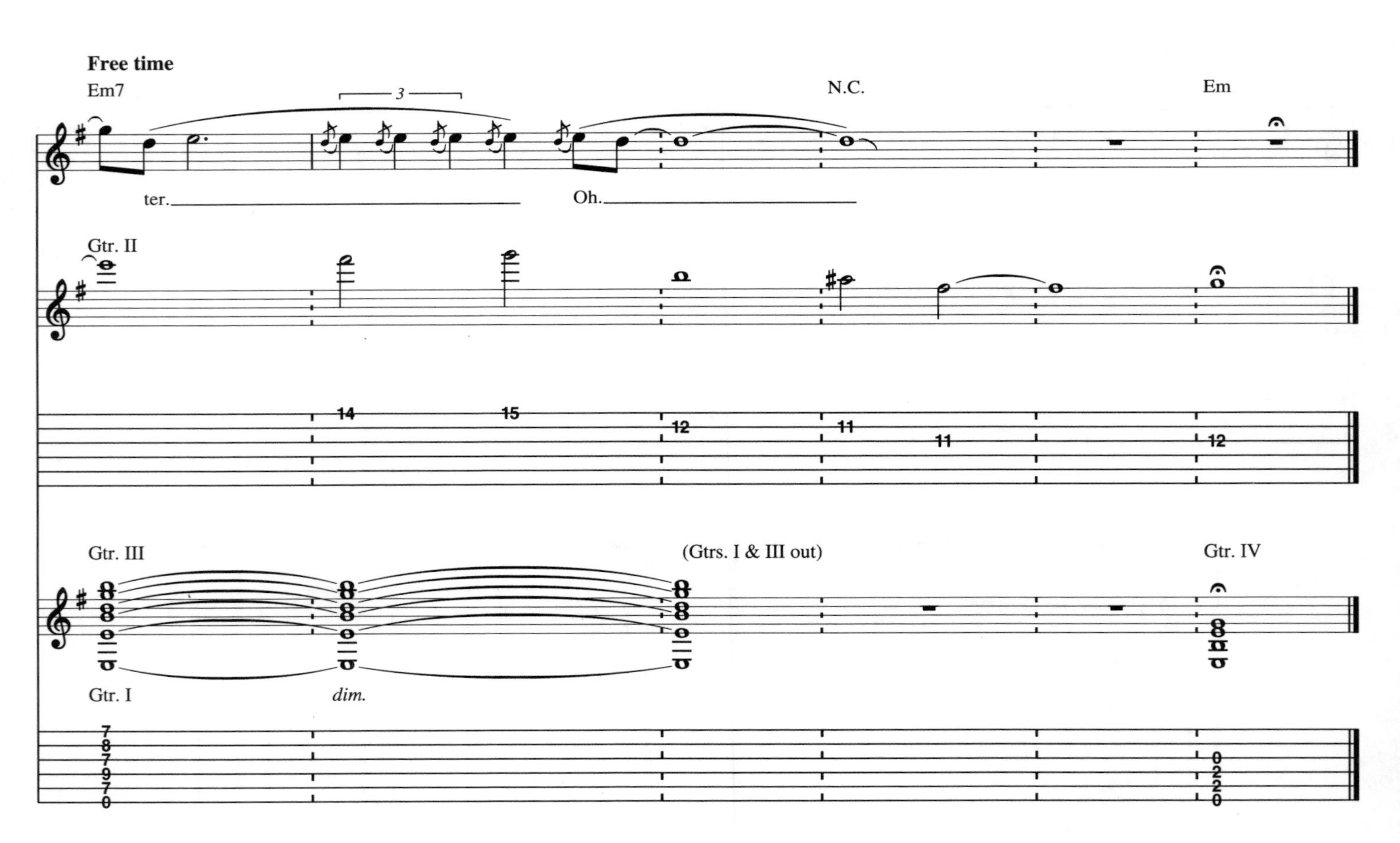
Free time
Em7
N.C.
Em
ter.
Oh.
Gtr. II
Gtr. III
(Gtrs. I & III out)
Gtr. IV
Gtr. I
dim.

NOTHING ELSE MATTERS

Words and Music by
James Hetfield and Lars Ulrich

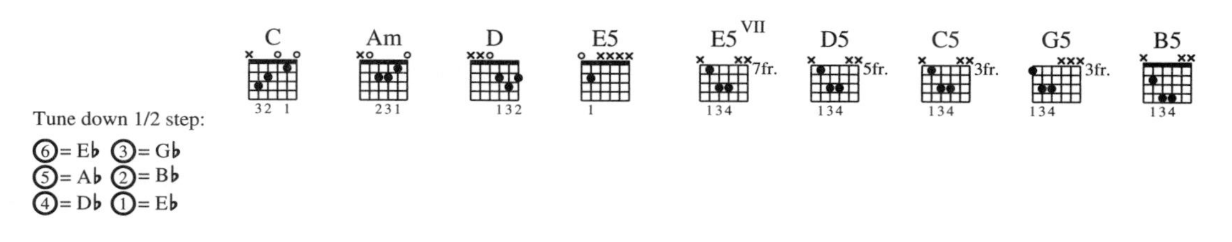

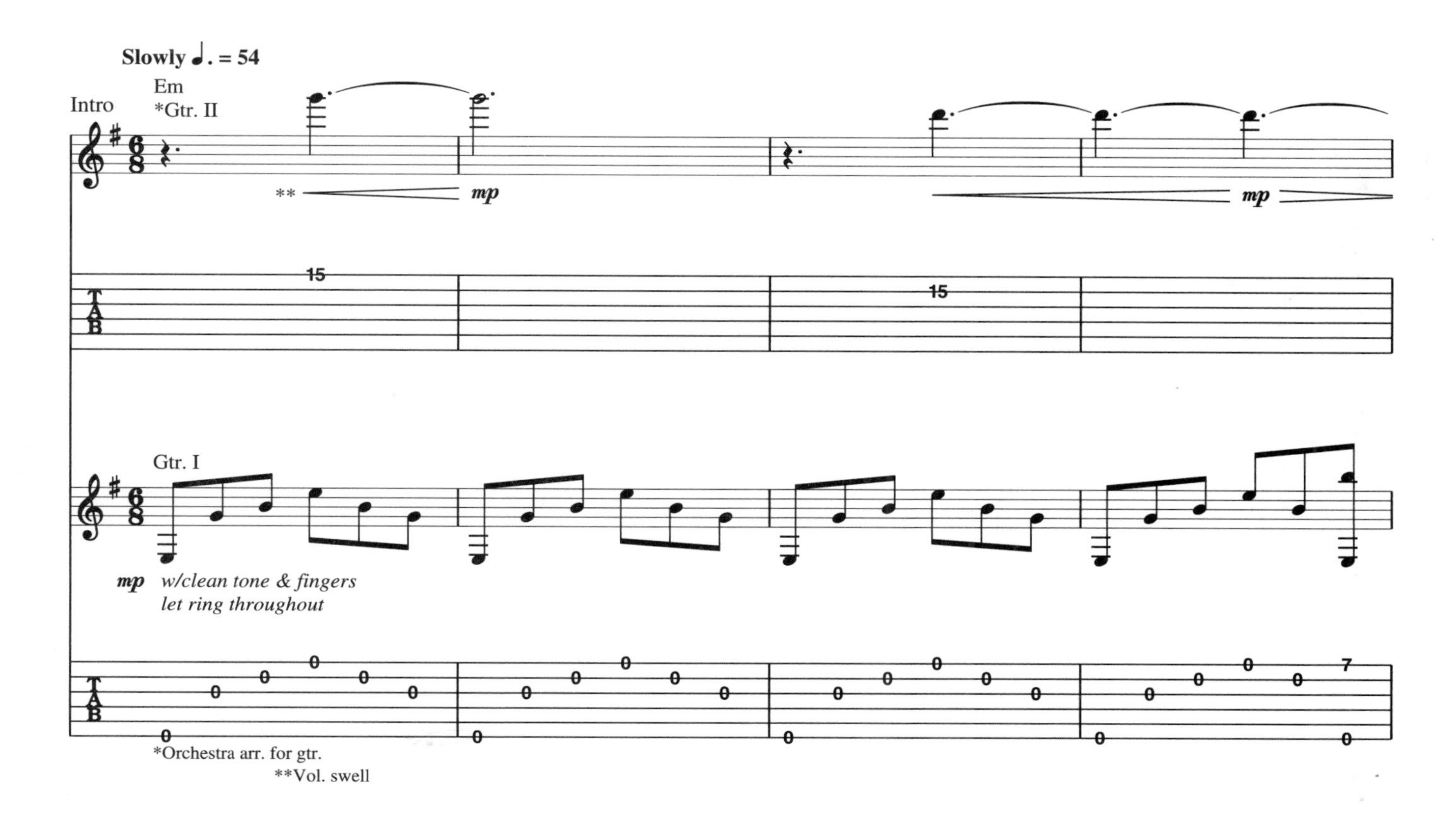

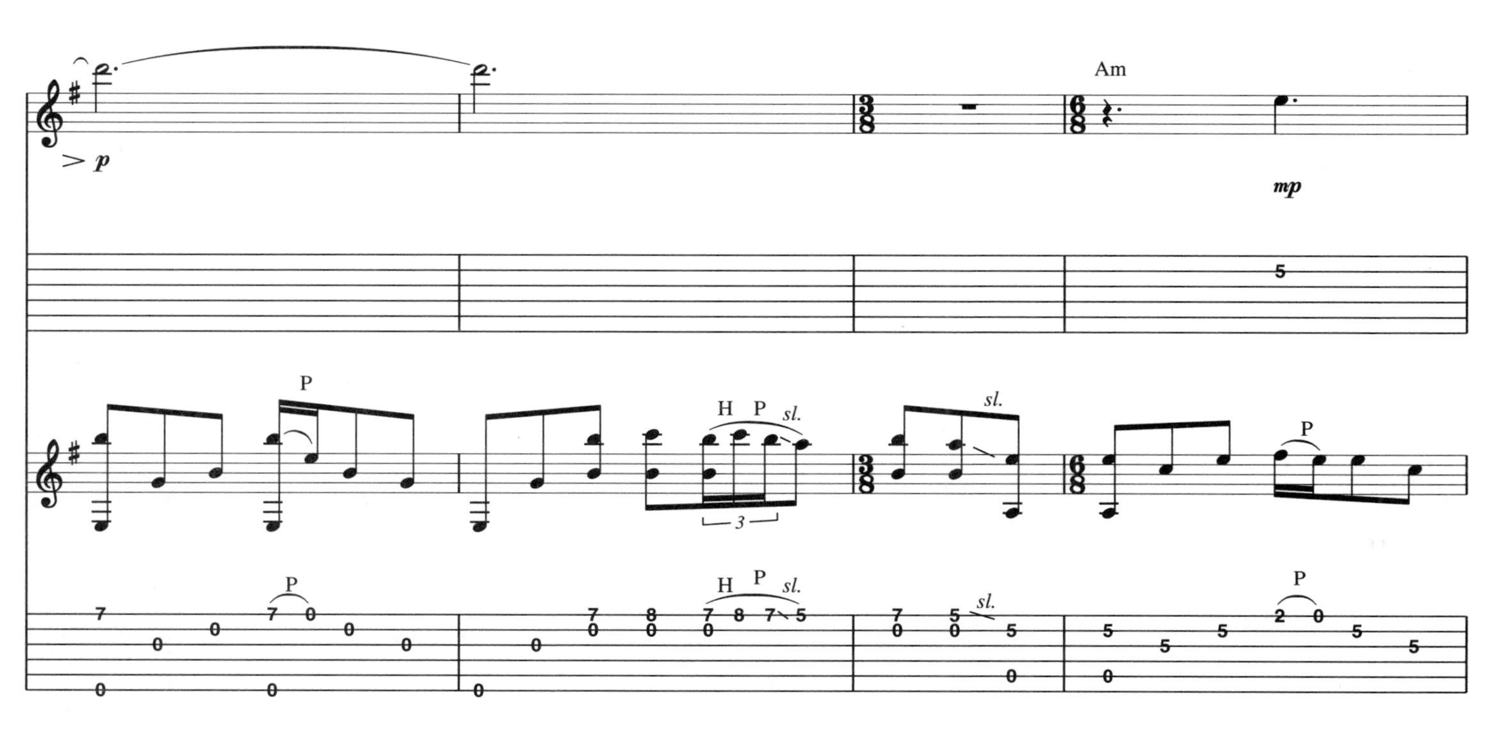

C
Dadd2
P
H P
P
P
Em
p
Harm.
Harm.
D
C
Em
D
C
Gtrs. I & *III
w/pick
*clean tone

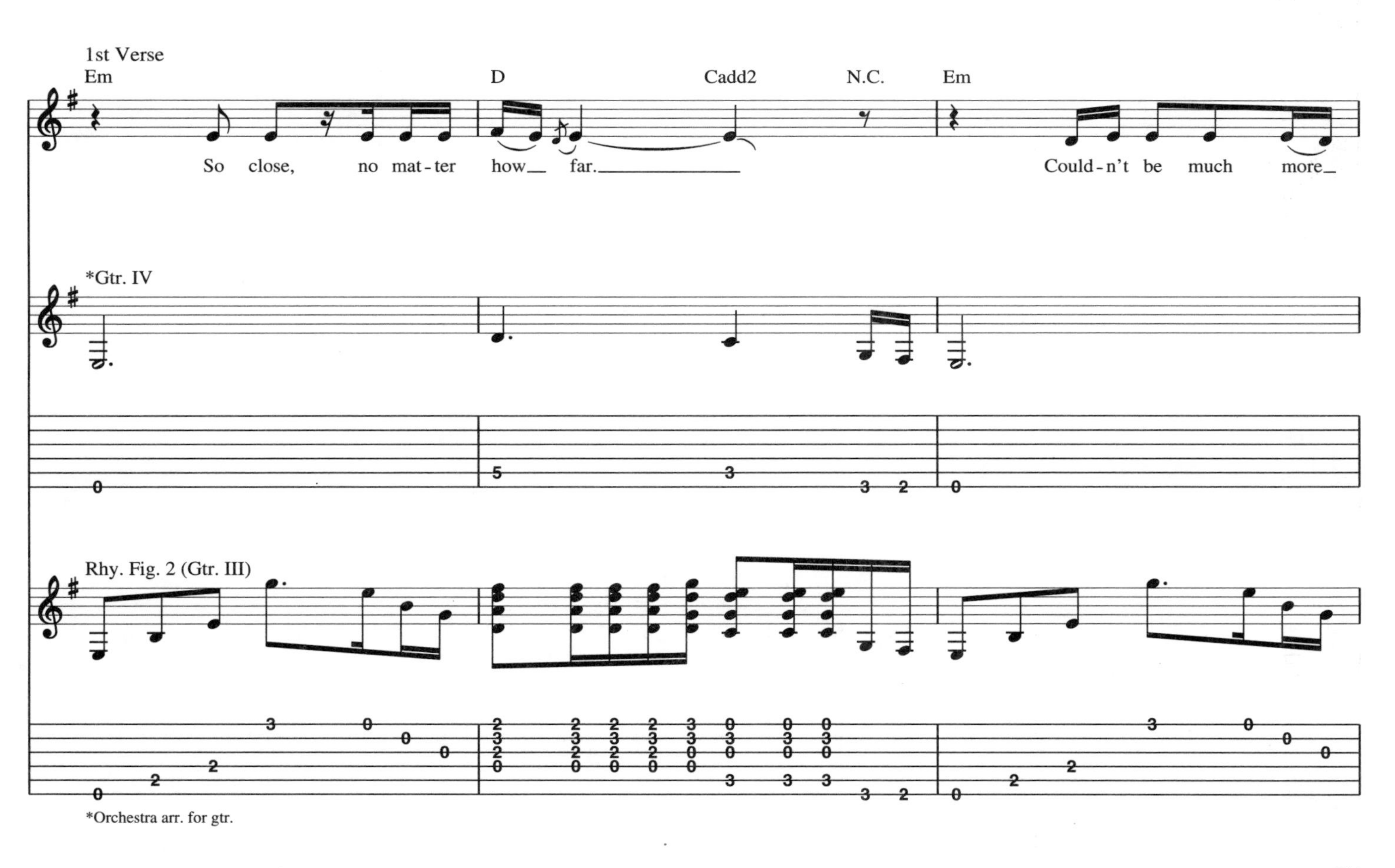

*Orchestra arr. for gtr.

D
Cadd2
N.C.
Em
D
Cadd2
from the heart.
For - ev - er trust - ing who we are.
G
B7
Em
N.C.
And noth - ing else mat - ters.
Gtr. II
Gtr. IV
P
(end Rhy. Fig. 2)
2nd Verse
w/Rhy. Fig. 2
Em
D
Cadd2
N.C.
Em
I nev - er o - pened my - self this way.
Life is ours, we live it
Gtr. II
H
(Gtr. IV out)

D
Cadd2
N.C.
Em
D
Cadd2
our way.
All these words I don't just say.
H
H
G
B7
Em
N.C.
And noth - ing else mat - ters.
Yeah!
3rd Verse
w/Rhy. Fig. 2 (1st 8 bars only)
Em
D
Cadd2
N.C.
Em
Trust I seek and I find in you.
Ev - 'ry day for us
H
H
Rhy. Fig. 3 (Gtr. I)
sl.
sl.
sl.
sl.

D
Cadd2
N.C.
Em
D
Cadd2
some - thing new.
O - pen mind for a dif - f'rent view.
H
H
sl.
sl.
sl.
sl.
G
B7
Em
C
Am
Gtr. III
And noth - ing else matters.
(cont. in slashes)
(end Rhy. Fig. 3)
Chorus
D
Gtrs. I & III
C
Am
D
Nev - er cared for what they do.
Nev - er cared for what they
Gtr. II

C
Am
D
w/Rhy. Fig. 1 (Gtrs. I & III)
Em
know, oh, and I know.
Gtr. II
Gtr. IV
4th Verse
w/Rhy. Fig. 2 (1st 8 bars only) (Gtrs. I & III)
Em
D
Cadd2
N.C.
Em
So close, no mat-ter how far.
Could-n't be much more
(Gtr. IV out)
Gtr. II
H
D
Cadd2
N.C.
Em
D
Cadd2
from the heart.
For-ev-er trust-ing who we are.
G
B7
Em
Gtrs. I & III
C
Am
Chorus
D
Rhy. Fig. 4
And noth-ing else mat-ters.
Nev-er cared for what they do.
*Vol. swell

C
Am
(end Rhy. Fig. 4)
D
Rhy. Fig. 5
C
Am
D
(end Rhy. Fig. 5)
Nev- er cared for what they know,
oh, and I know,
w/Rhy. Fig. 1 (Gtrs. I & III)
Em
oh, yeah. That's right.
Interlude
Em
Gtr. II
8va
**8va
Gtr. I
Gtr. III
let ring
*Gtr. I notated to left of slashes.
**8va refers to both gtrs.
Am
8va
C
Dadd2
Em
loco
loco
sl.
sl.

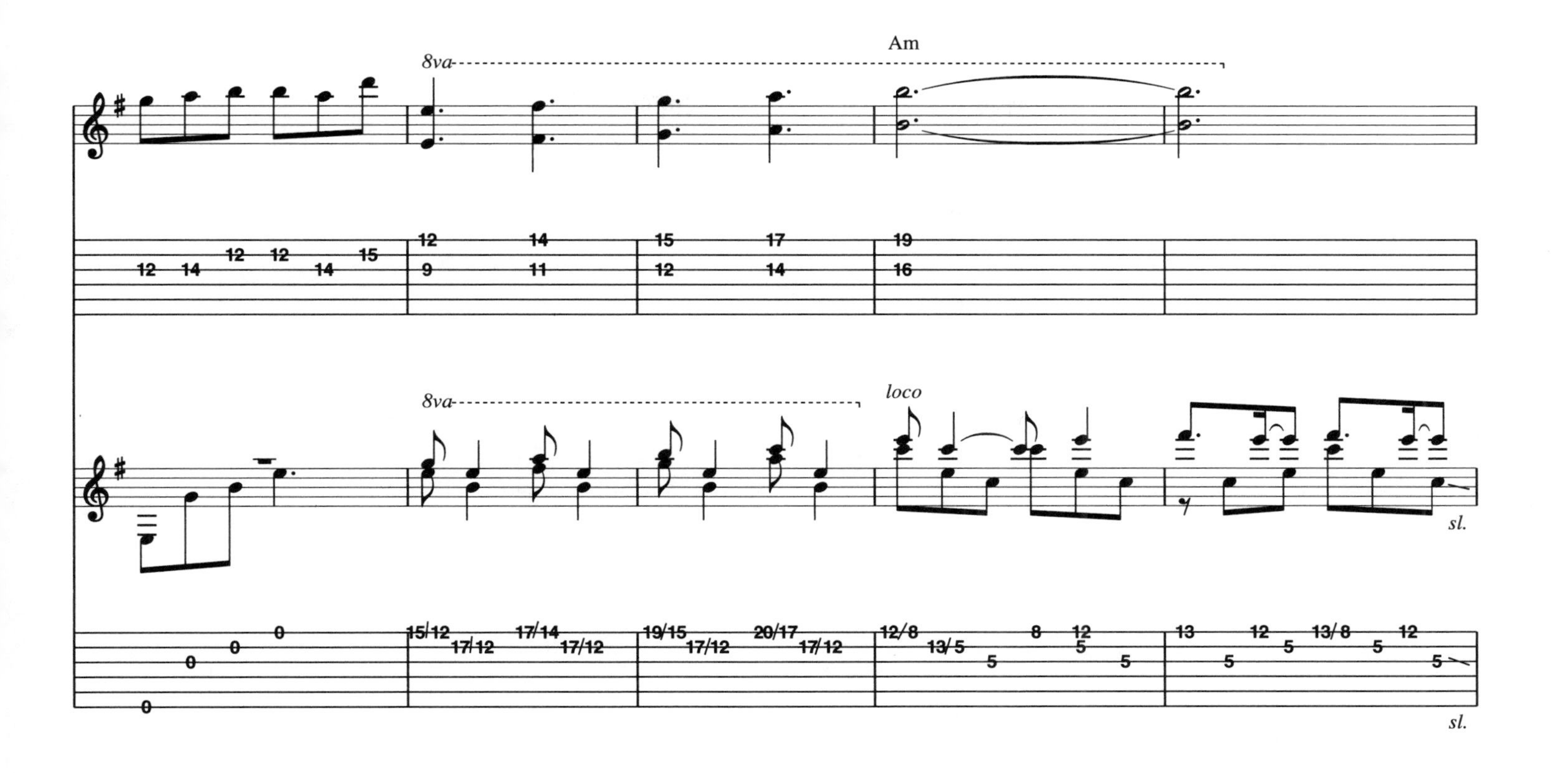
Am
8va
8va
loco
sl.
sl.

C
Dsus2
Em
N.C.
Gtr. II
loco
*
Gtr. I
Full
Full
Full
Full
Full
P
3
Gtr. III
*Vol. swell

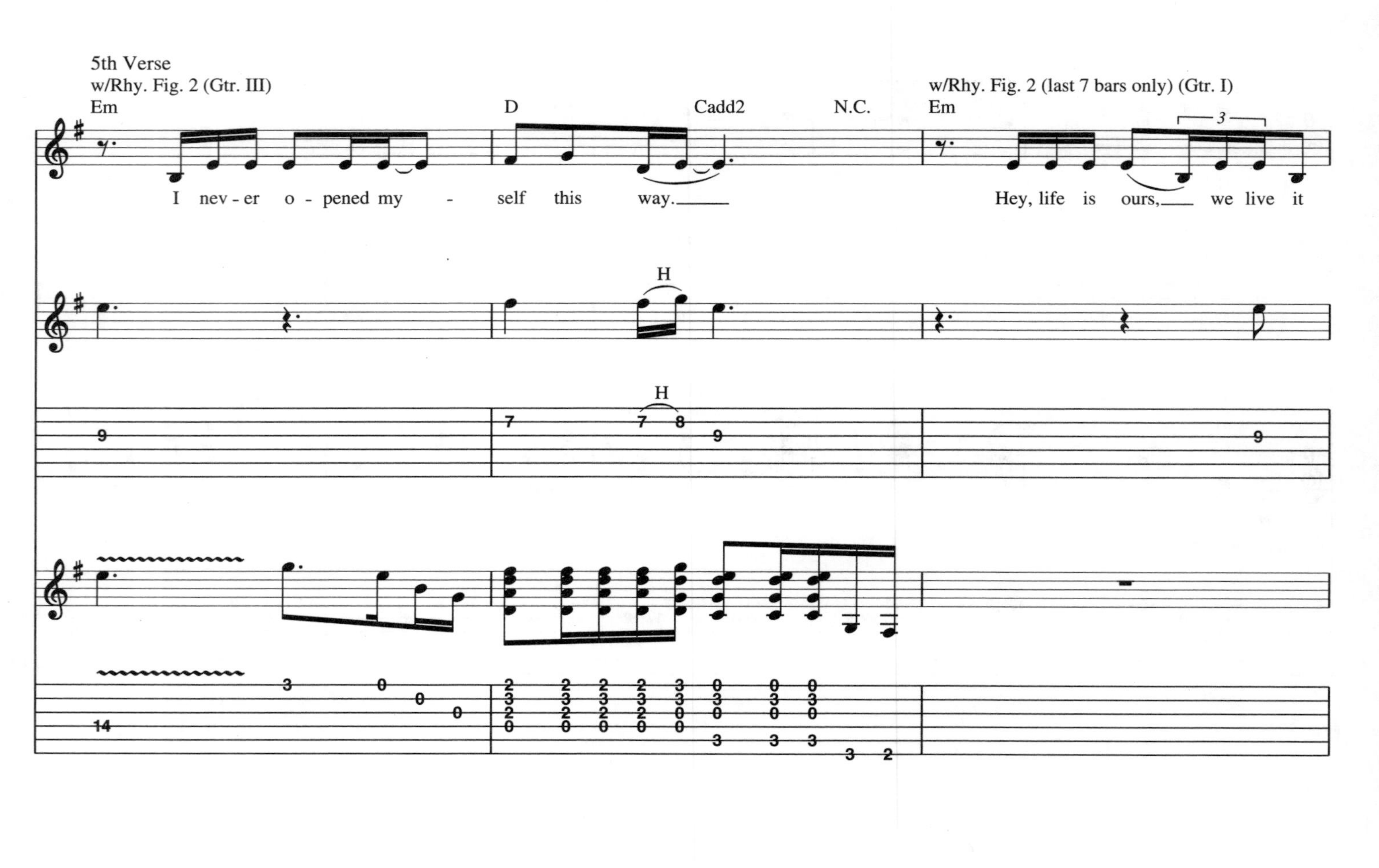
5th Verse
w/Rhy. Fig. 2 (Gtr. III)
Em
D
Cadd2
N.C.
w/Rhy. Fig. 2 (last 7 bars only) (Gtr. I)
Em
I nev - er o - pened my - self this way.
Hey, life is ours, we live it
H

D
Cadd2
N.C.
Em
D
Cadd2
our way.
All these words I don't just say.
Gtr. II
H

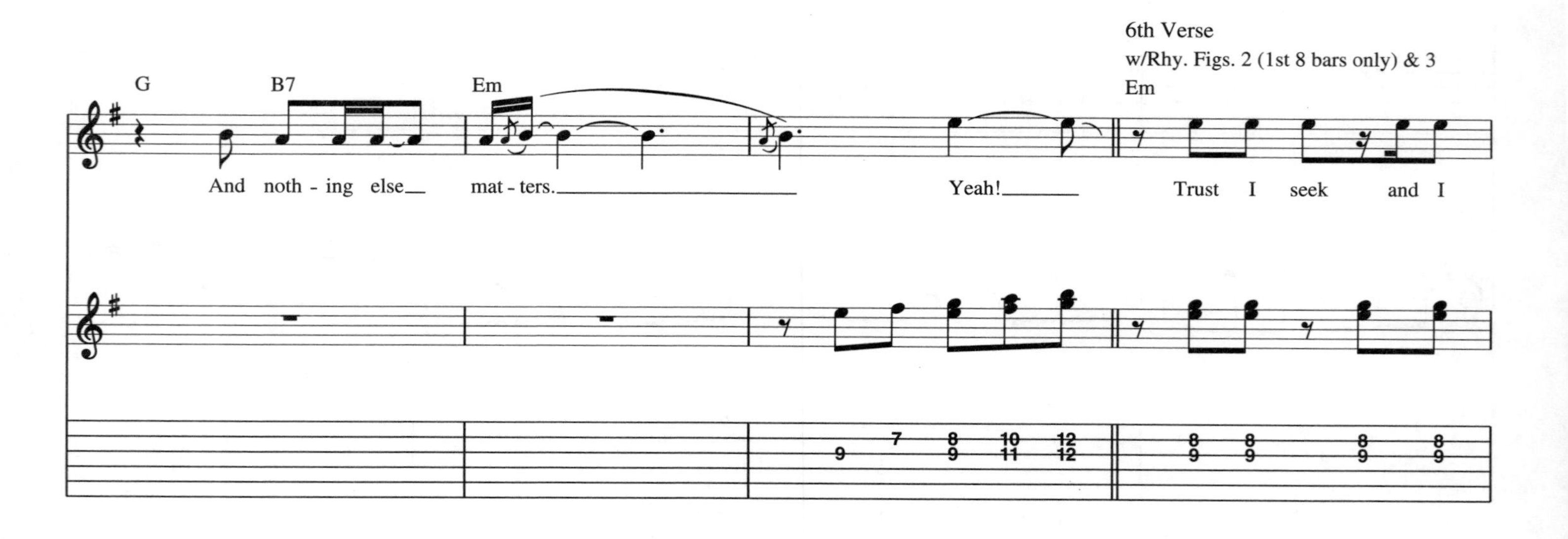
6th Verse
w/Rhy. Figs. 2 (1st 8 bars only) & 3
G
B7
Em
Em
And noth - ing else mat - ters.
Yeah!
Trust I seek and I

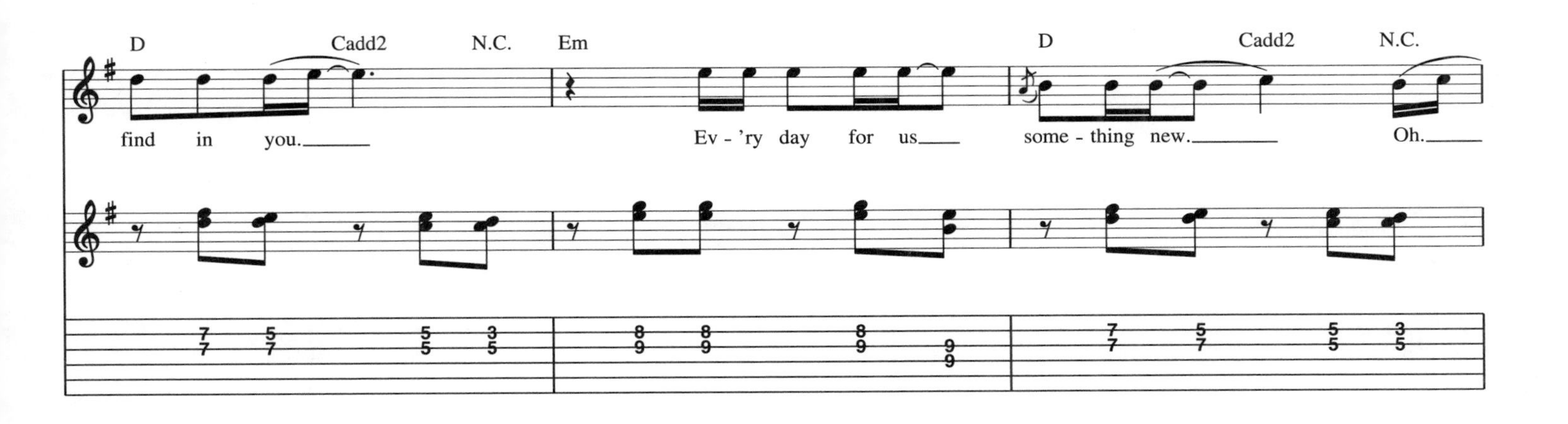
D Cadd2 N.C. Em D Cadd2 N.C.
find in you. Ev - 'ry day for us some - thing new. Oh.

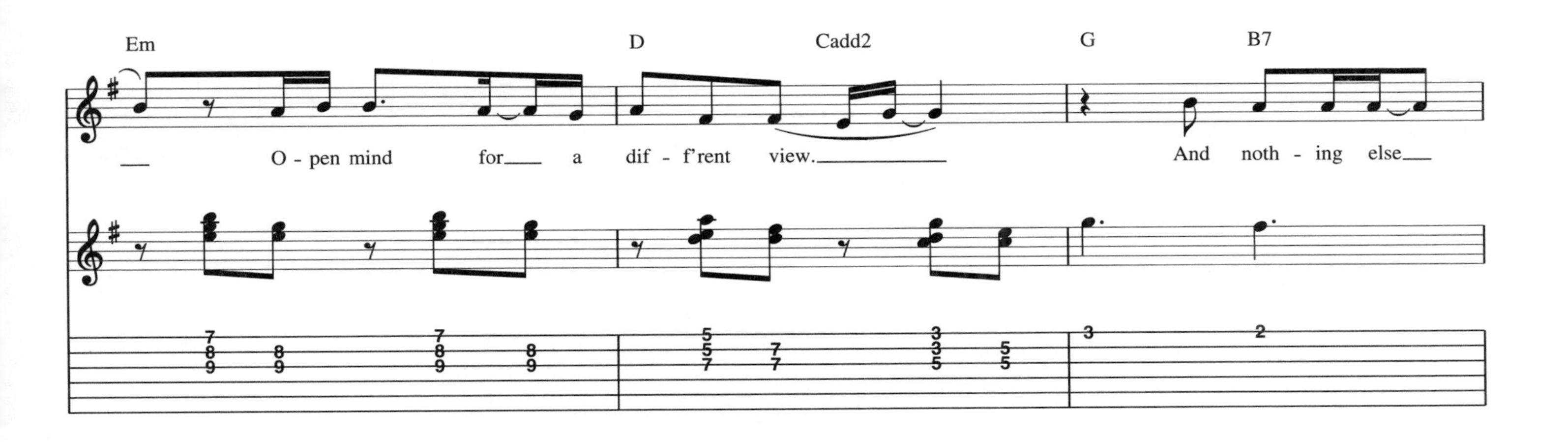
Em D Cadd2 G B7
O - pen mind for a dif - f'rent view. And noth - ing else

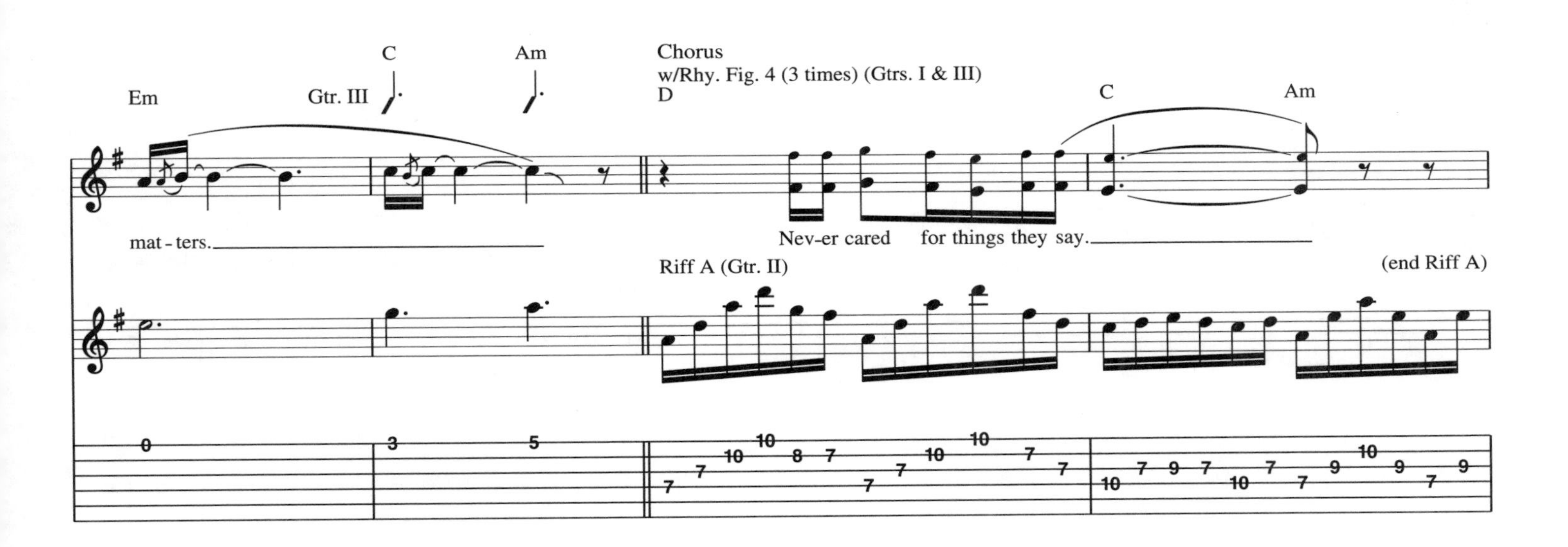
Em Gtr. III C Am
Chorus
w/Rhy. Fig. 4 (3 times) (Gtrs. I & III)
D C Am
mat - ters. Nev-er cared for things they say.
Riff A (Gtr. II)
(end Riff A)

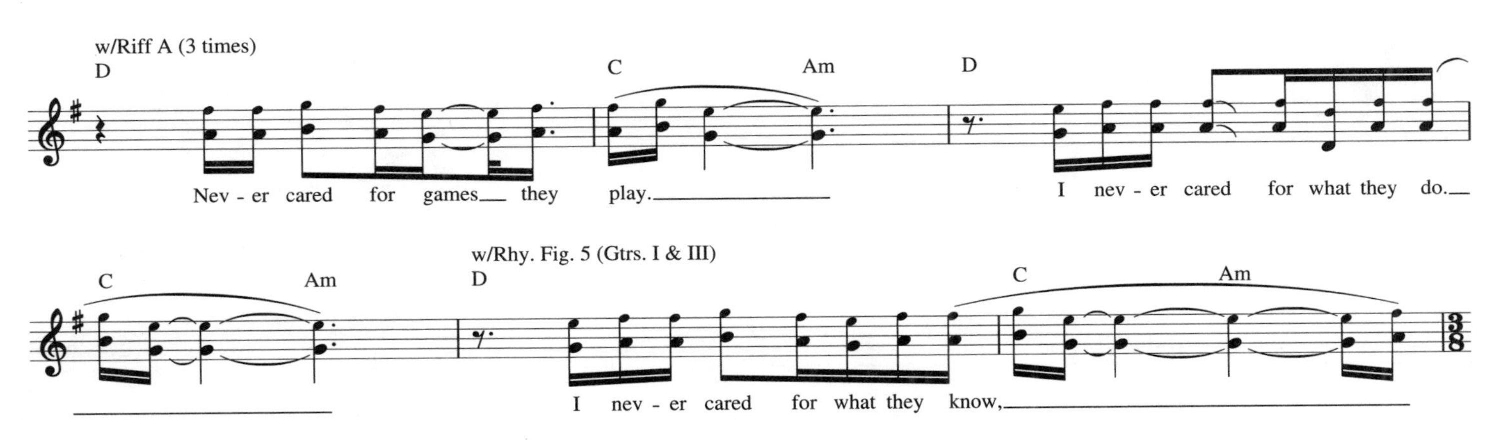
w/Riff A (3 times)
D C Am D
Nev - er cared for games they play. I nev - er cared for what they do.
C Am
w/Rhy. Fig. 5 (Gtrs. I & III)
D C Am
I nev - er cared for what they know,

Guitar solo
D
Em
E5
E5 VII
Gtr. I
oh, and I know.
Yeah, yeah, yeah!
Gtr. II
Gtr. III
Gtrs. I & III
(Gtr. I cont. in slashes)
P.M.
w/dist.
D5
C5
G
F#
P.M.
Full
sl.

D5
C5
G5
B5
E5
Full
P
Full
P
Full
Full
P
Full
P
Full
mf
dim.
Freely
(cont. in notation)
H
sl.
H
(Gtr. III out)
H
sl.
H
A tempo
Em
dim.
Outro
Em
p
Gtr. I
Rhy. Fig. 6
P
mp w/clean tone & fingers
P

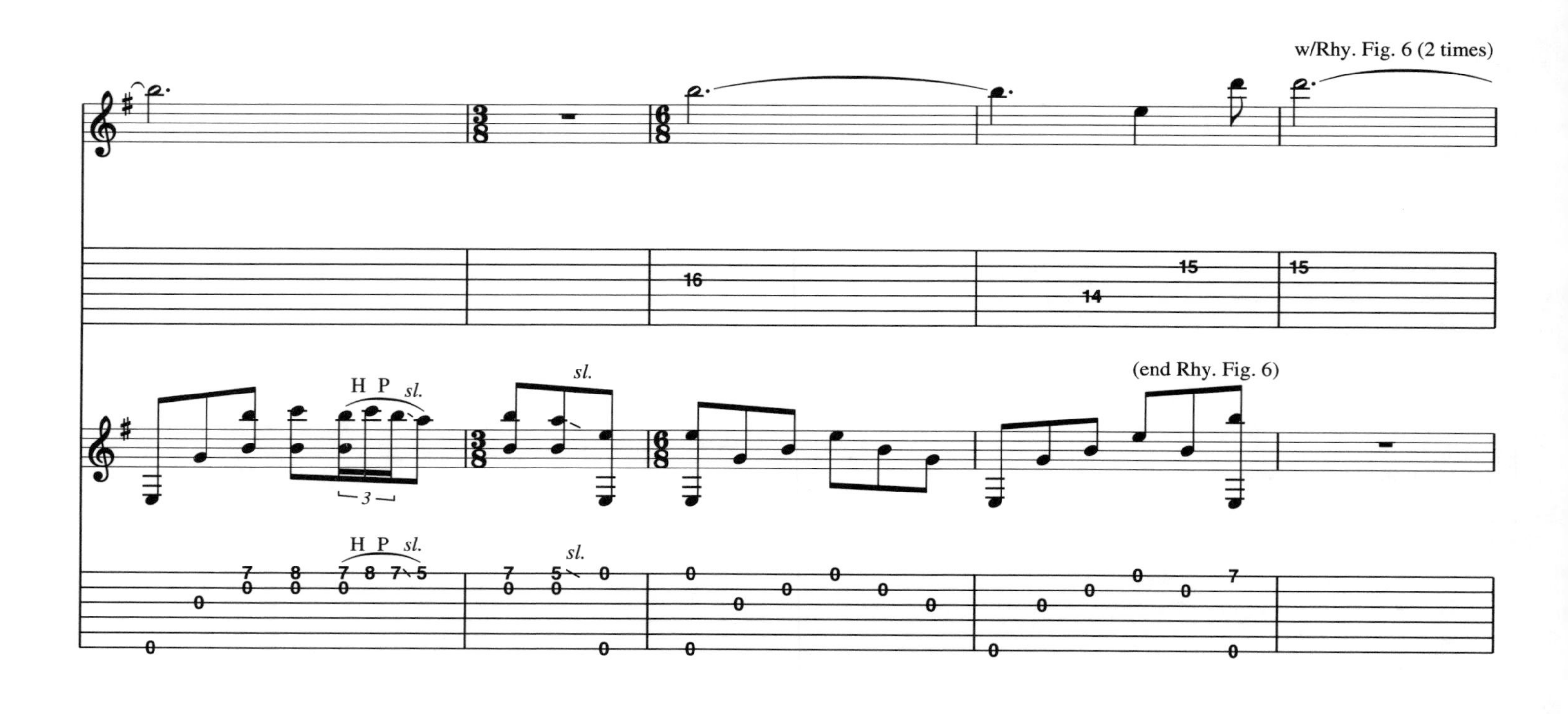
w/Rhy. Fig. 6 (2 times)
H P sl.
sl.
(end Rhy. Fig. 6)
H P sl.
sl.

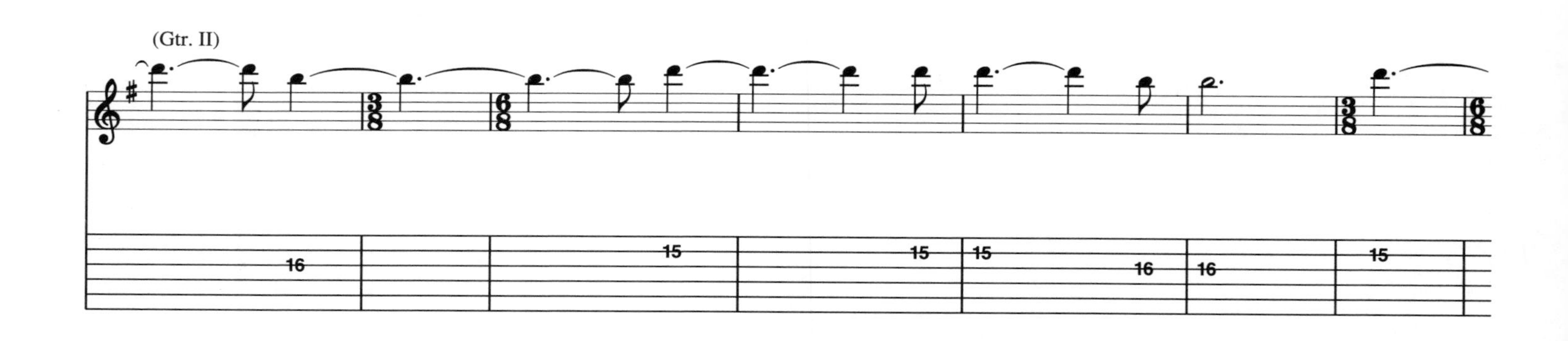
(Gtr. II)

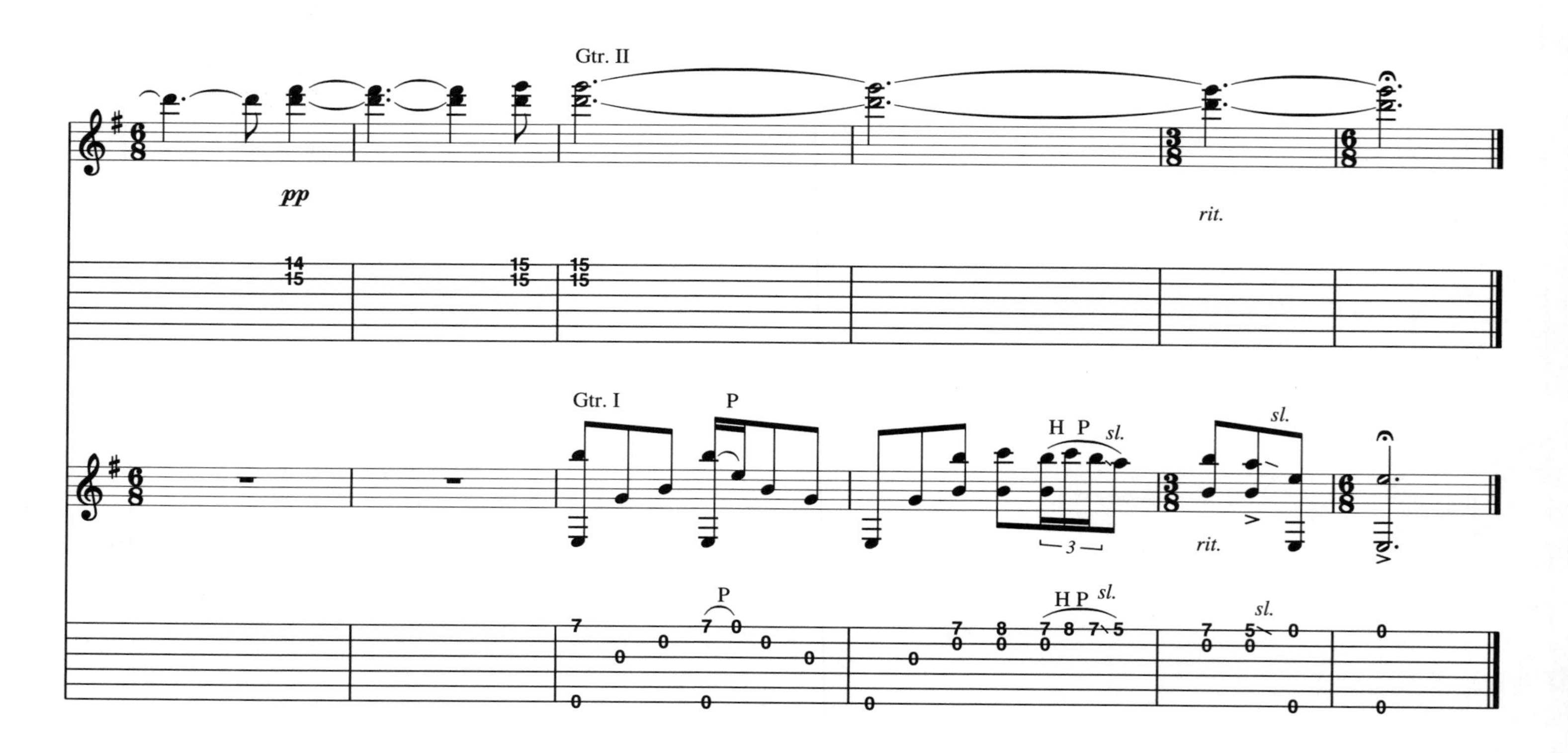
Gtr. II
pp
rit.
Gtr. I
P
H P sl.
sl.
rit.
P
H P sl.
sl.

UNTIL IT SLEEPS

Words and Music by
James Hetfield and Lars Ulrich

Chorus
Am
G
F
So tear_ me o - pen, pour me out.
There's things_ in - side_ that scream_ and shout._
sl.
15/17
12
14
15
13
12
14
Rhy. Fig. 2 (Gtr. II)
(end Rhy. Fig. 2)
P.M.
Rhy. Fig. 2A (Gtr. III)
(end Rhy. Fig. 2A)
w/Rhy. Figs. 2 & 2A (both 2 times)
And the pain_ still hates_ me,_
so hold_ me un - til_ it sleeps._
Gtr. I

A5
G
Rhy. Fig. 3 (Gtr. II)
clean tone
let ring
Rhy. Fig. 3A (Gtr. III)
dim.
clean tone
Fmaj7
2nd Verse
Am
Just like the curse, just like the stray.
(end Rhy. Fig. 3)
Rhy. Fill 1 (Gtr. II)
(end Rhy. Fill 1)
(end Rhy. Fig. 3A)
Rhy. Fill 1A (Gtr. III)
(end Rhy. Fill 1A)

w/Rhy. Fig. 1
N.C.
Am
You feed it once and now it stays,
Gtr. I
N.C.
now it stays.
Chorus
w/Rhy. Figs. 2 & 2A (both 3½ times)
Am
G
So tear me o -
F
Am
G
F
pen, but be - ware there's things in - side with - out a care.
Am
G
F
Am
G
And the dirt still stains me, so wash me

Bridge
F
E5 N.C.
E5 N.C.
un - til I'm clean. It grips you, so hold me.
Gtr. I
Rhy. Fill 2 (Gtr. II)
Rhy. Fig. 4
(end Rhy. Fig. 4)
P.M.
sl.
Rhy. Fill 2A (Gtr. III)
Rhy. Fig. 4A
(end Rhy. Fig. 4A)
w/Rhy. Figs. 4 (2½ times) & 4A (3 times)
E5 N.C
E5 N.C.
E5 N.C.
It stains you, so hold me.
It hates you, so hold me.
Gtr. I

w/Rhy. Fill 3
E5 N.C.
E5 N.C.
E5 N.C.
It holds you, so hold me until it sleeps.
w/Rhy. Figs. 3 & 3A
A5
G
Fmaj7
(Until it sleeps). Until it sleeps. (Until it sleeps).
3rd Verse
w/Rhy. Fills 1 & 1A
Am
w/Rhy. Fig. 1
N.C.
So tell me why you've chosen me.
Am
N.C.
Don't want your grip, don't want your greed.
I don't want it.
Rhy. Fill 3 (Gtr. II)
P.M.
P.M.

Chorus
w/Rhy. Figs. 2 & 2A (both 3½ times)
Am G F Am G F
So tear_ me o - pen,_ make you gone. No long - er will you_ hurt an - y - one._
8va
loco
Am G F Am G F
w/Rhy. Fills 2 & 2A
_ And the pain_ still shakes_ me,_ so hold_ me un - til_ it sleeps._
*Gtr. IV
Gtr. I
*Orchestra arr. for gtr.
Bridge
w/Rhy. Figs. 4 & 4A (both 3½ times)
E5 N.C. E5 N.C. E5 N.C. E5 N.C.
_ It grips_ you, so_ hold me._ It stains_ you, so_ hold me._ Ooh yeah._
(Gtr. IV out) Gtr. I
E5 N.C. E5 N.C. E5 N.C.
It hates_ you, so_ hold me._ It holds_ you, holds_ you, holds_

Guitar solo
E5
Am
you until it sleeps. (Until it sleeps.
Until it sleeps.
Until it sleeps).
Gtr. I
Gtr. III
Gtr. II
8va
loco
H
sl.
P
Full
P.M.
w/wah as filter
clean tone
let ring

8va
sl.
P
Full
Full
H
let ring
Cmaj7
I don't want it, no.
loco
sl.
1/2
trem. bar
let ring

C
Am
I don't want__ it, want__ it, want__ it, want__ it, want__ it, no.
H
H
sl.
sl.
sl.
* trem. bar
8va
loco
(wah off)
let ring
(dist. on)
*Depress bar before striking notes.
Chorus
w/Rhy. Figs. 2 & 2A (both 4 times)
Am G F Am G F
So tear__ me o - pen, but be-ware there's things__ in - side__ with - out__ a care.__
Gtr. I
Am G F Am G F
And the dirt__ still stains_ me, so wash_ me till I'm clean,_ ah.
8va

w/Rhy. Fig. 2A (4 times) (Gtrs. II & III)
A5
D5/A
F/A
A5
D5/A
F/A
I'll tear me o - pen, I'll make you gone.
No long - er will you hurt an - y - one.
8va
loco
A5
D5/A
F/A
A5
D5/A
F/A
And the pain still shakes me,
so hold me un - til it sleeps.
Outro
A5
(Un - til it sleeps.) Un - til it sleeps.
Un - til it
8va
clean tone
let ring
H
H
Gtr. III
(Gtr. III out)
dim.

Am
sh - sh - sh - sh - sh...
Un-til it sleeps.
Gtr. I
8va
rit.
Gtr. II
rit.

Free time

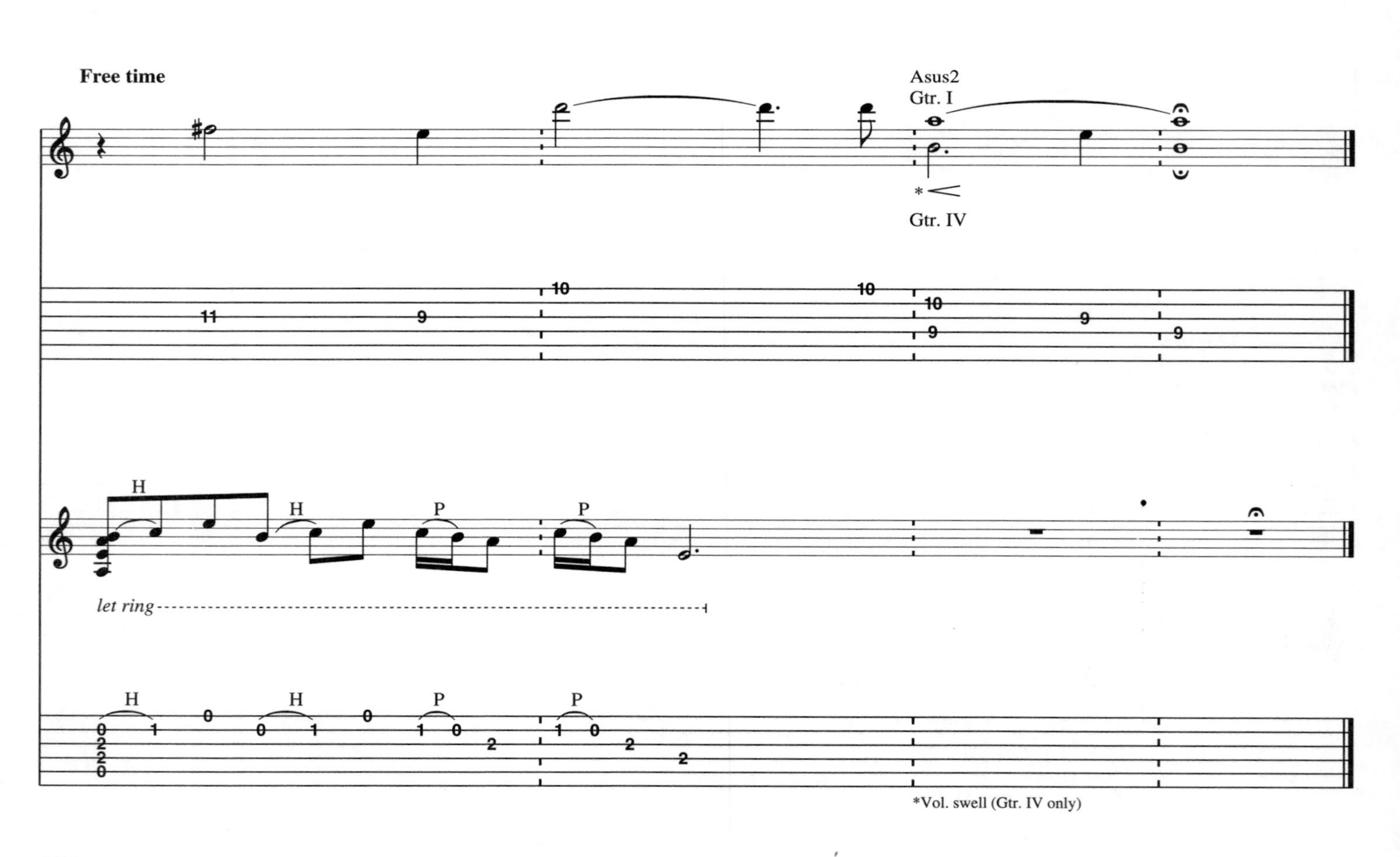
Asus2
Gtr. I
Gtr. IV
H
H
P
P
let ring
*Vol. swell (Gtr. IV only)

HUMAN

Words and Music by
James Hetfield and Lars Ulrich

N.C.
D5
8va
N.C.
w/Rhy. Fig. 2 (Gtr. II)
D5
P
(end Rhy. Fig. 2)
Rhy. Fig. 2A (Gtr. III)
H
N.C.
D5
N.C.
D5
sl.
1st Verse
D5
F5
Don't you leave me, Fa - ther Time.
mp
(end Rhy. Fig. 2A)
Rhy. Fig. 3 (Gtrs. II & III)

G5
D5
N.C.
D5
Take me with you.
Tell me, does your sun
8va
loco
sl.
P
mf
mp
H
F5
G5
A5
still shine?
Come squeeze the world and drip it down my throat a - gain,
(end Rhy. Fig. 3)
P.M.
P.M.

w/Rhy. Fig. 2
D5
N.C.
D5
N.C.
uh.
Down my throat a -
(Gtr. I)
f

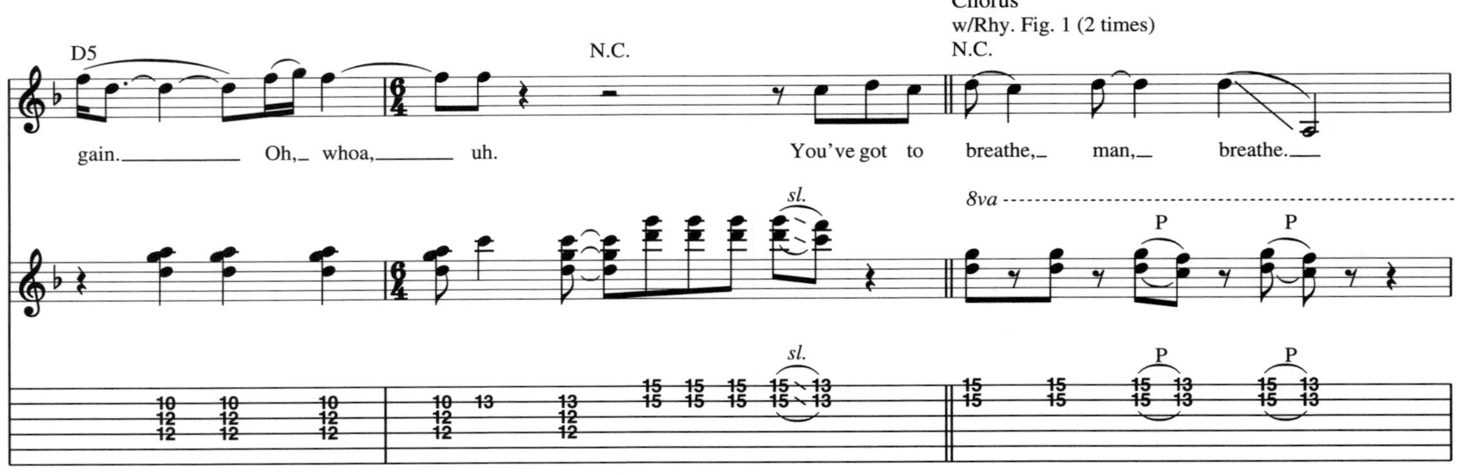
Chorus
w/Rhy. Fig. 1 (2 times)
D5
N.C.
N.C.
gain. Oh, whoa, uh.
You've got to breathe, man, breathe.
8va
sl.
P
P

F5
N.C.
F5
Breathe, man, breathe.
(Com-in' up for air.
Com-in' up for...)
8va
H
P
H

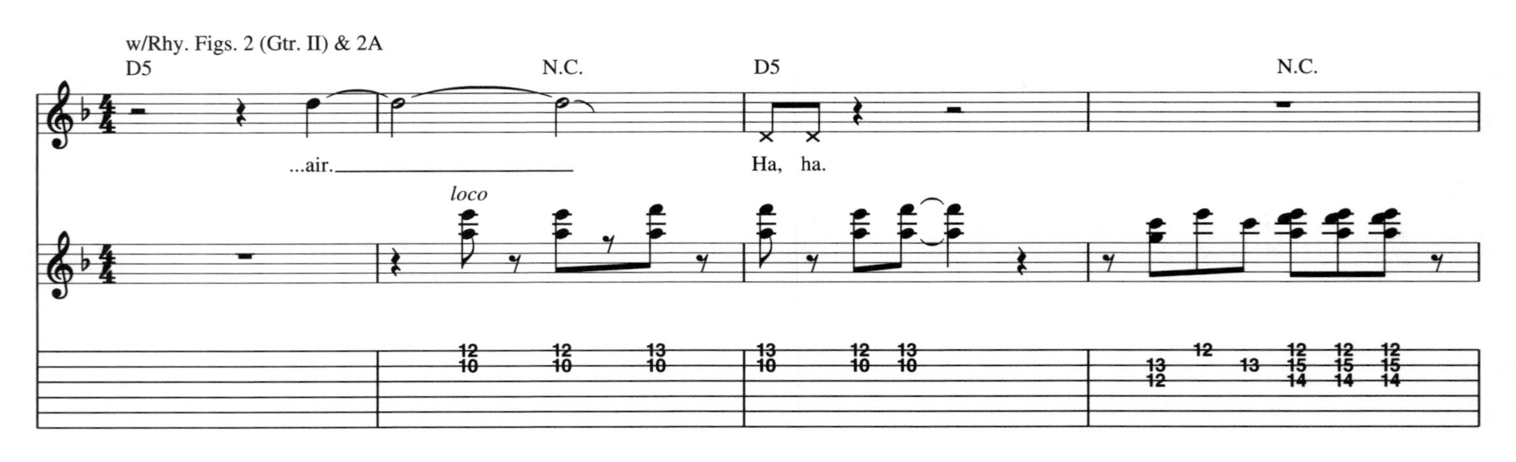
w/Rhy. Figs. 2 (Gtr. II) & 2A
D5
N.C.
D5
N.C.
...air.
Ha, ha.
loco

D5
N.C.
2nd Verse
w/Rhy. Fig. 3
D5
F5
Touch me so I think I'm here.
H
mf

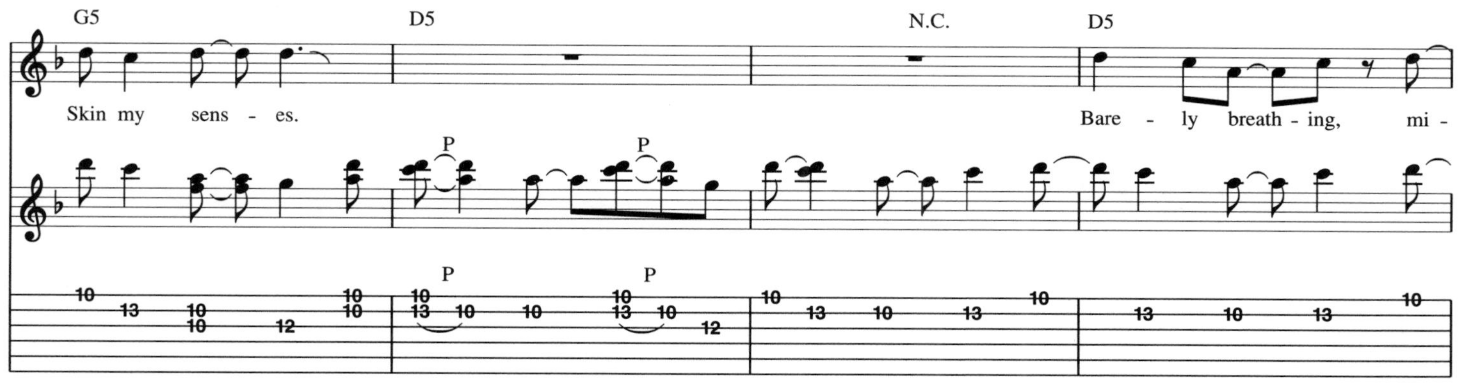
G5
D5
N.C.
D5
Skin my sens - es.
Bare - ly breath - ing, mi -
P

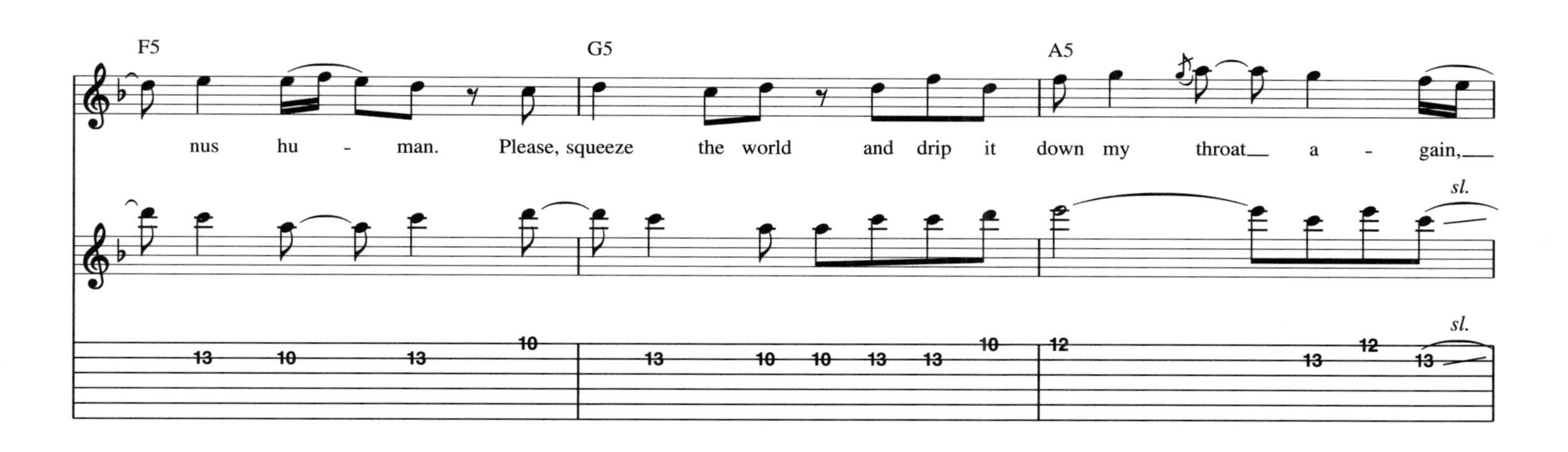
F5
G5
A5
nus hu - man. Please, squeeze the world and drip it down my throat a - gain,
sl.

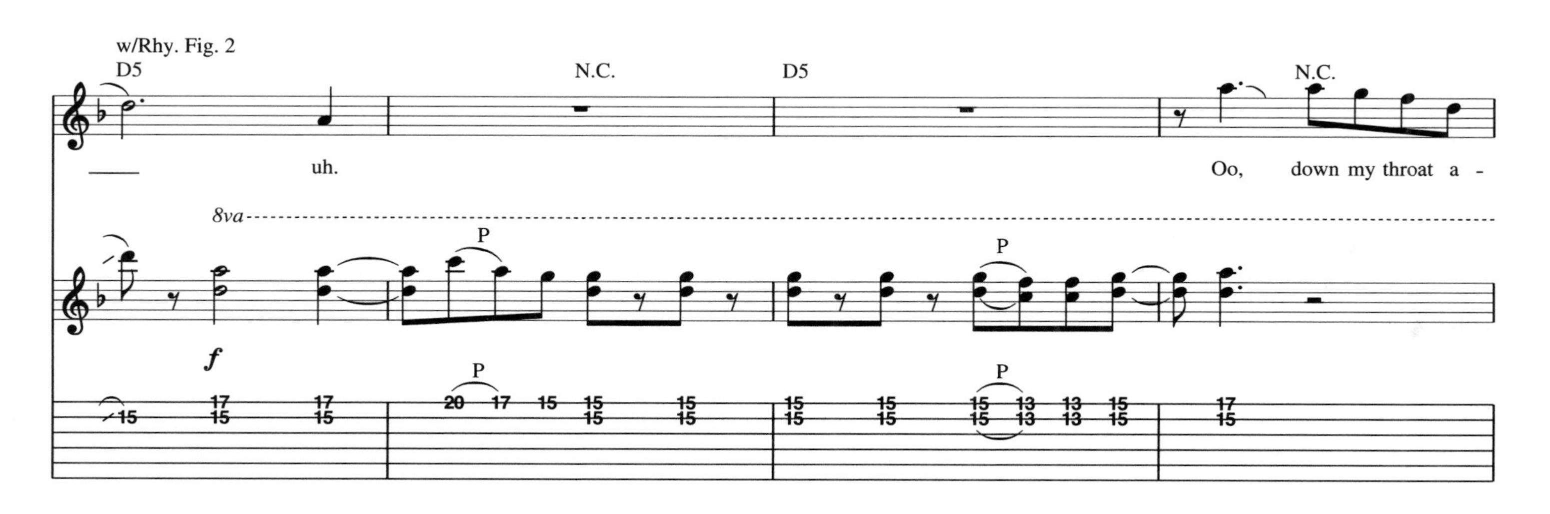
w/Rhy. Fig. 2
D5
N.C.
D5
N.C.
uh.
Oo, down my throat a -
8va
P
f

Chorus
w/Rhy. Fig. 1 (2 times)
D5
N.C.
N.C.
gain. Oh, whoa, whoa.
You've got to breathe, man, breathe.
loco
H
H

F5
N.C.
F5
Breathe, man, breathe.
(Com-in' up for air.
Com-in' up for...)
(Gtr. I out)

Half time feel
Guitar solo
D5
Gtr. II
...air.
Gtr. III
Harm.
(8va)
w/wah
1/2
Harm.
(8va)
Harm.
Harm.

trem. pick
Full
Gtr. I
trem. pick
A
7fr.
sl.
(end half time feel)
You've got to
(cont. in Rhy. Fill 1)
Full

Outro-Chorus
w/Rhy. Fig. 1
Gtr. III substitute Rhy. Fill 1
N.C.
F5
breathe, man, breathe.
(Com - in' up for
8va
Gtr. I

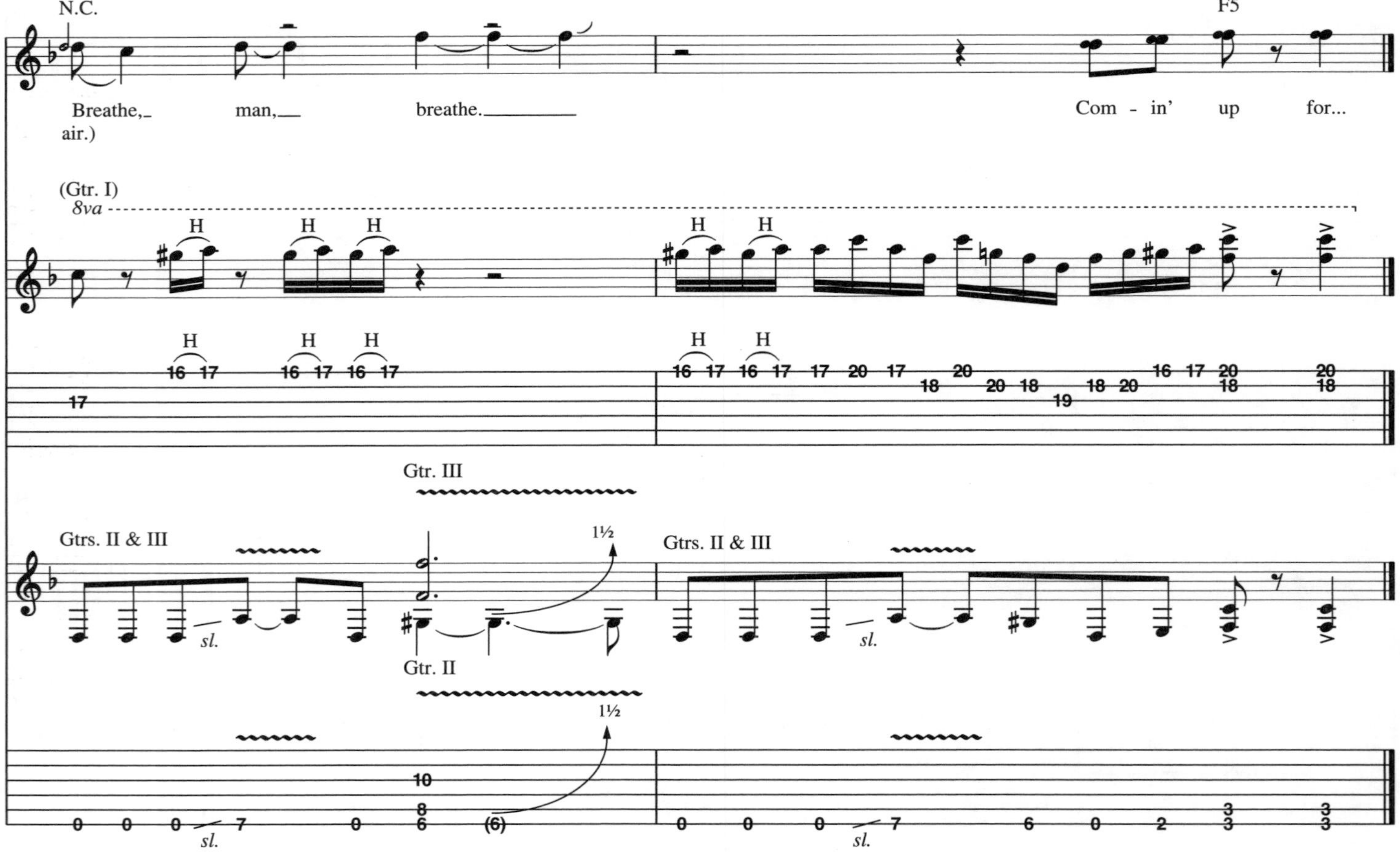
N.C.
F5
Breathe, man, breathe.
air.)
Com - in' up for...
(Gtr. I)
8va
Gtr. III
Gtrs. II & III
Gtr. II
sl.

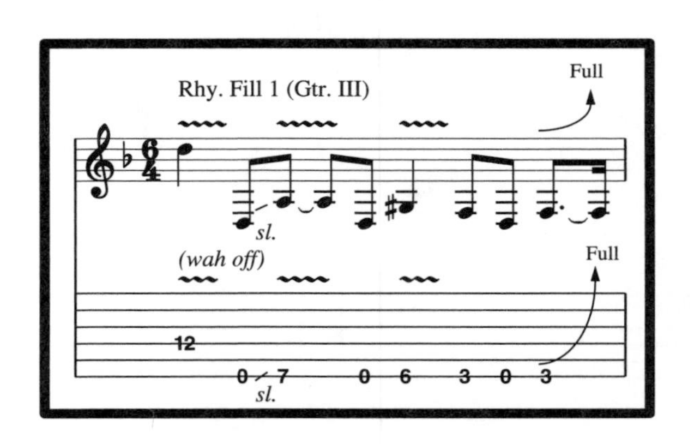
Rhy. Fill 1 (Gtr. III)
Full
(wah off)
sl.

THE OUTLAW TORN

Words and Music by
James Hetfield and Lars Ulrich

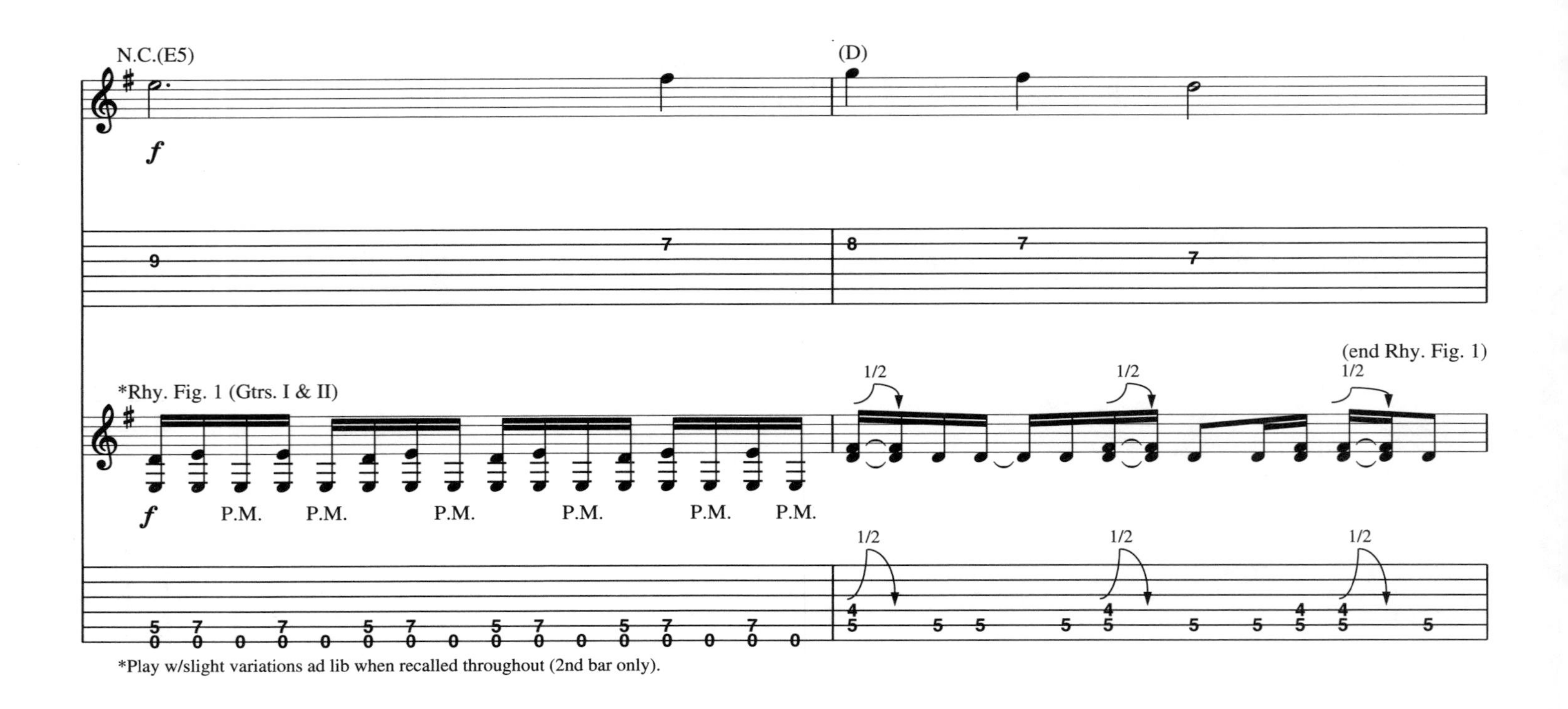
N.C.(E5)
(D)
f
*Rhy. Fig. 1 (Gtrs. I & II)
(end Rhy. Fig. 1)
1/2
P.M.
*Play w/slight variations ad lib when recalled throughout (2nd bar only).

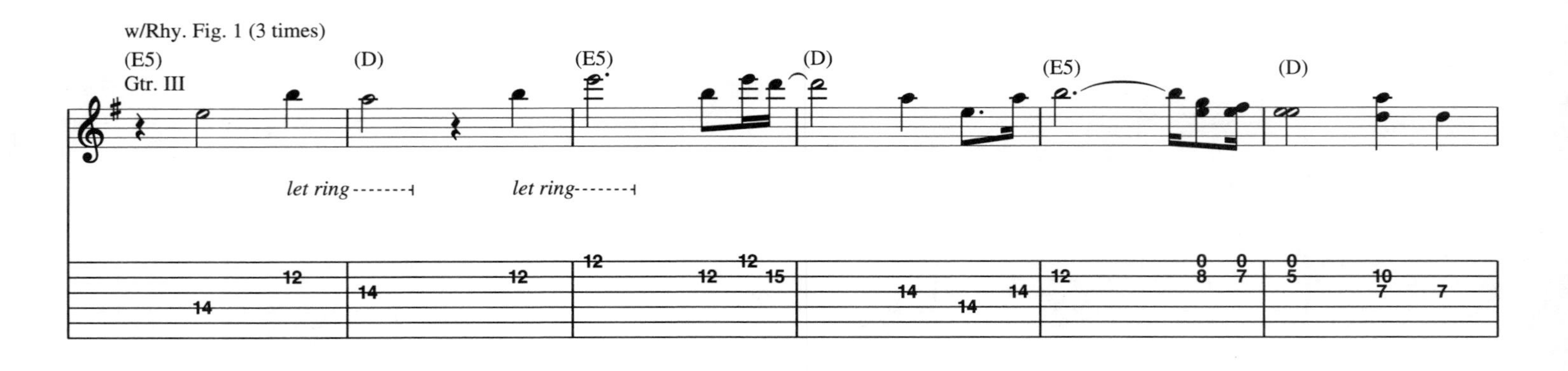
w/Rhy. Fig. 1 (3 times)
(E5)
(D)
Gtr. III
let ring
let ring

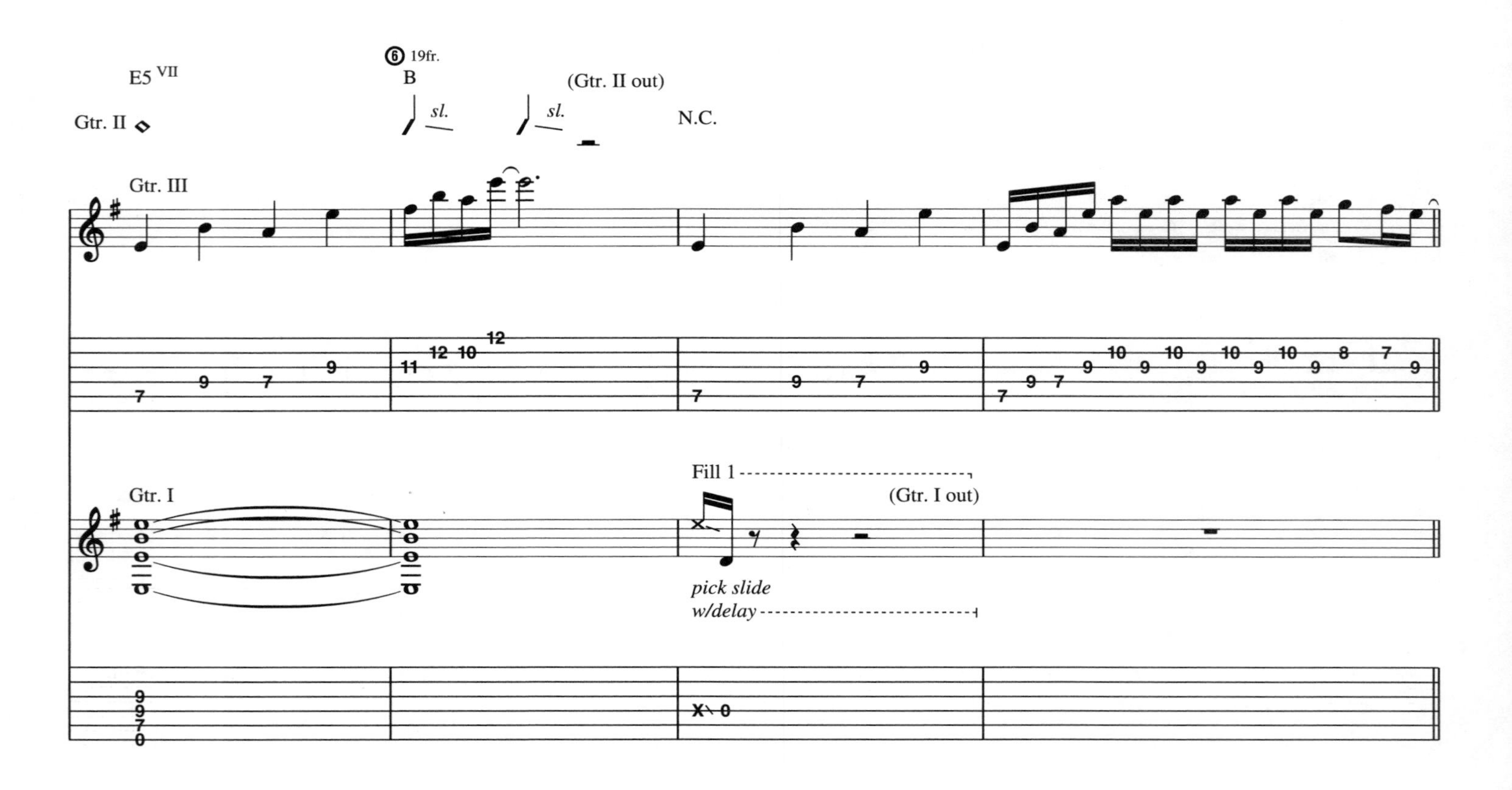
E5 VII
Gtr. II
19fr.
B
sl.
sl.
(Gtr. II out)
N.C.
Gtr. III
Gtr. I
Fill 1
(Gtr. I out)
pick slide
w/delay

1st Verse
*N.C.(E5)
And now I wait my whole life - time for you.
*Chords implied by bass when gtrs. are tacet (throughout).
And now I wait my whole life - time for
D5 E5VII
Gtrs. I & II
you.
**Gtr. IV
Gtr. III
(Gtr. IV out) Gtr. III
w/Fill 1 (Gtr. I)
⑥ 12fr.
E
Gtr. II
sl.
(Gtrs. I & II out)
**Orchestra arr. for gtr.
N.C.(E5)
I ride the dirt, I ride the tide for you.
Gtr. IV
Gtr. III

I search the out - side, search_ in - side
for
*Gtr. IV to left of slashes in TAB.

D5 B5
Gtrs. I & II
(Gtrs. I & II out)
you to take back what you_ left me.
You know I'll al - ways burn_ to be_
P.M.

N.C.(A5)
the one who seeks so I_ may_ find.
So on I wait my whole_ life - time.
(Gtr. IV out)
*P.M.
*P.M. refers to Gtr. III only.

Chorus
w/Rhy. Fig. 1 (4 times)
N.C.(E5)
(D)
(E5)
Out - law of torn.
Gtr. III
(D)
(E5)
(D)
Out - law of torn.
Out - law of
(E5)
(D)
E5 VII
Gtrs. I & II
(Gtr. II out)
torn.
And I'm torn.
mf
w/Fill 1
N.C.
(Gtr. I out)
2nd Verse
N.C.(E5)
So on I wait my whole life - time
mp

for you.
So on I wait my whole life - time
mp
*Vol. swell
(Gtr. II out)
22fr.
D5 E5 VII
D
Gtr. II
sl.
D5E5
f
for you.
(w/delay repeats)
Gtr. III
Gtr. I
(Gtr. I out)
1/2 1/2 1/2 1/2
w/delay
**Vol. swell
N.C.(E5)
The more I search, the more my need for you.
(Gtr. III)

The more I bless, the more I bleed for
D5 B5
Gtrs. I & II
⑤ open
A B5
you. You make me smash the clock and feel. I'd rath - er die be - hind the wheel.
A5
⑥ 3fr.
G A5
Time was nev - er on my side, so on I wait my whole life - time.

Chorus
w/Rhy. Fig. 1 (2 times)
N.C.(E5)
(D)
(E5)
(D)
Out - law of torn.
Out - law...

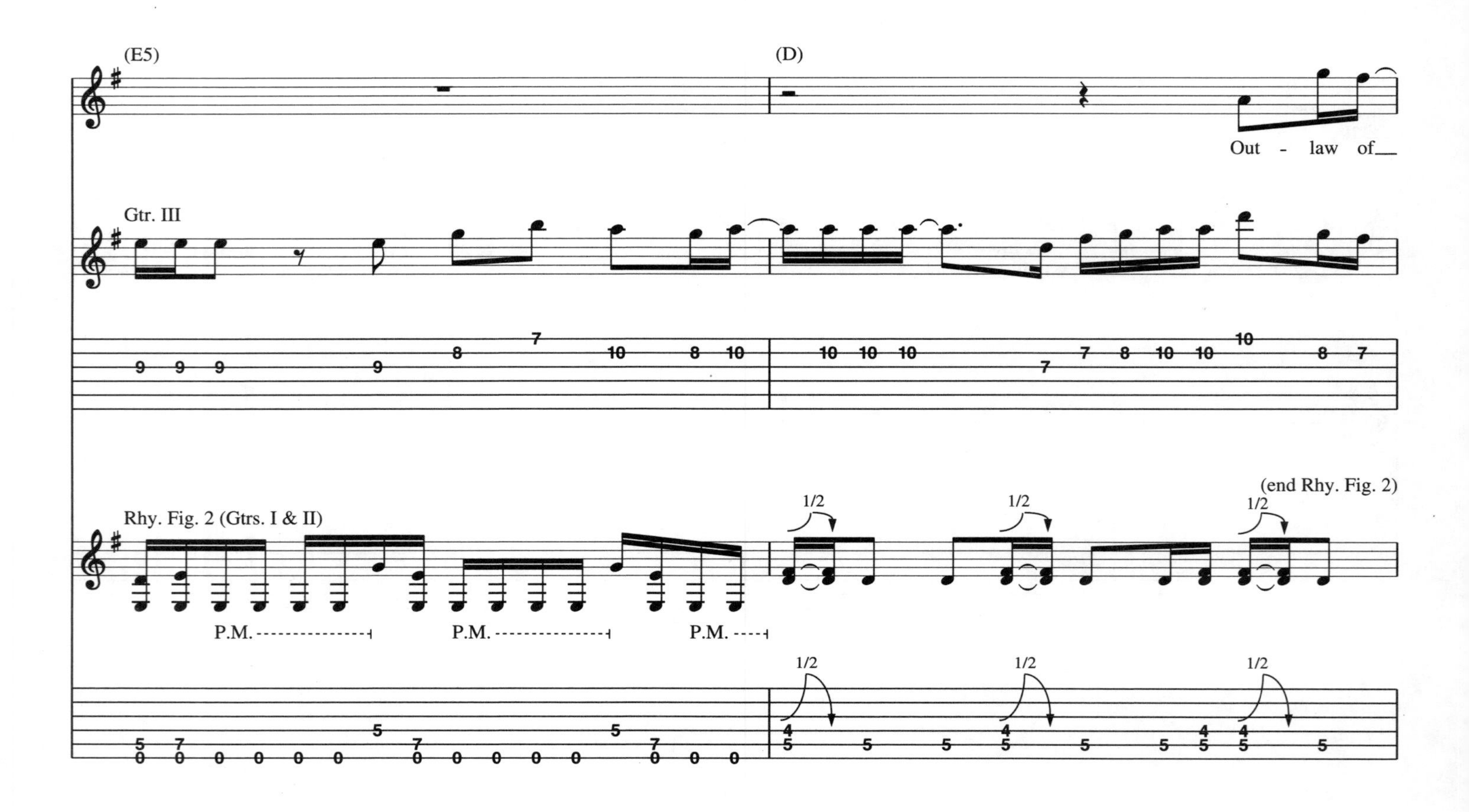
(E5)
(D)
Out - law of
Gtr. III
Rhy. Fig. 2 (Gtrs. I & II)
(end Rhy. Fig. 2)
1/2
P.M.

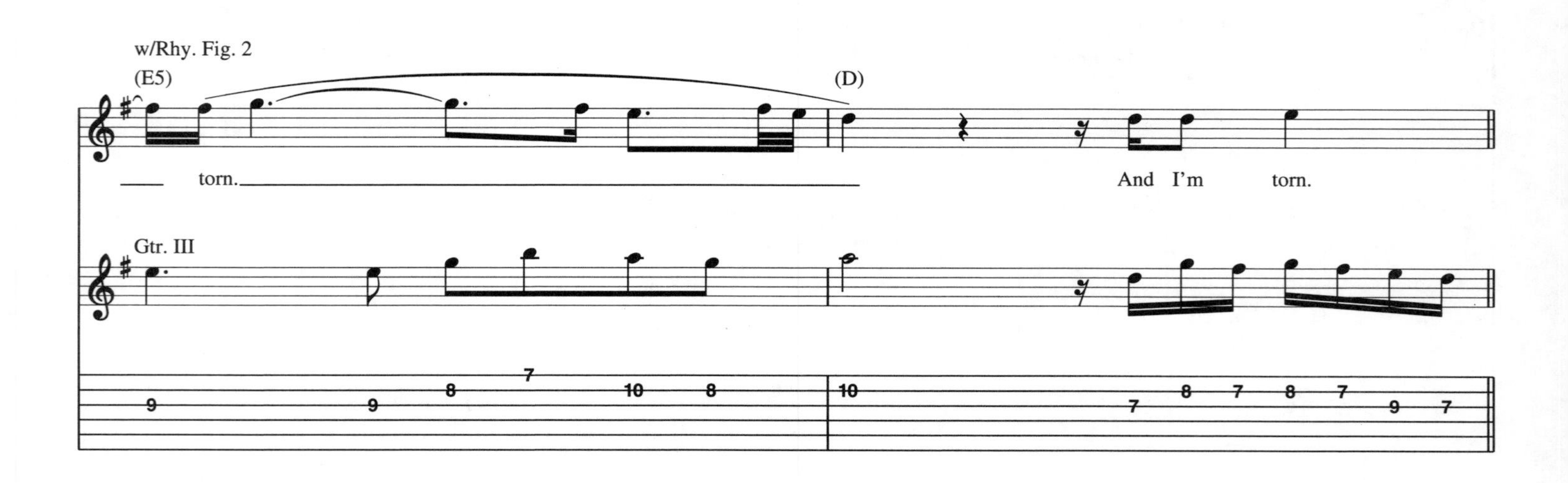
w/Rhy. Fig. 2
(E5)
(D)
torn.
And I'm torn.
Gtr. III

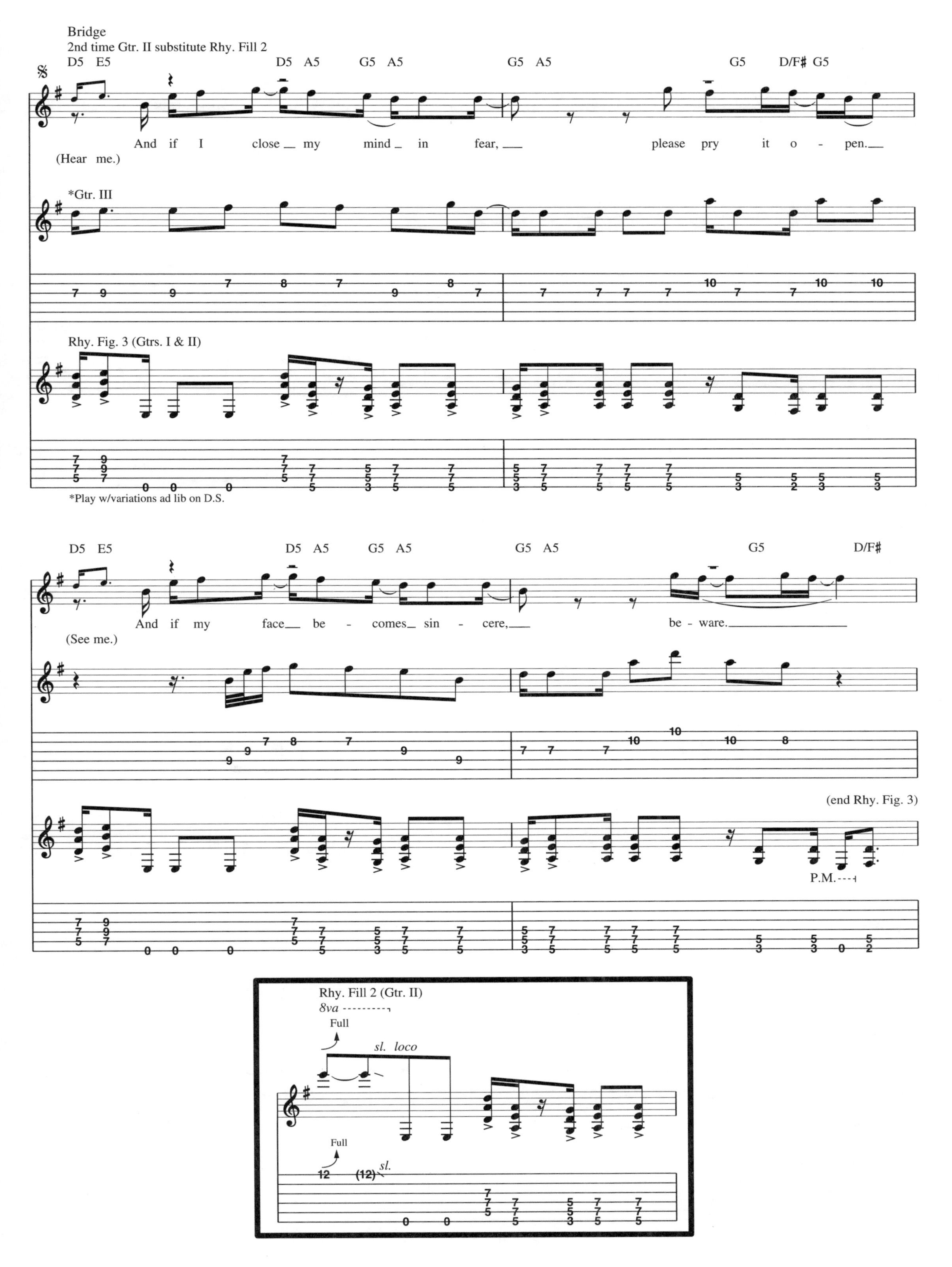
Bridge
2nd time Gtr. II substitute Rhy. Fill 2
D5 E5
D5 A5
G5 A5
G5 A5
G5
D/F♯ G5
And if I close my mind in fear, please pry it o - pen.
(Hear me.)
*Gtr. III
Rhy. Fig. 3 (Gtrs. I & II)
*Play w/variations ad lib on D.S.
D5 E5
D5 A5
G5 A5
G5 A5
G5
D/F♯
And if my face be - comes sin - cere, be - ware.
(See me.)
(end Rhy. Fig. 3)
P.M.
Rhy. Fill 2 (Gtr. II)
8va
Full
sl. loco
Full
sl.

w/Rhy. Fig. 3
D5 E5
D5 A5 G5 A5
G5 A5
G5 D/F♯ G5
And if I start to come un - done, stitch me to - geth - er.
(Hold me.)
Gtr. III
D5 E5
D5 A5 G5 A5
G5 A5
G5 D/F♯
To Coda
And if you see me strut, re - mind me of what left this out - law torn.
(Save me.)
⑥ open
E
Rhy. Fill 1 (Gtrs. I & II)
(end Rhy. Fill 1)
(Gtr. II out)
w/Fill 1
N.C.
(Gtr. I out)
Interlude
N.C.(E5)
Gtr. III
Gtr. I
Full
mp
sim.
w/delay
sl.
*Vol. swell

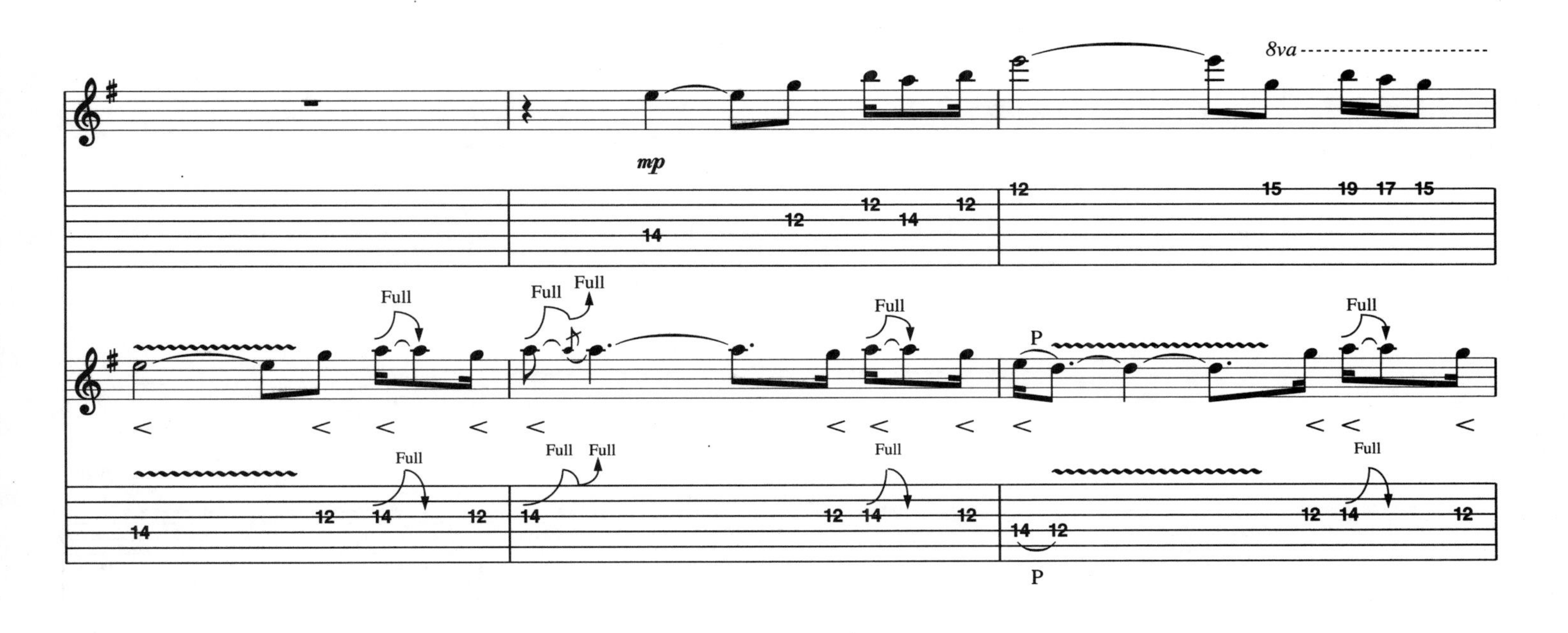
8va
mp
Full
Full Full
Full
P
Full
P

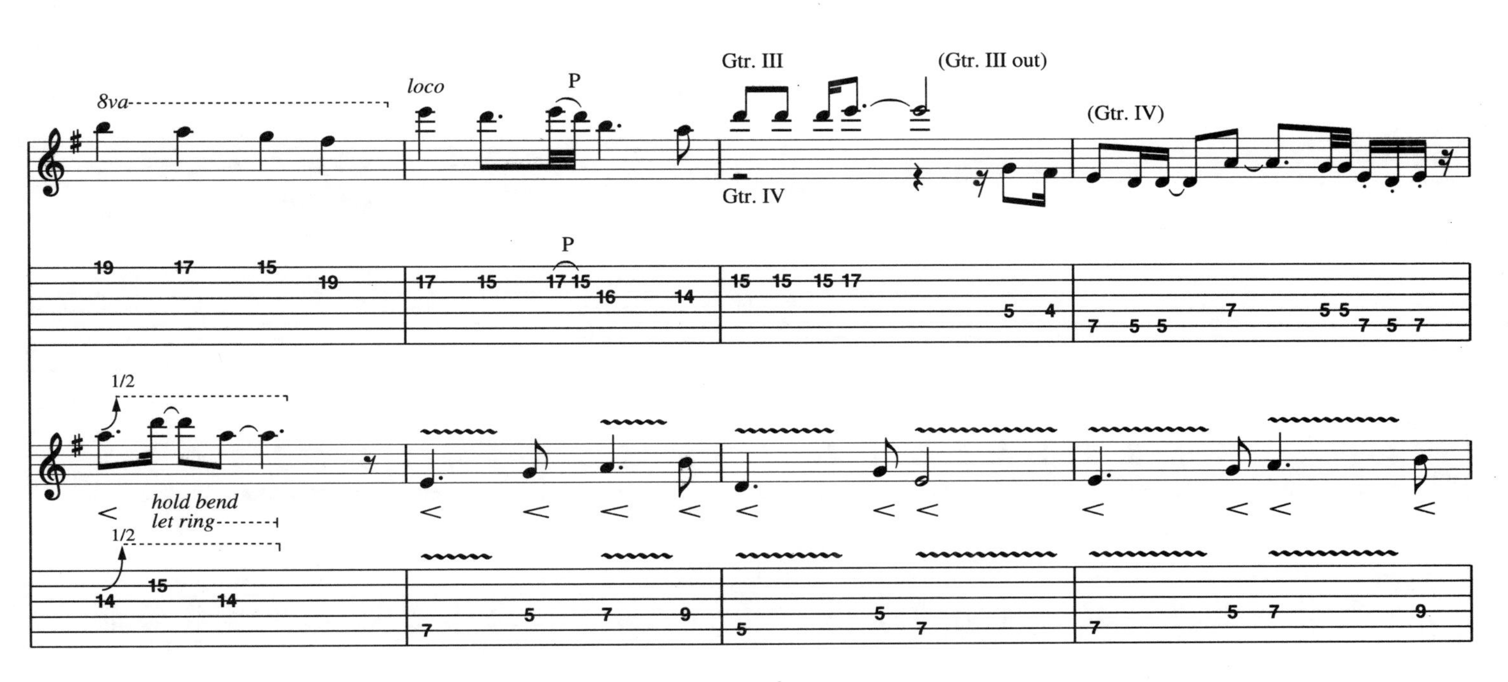
8va
loco
P
Gtr. III
(Gtr. III out)
Gtr. IV
(Gtr. IV)
1/2
hold bend
let ring

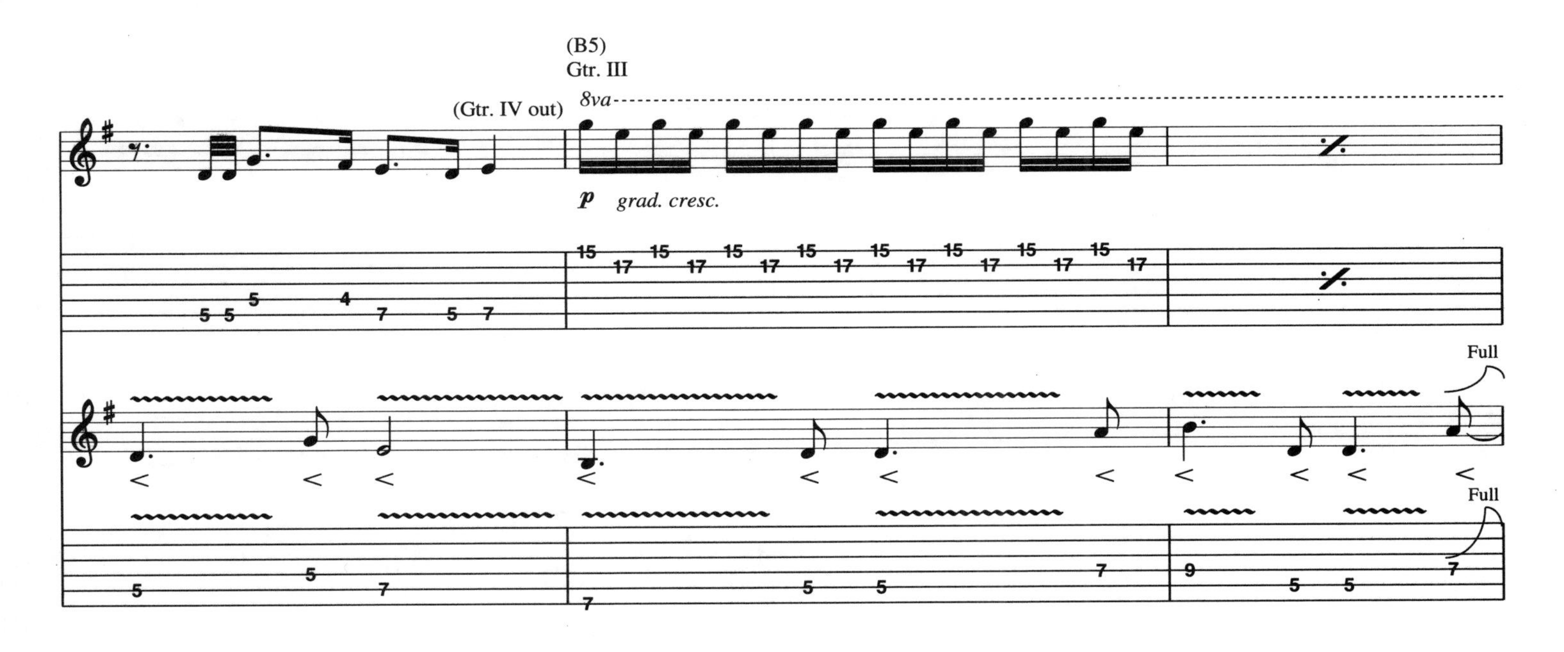
(B5)
Gtr. III
(Gtr. IV out)
8va
p grad. cresc.
Full

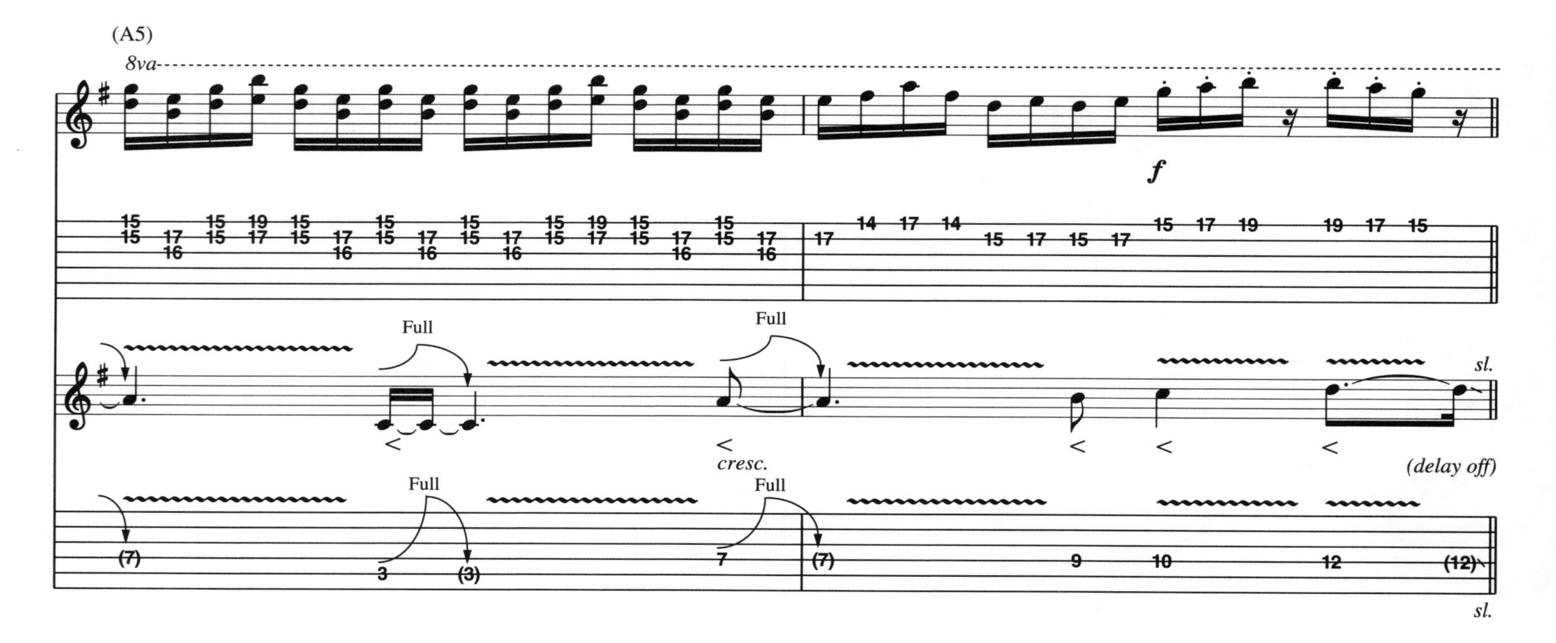
(A5)
8va
f
Full
Full
cresc.
sl.
(delay off)
sl.

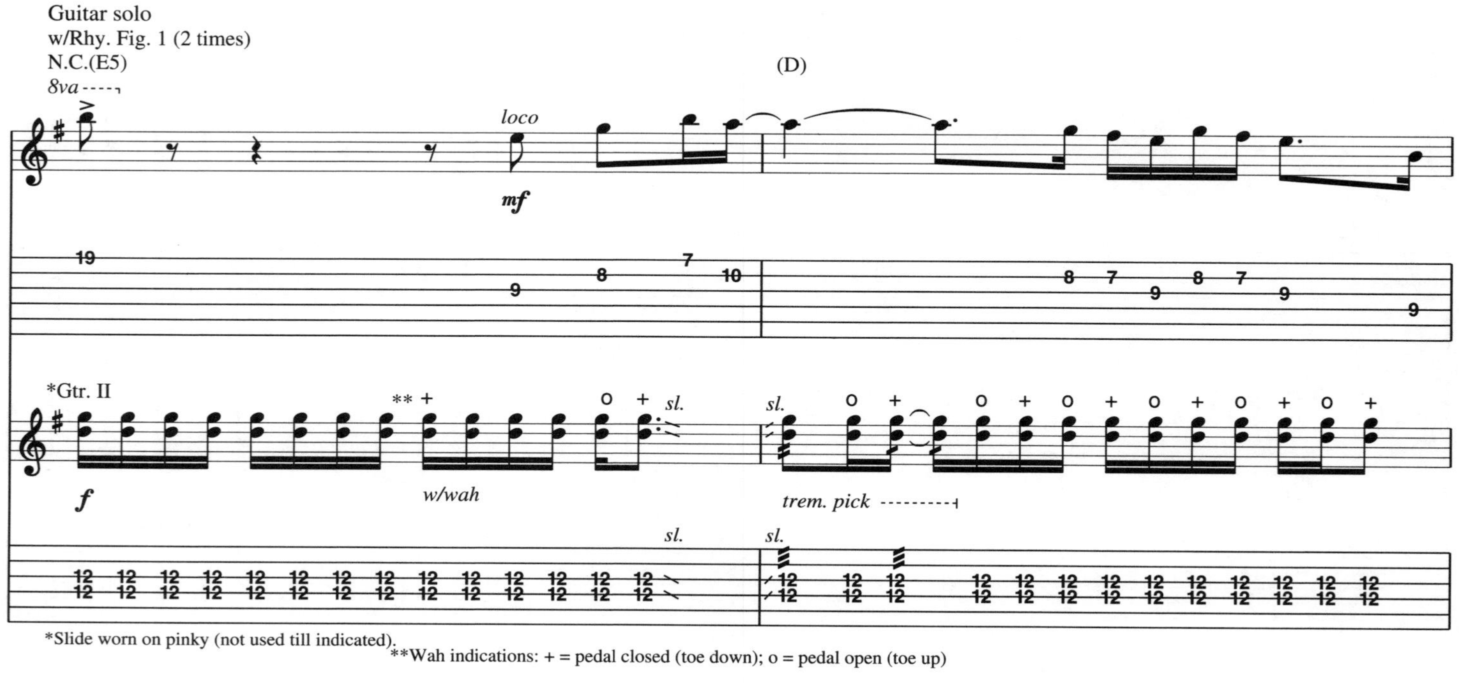
Guitar solo
w/Rhy. Fig. 1 (2 times)
N.C.(E5)
8va
(D)
loco
mf
*Gtr. II
f
w/wah
sl.
trem. pick
*Slide worn on pinky (not used till indicated).
**Wah indications: + = pedal closed (toe down); o = pedal open (toe up)

(E5)
(D)
1/2
Full

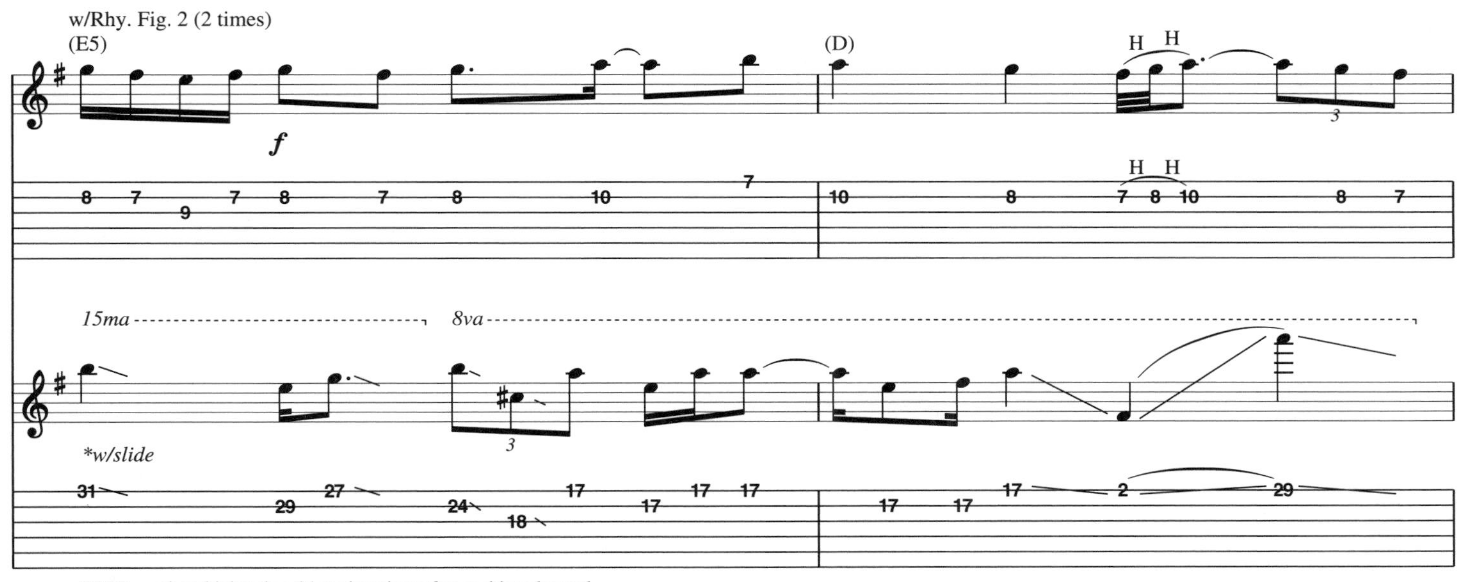

*TAB numbers higher than 24 are imaginary fret positions located past fretboard. Pitches shown are approximate (next 2 bars only).

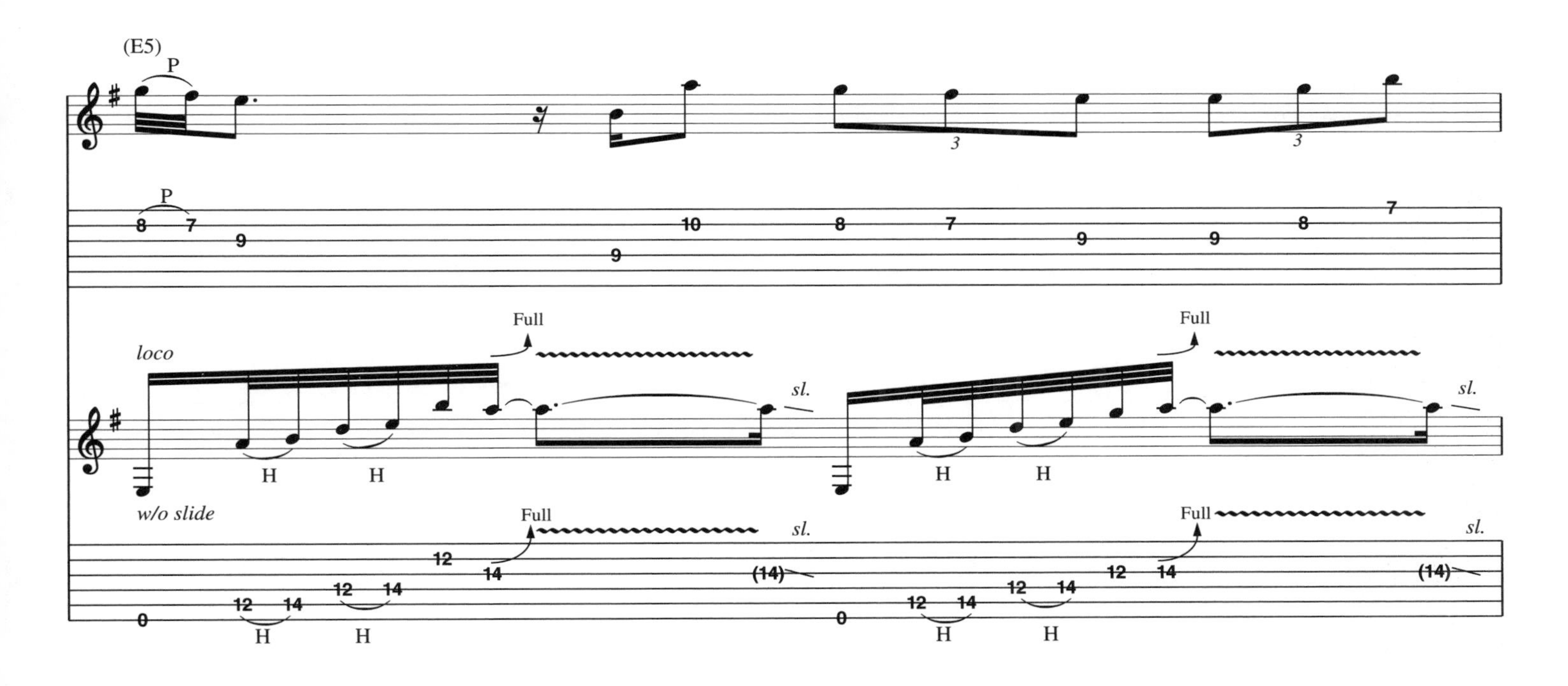

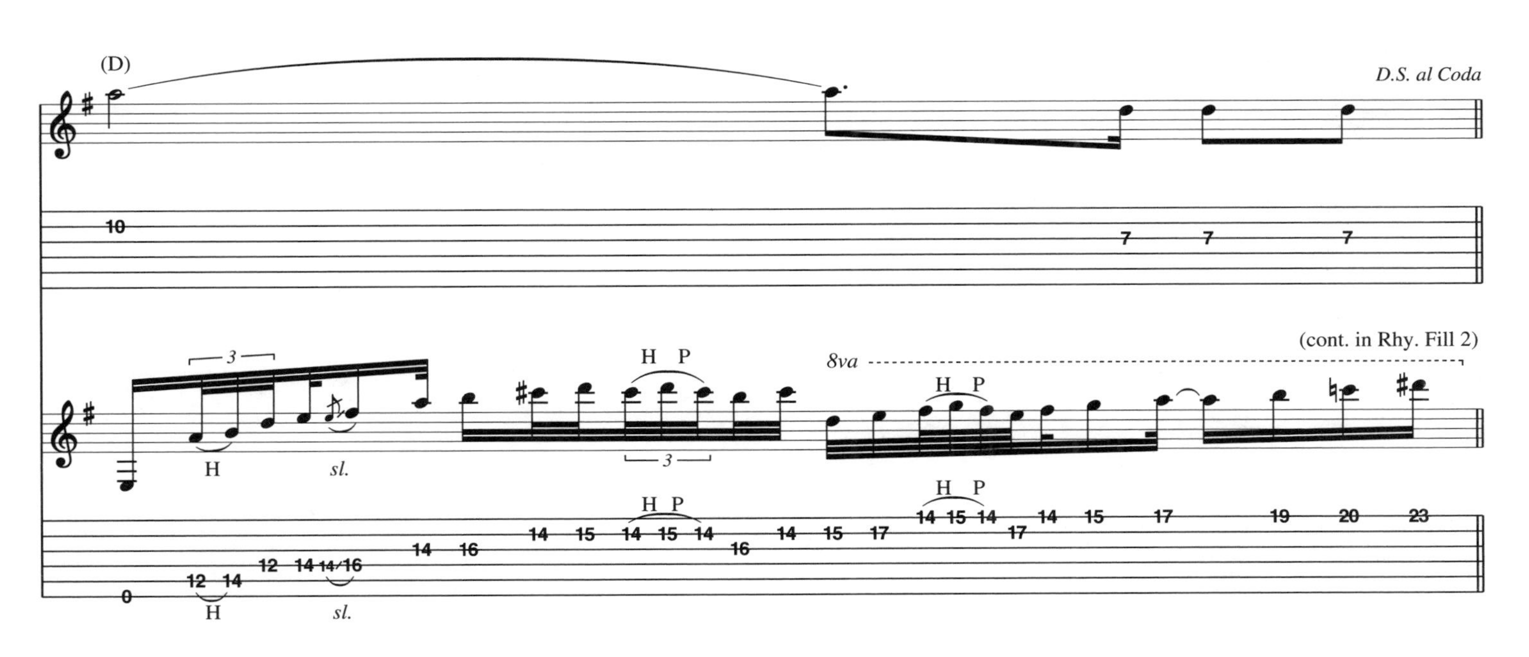

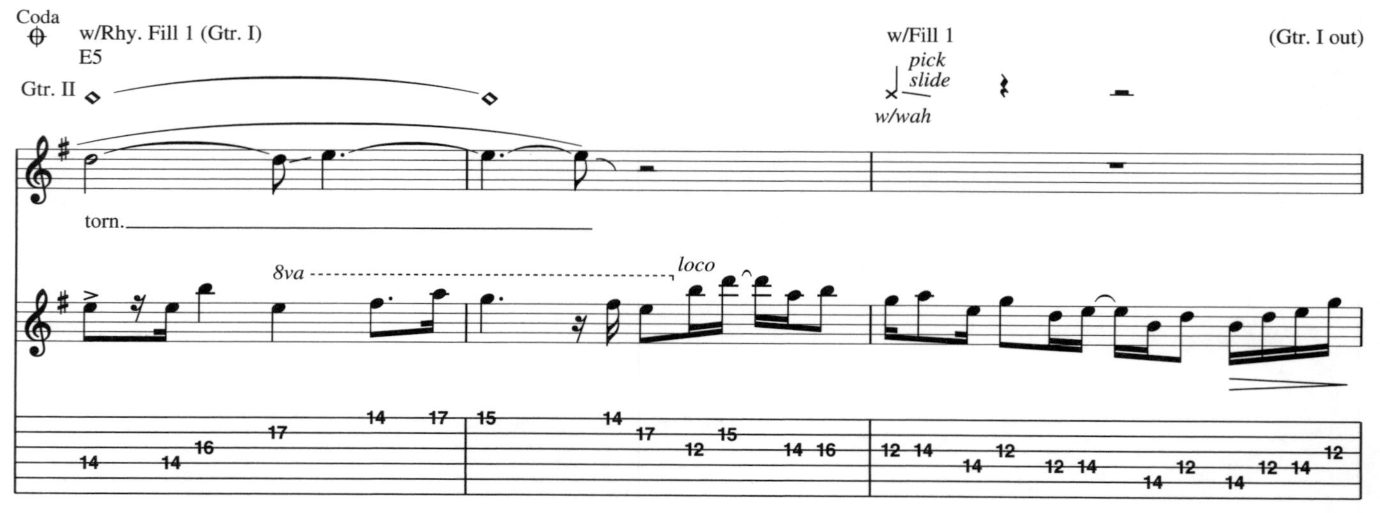
Coda
w/Rhy. Fill 1 (Gtr. I)
E5
Gtr. II
w/Fill 1
pick slide
w/wah
(Gtr. I out)
torn.
8va
loco

Rhy. Fig. 4
E5
w/Rhy. Fig. 4 (4 times)
Gtr. III
mp
P.M.
Gtr. I
Full
** mp
w/delay
sim.
sl.
*Vol. swell
**Vol. swell
Outro
w/Rhy. Fig. 4 (4 times)
E5
grad. bend
f

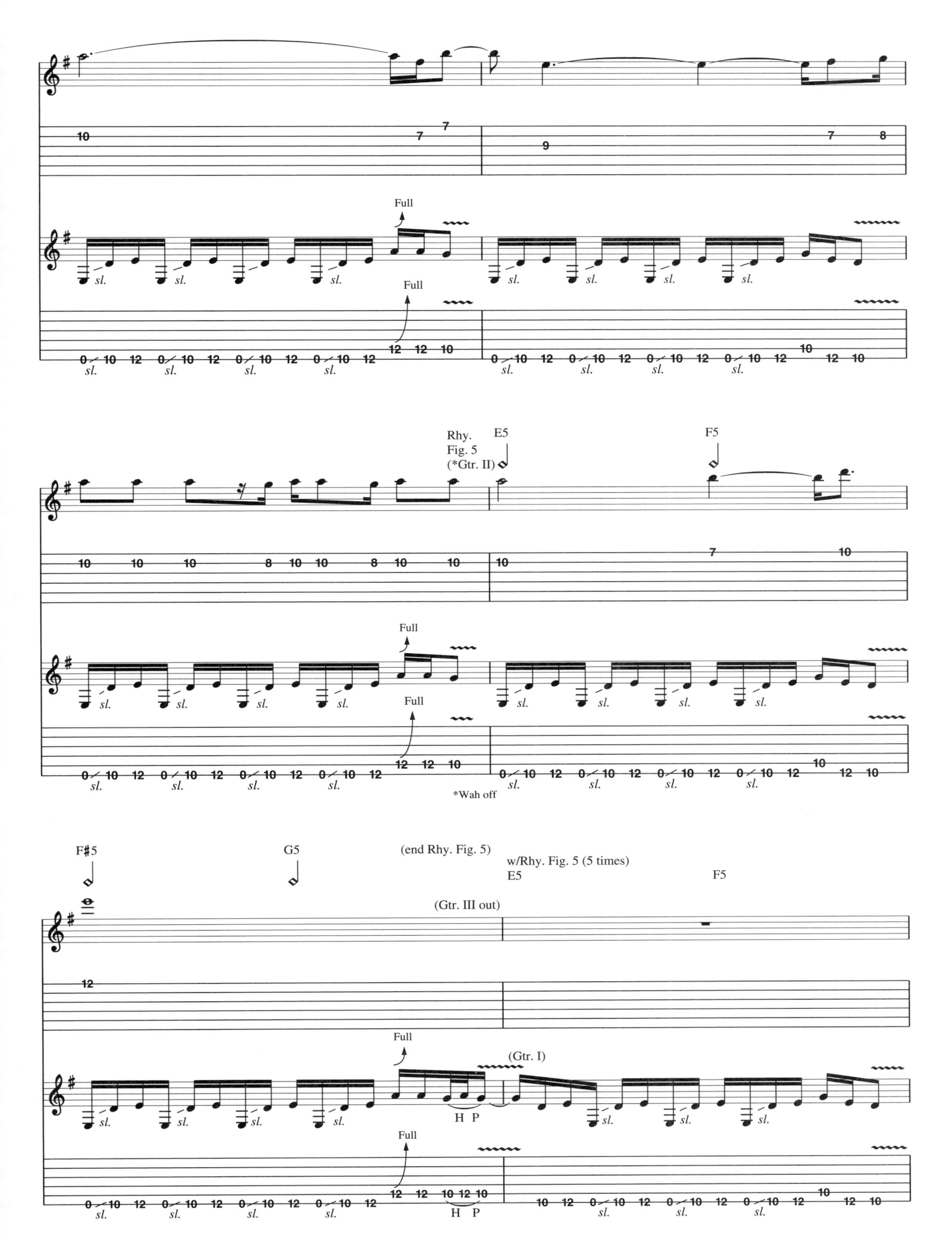
Full
Full
Rhy.
Fig. 5
(*Gtr. II)
E5
F5
Full
Full
*Wah off
F#5
G5
(end Rhy. Fig. 5)
w/Rhy. Fig. 5 (5 times)
E5
F5
(Gtr. III out)
Full
(Gtr. I)
H P
Full
H P

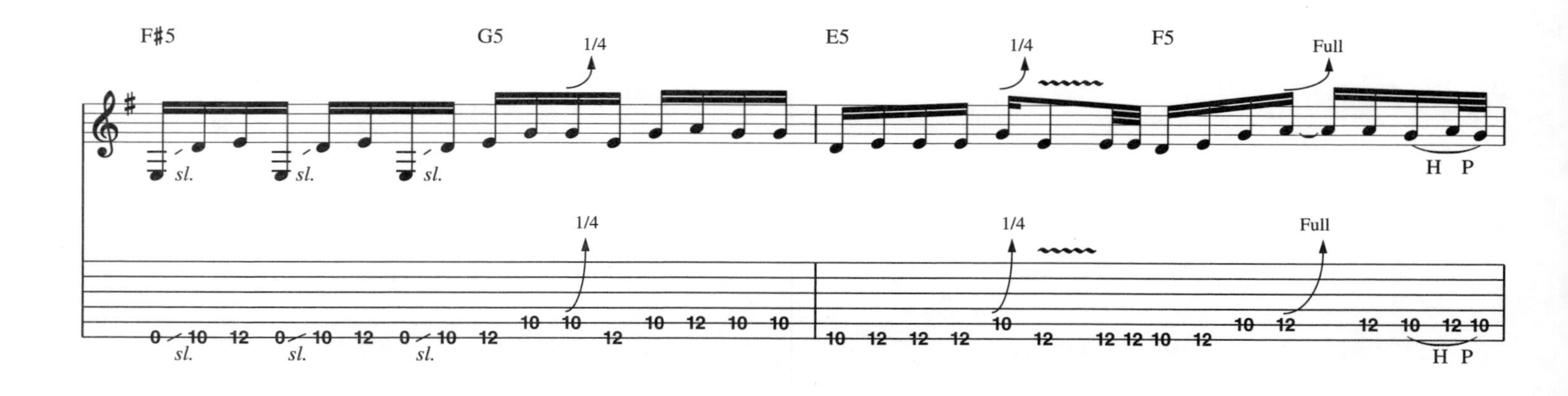

F#5
G5
E5
F5
1/4
Full
sl.
H P

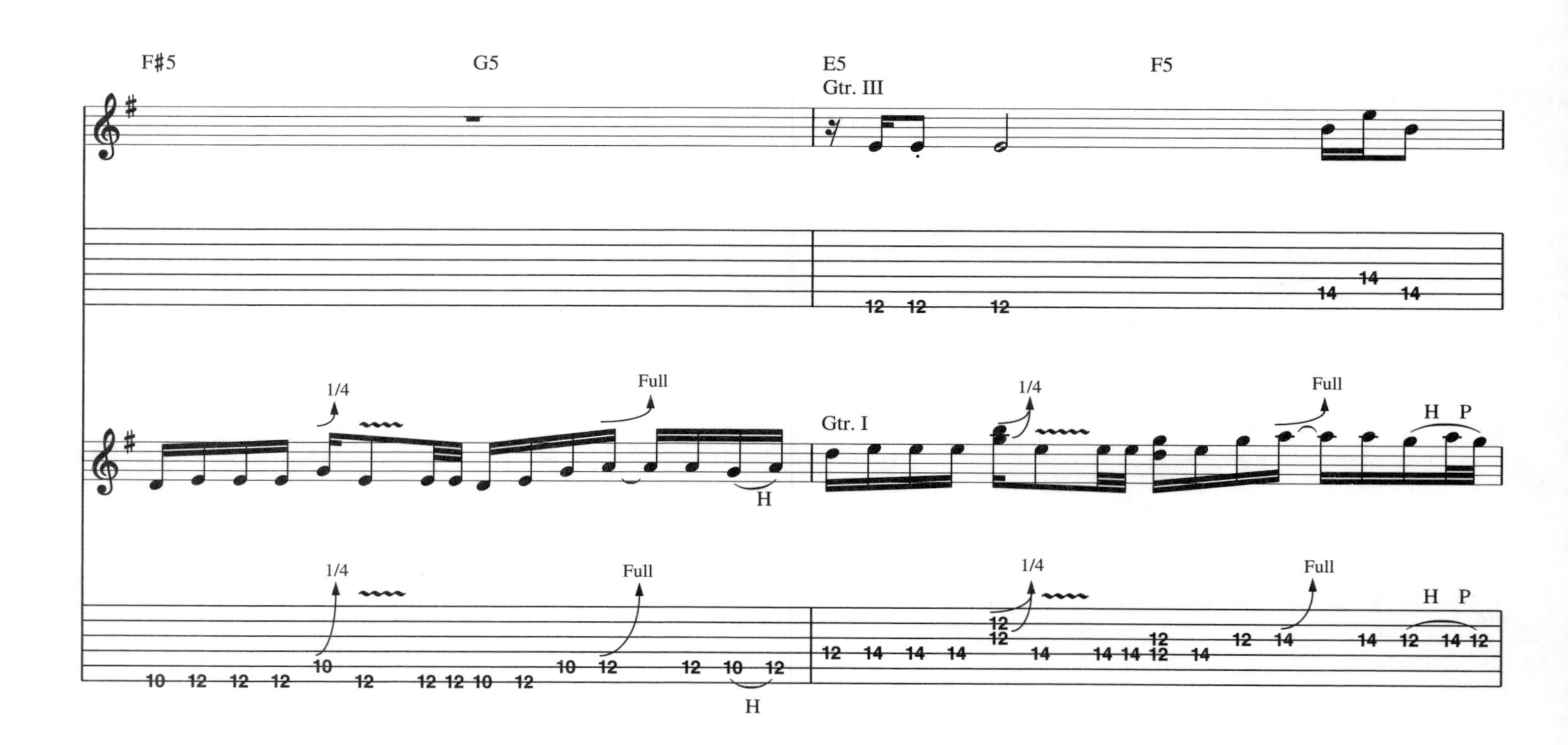

F#5
G5
E5
F5
Gtr. III
Gtr. I
1/4
Full
H P
H

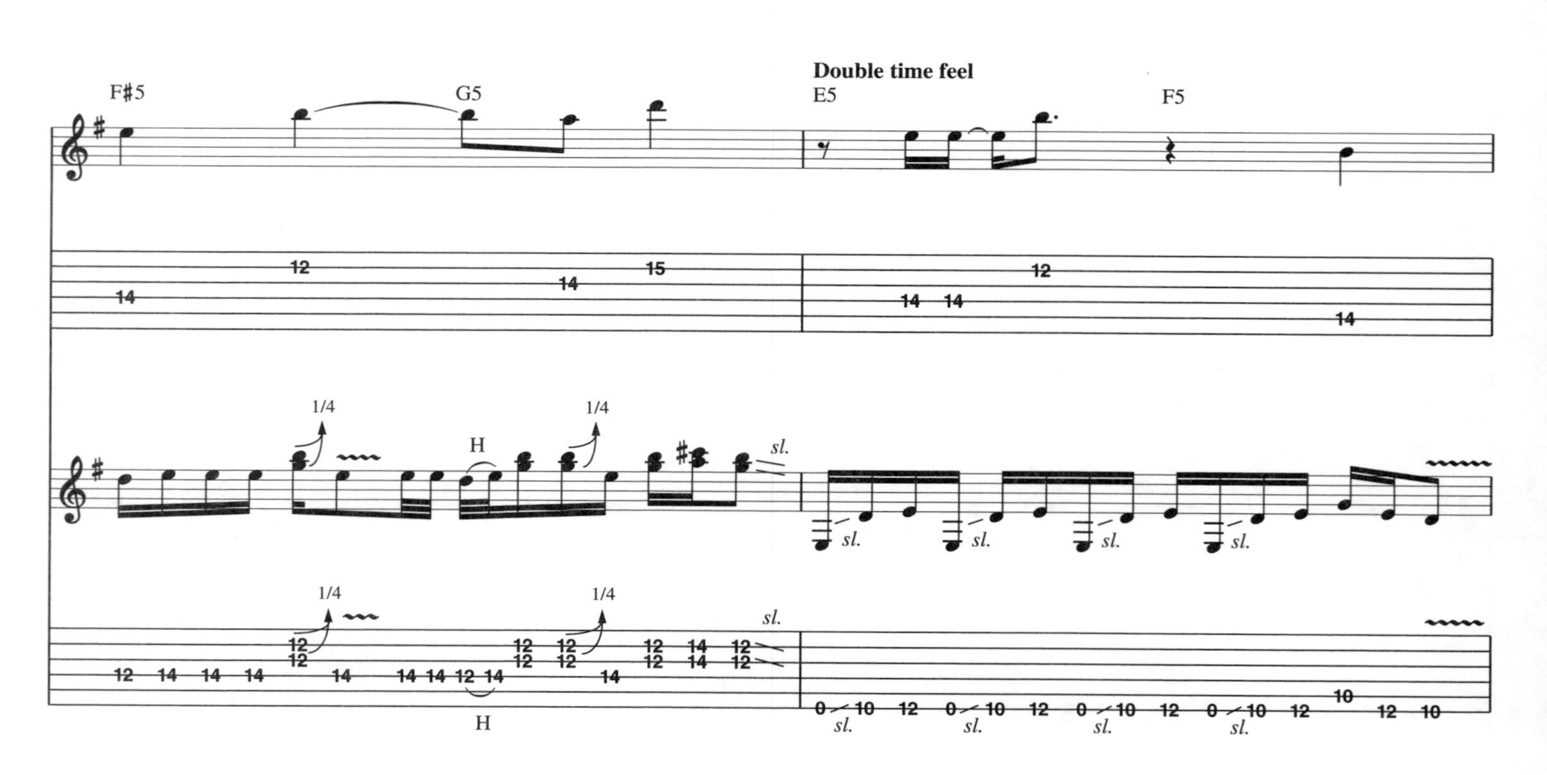

Double time feel
F#5
G5
E5
F5
1/4
H
sl.

F#5
G5
E5
F5
Full
sl.
Rhy.
Fig. 6
(Gtr. II)
*P.M.
P.M.
Gtr. III
Gtr. IV
1/4
P
H
*Throughout Rhy. Fig. 6, play only lowest note of chord
when P.M. is indicated.
(end Rhy. Fig. 6)
w/Rhy. Fig. 6 (5 times)

F#5
G5
E5
F5
(Gtr. IV out)
Gtr. III
hold bend
A.H.
(15ma)
Full
1/2
sl.
H
P

F♯5
Gtr. III
G5
E5
F5
Full
sl.
Free time
(end double time feel)
Gtr. II
H
P
E5 (type2)

ONE

Words and Music by
James Hetfield and Lars Ulrich

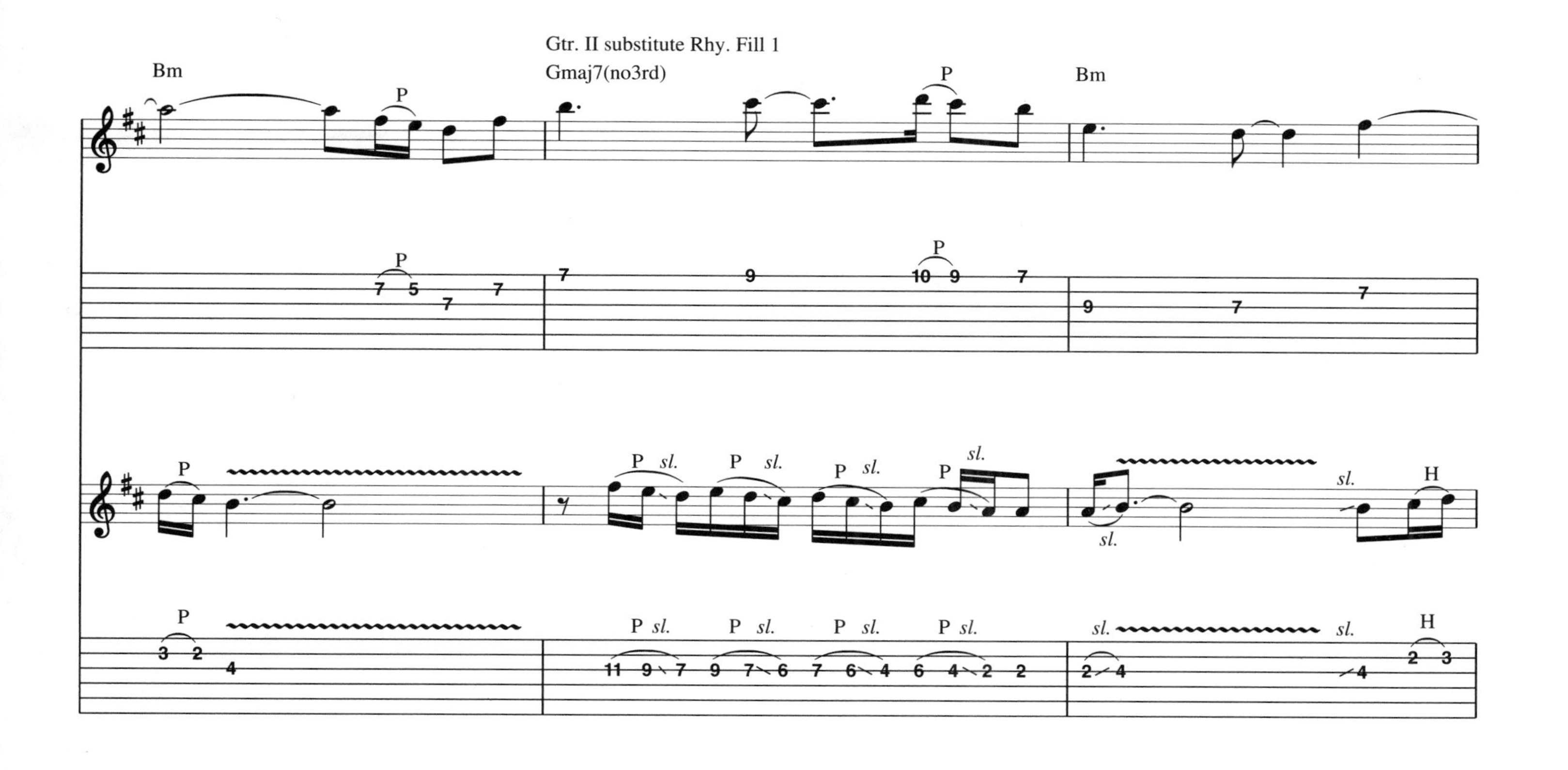
Gtr. II substitute Rhy. Fill 1
Bm
Gmaj7(no3rd)
Bm

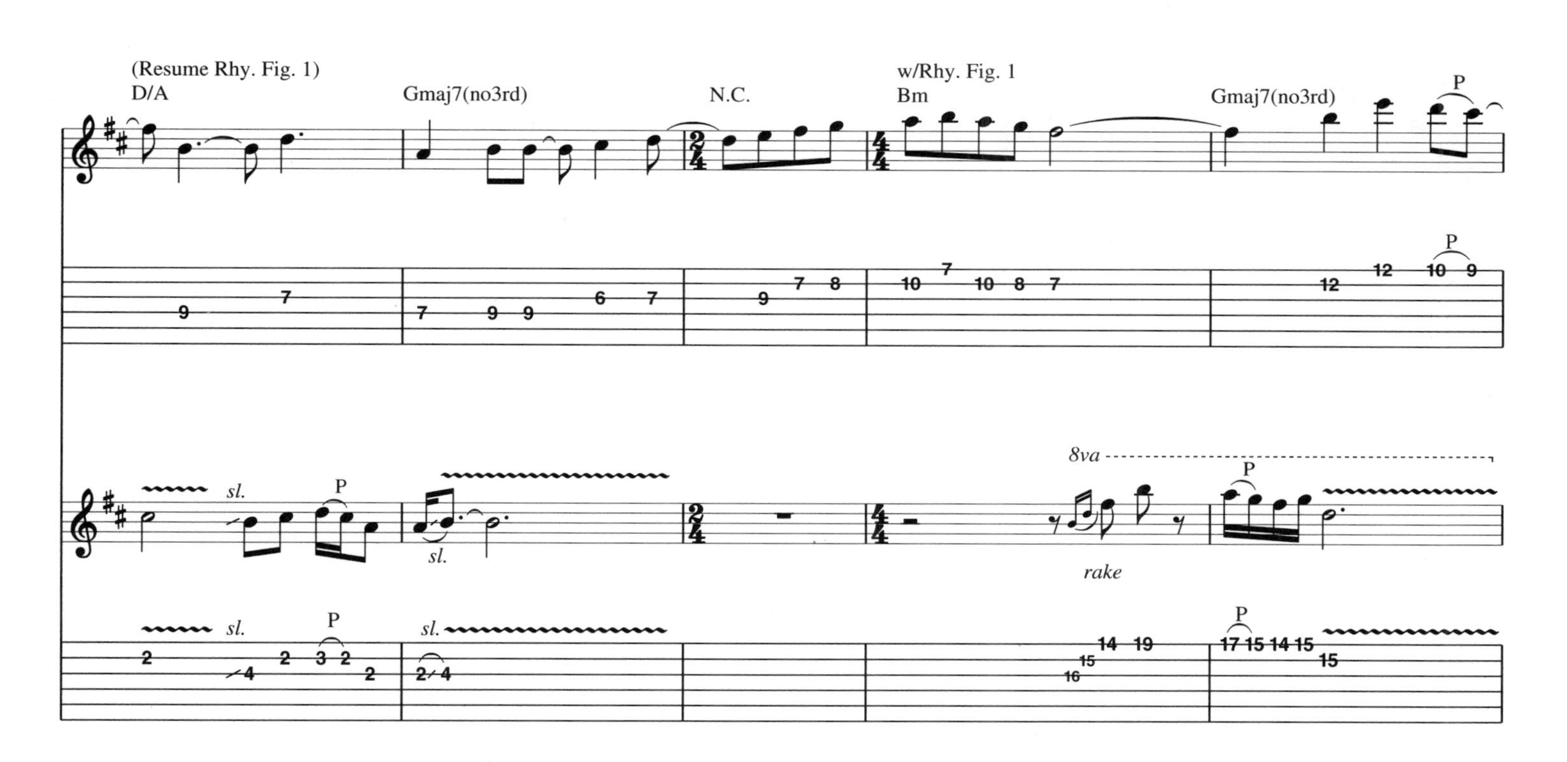
(Resume Rhy. Fig. 1)
D/A
Gmaj7(no3rd)
N.C.
w/Rhy. Fig. 1
Bm
Gmaj7(no3rd)
8va
rake

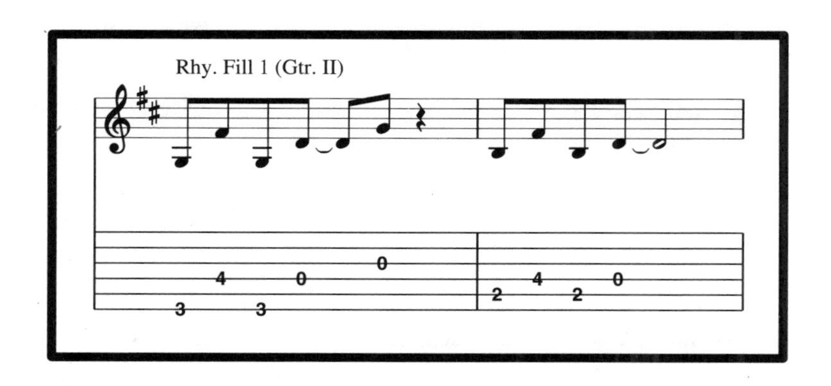
Rhy. Fill 1 (Gtr. II)

Gtr. II substitute Rhy. Fill 1
(Resume Rhy. Fig. 1)
Bm
Gmaj7(no3rd)
sl.
Bm
D/A
loco
P
Gmaj7(no3rd)
Gtr. II substitute Rhy. Fill 2
N.C.
Bm
Gmaj7(no3rd)
H P
Bm
1/2
Gtrs. II & III
let ring throughout

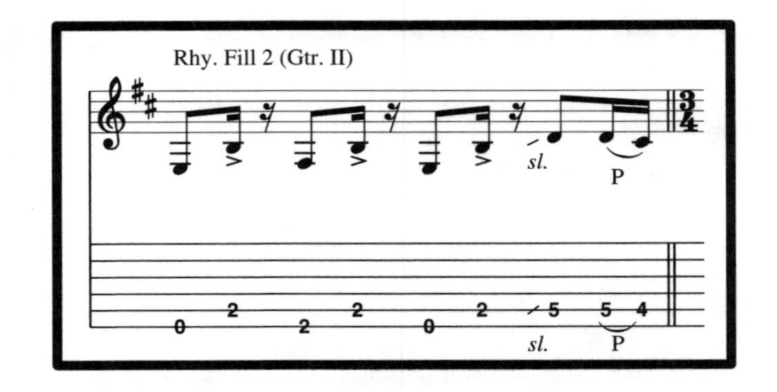
Rhy. Fill 2 (Gtr. II)
sl.
P

Gmaj7(no3rd)
Bm
D/A
H P
Gmaj7(no3rd)
H P
E5
Gtr. I
F#5
G5
A5
Dsus4
G
Fsus2
Gtr. II
H
Riff A (Gtr. II)
H P
H P
let ring throughout
Gtr. III
Riff A1 (Gtr. III)
H P
sl.

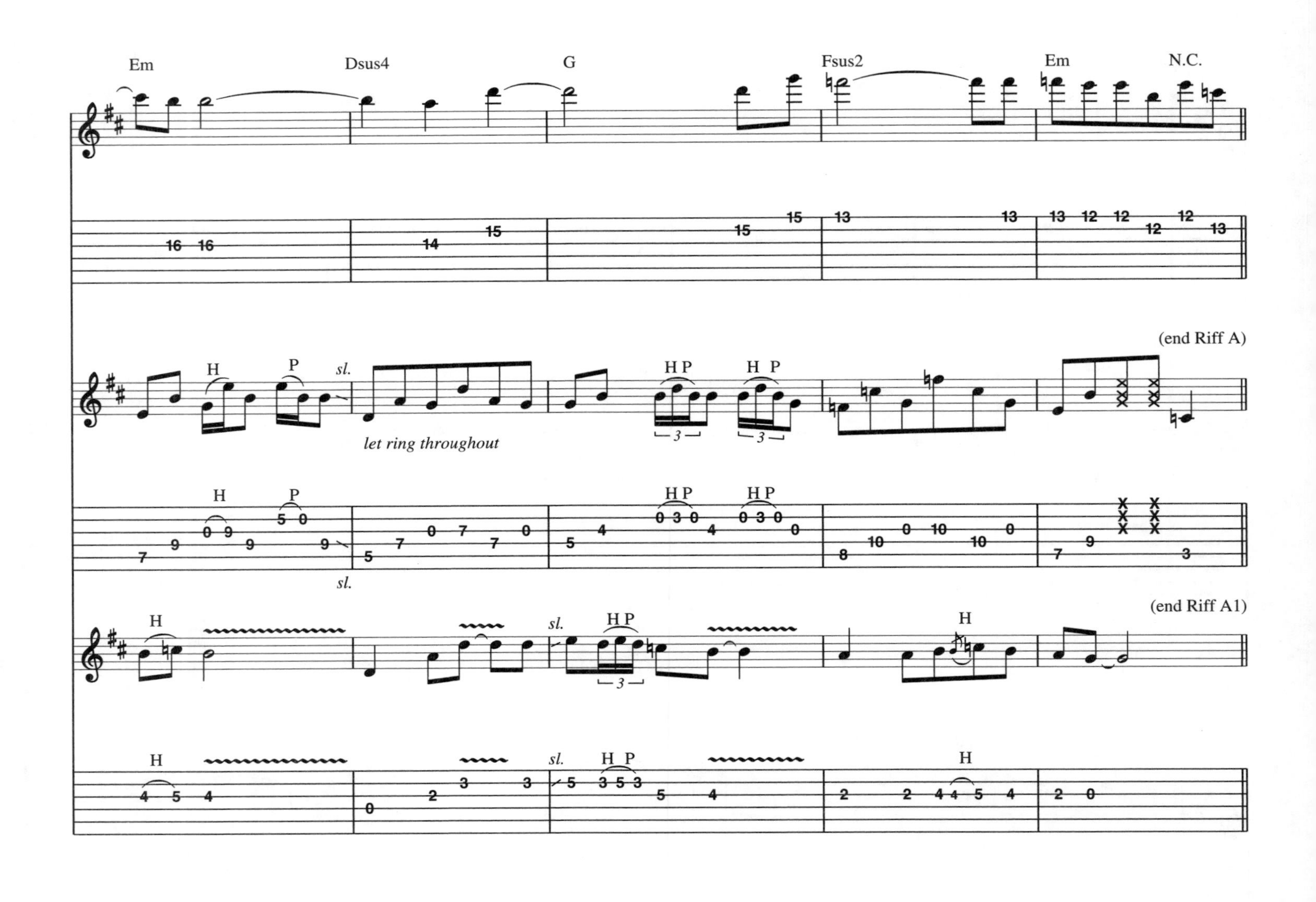

Em
Dsus4
G
Fsus2
Em
N.C.
(end Riff A)
H
P
sl.
let ring throughout
H P
(end Riff A1)

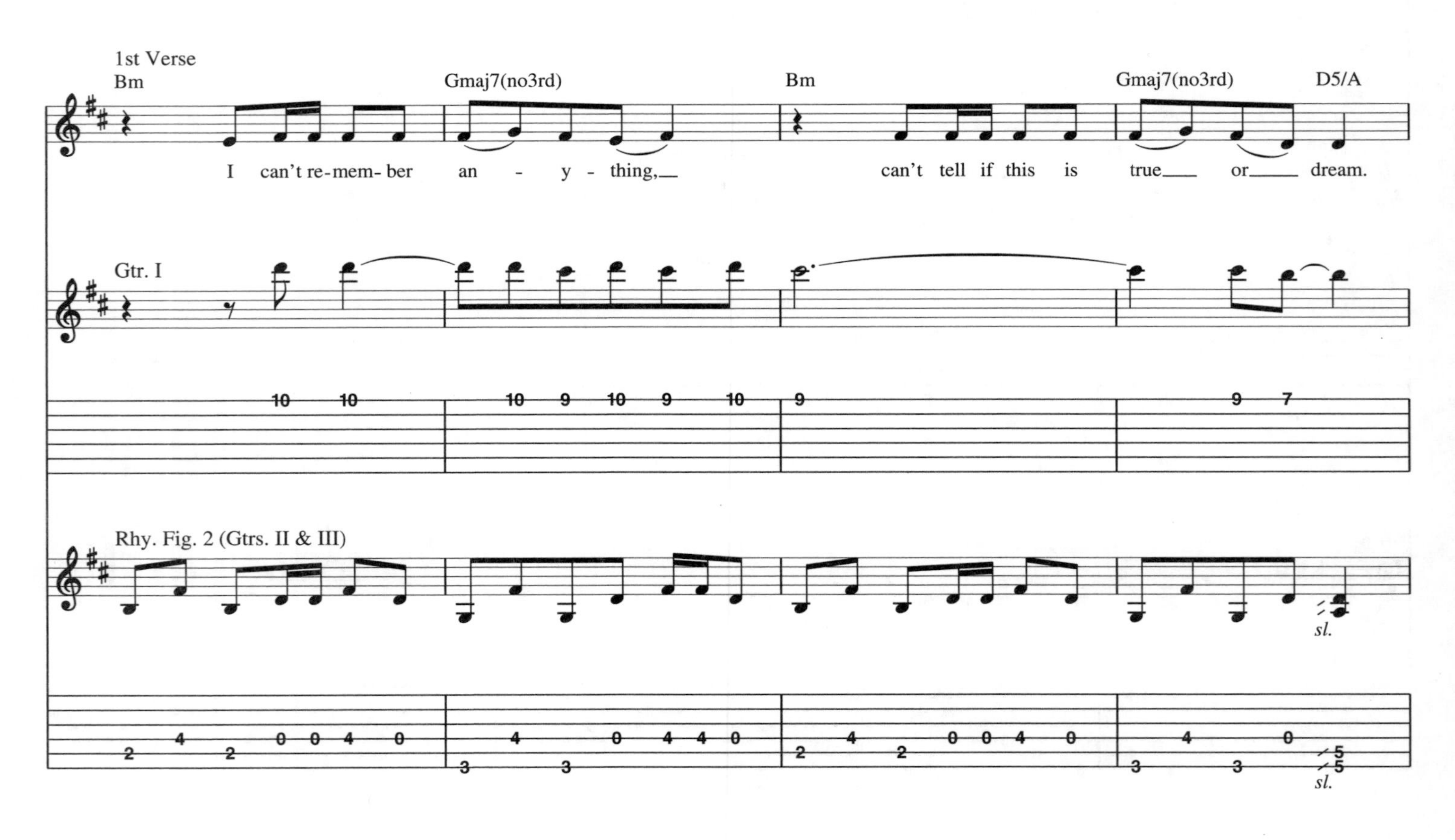

1st Verse
Bm
Gmaj7(no3rd)
Bm
Gmaj7(no3rd)
D5/A
I can't re-mem- ber an - y - thing,
can't tell if this is true or dream.
Gtr. I
Rhy. Fig. 2 (Gtrs. II & III)
sl.

Bm
D/A
Gmaj7(no3rd)
N.C.
Deep down in-side I feel to scream, this ter-ri-ble si-lence stops me.
(end Rhy. Fig. 2)
w/Rhy. Fig. 2
Bm
Gmaj7(no3rd)
Bm
Gmaj7(no3rd)
Now that the war is through with me, I'm wak-ing up, I can-not see
Gtr. I
Bm
D/A
Gmaj7(no3rd)
N.C.
that there's not much left to me. Noth-ing is real but pain now!

G5
A5
B5
A5
G5
F#5
B5
A5
B5
C#5
B5
A5
N.C.
Hold my breath as I wish for death.
Oh please, God, wake
Rhy. Fig. 3 (Gtrs. I & II)
(end Rhy. Fig. 3)
P.M.
w/dist.

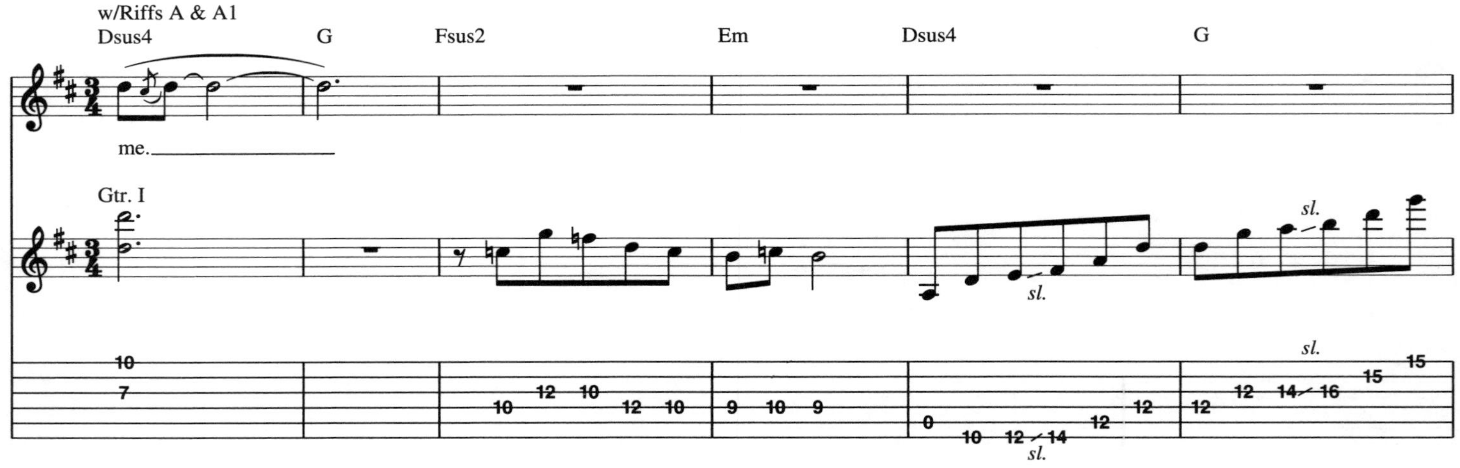
w/Riffs A & A1
Dsus4
G
Fsus2
Em
Dsus4
G
me.
Gtr. I
sl.

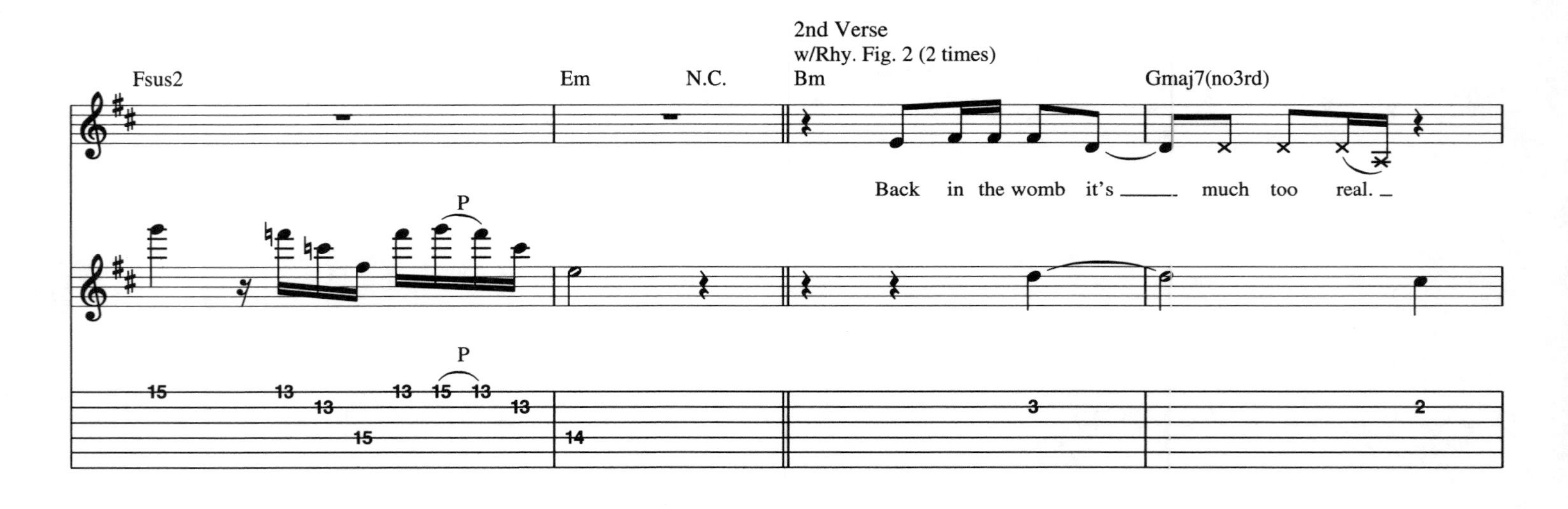
Fsus2
Em
N.C.
2nd Verse
w/Rhy. Fig. 2 (2 times)
Bm
Gmaj7(no3rd)
Back in the womb it's much too real.
P

Bm
Gmaj7(no3rd)
Bm
In pumps life that I must feel, but can't look for - ward
P
P
D/A
Gmaj7(no3rd)
N.C.
to re - veal, look to the time when I'll live.
*Gtr. IV
Gtr. IV
Gtr. I
**
(Gtr. I out)
*Orchestra arr. for gtr.
**Gtr. IV to left of slash in TAB.
Bm
Gmaj7(no3rd)
Bm
Fed through the tube that sticks in me, just like a war - time
(Gtr. IV out) Gtr. I
Gmaj7(no3rd)
Bm
D/A
nov - el - ty; tied to ma-chines that make me be.

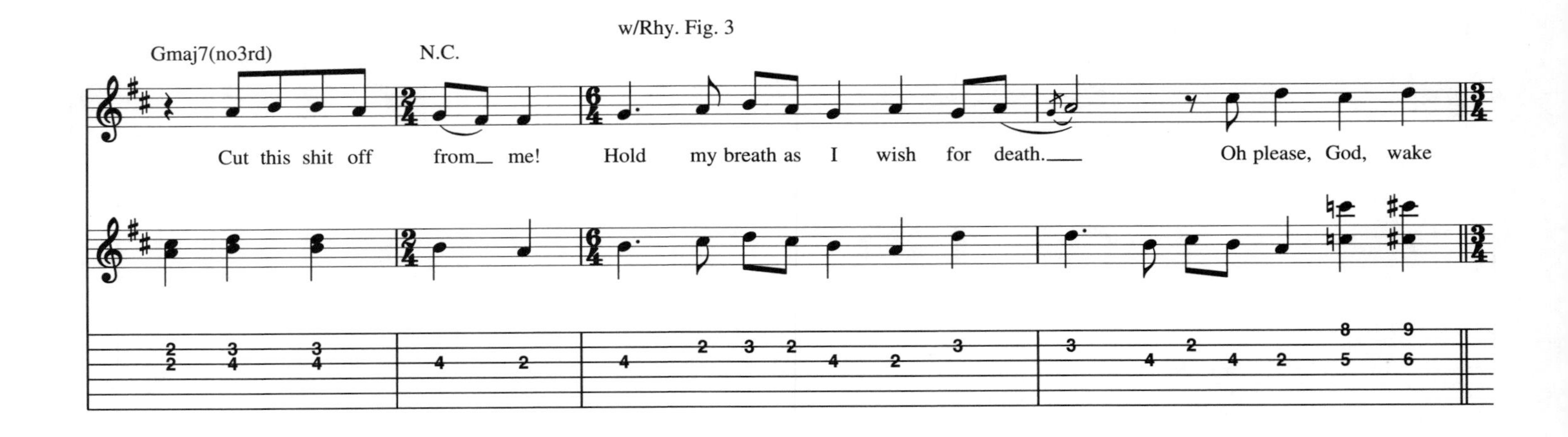
w/Rhy. Fig. 3
Gmaj7(no3rd)
N.C.
Cut this shit off from_ me! Hold my breath as I wish for death.___ Oh please, God, wake

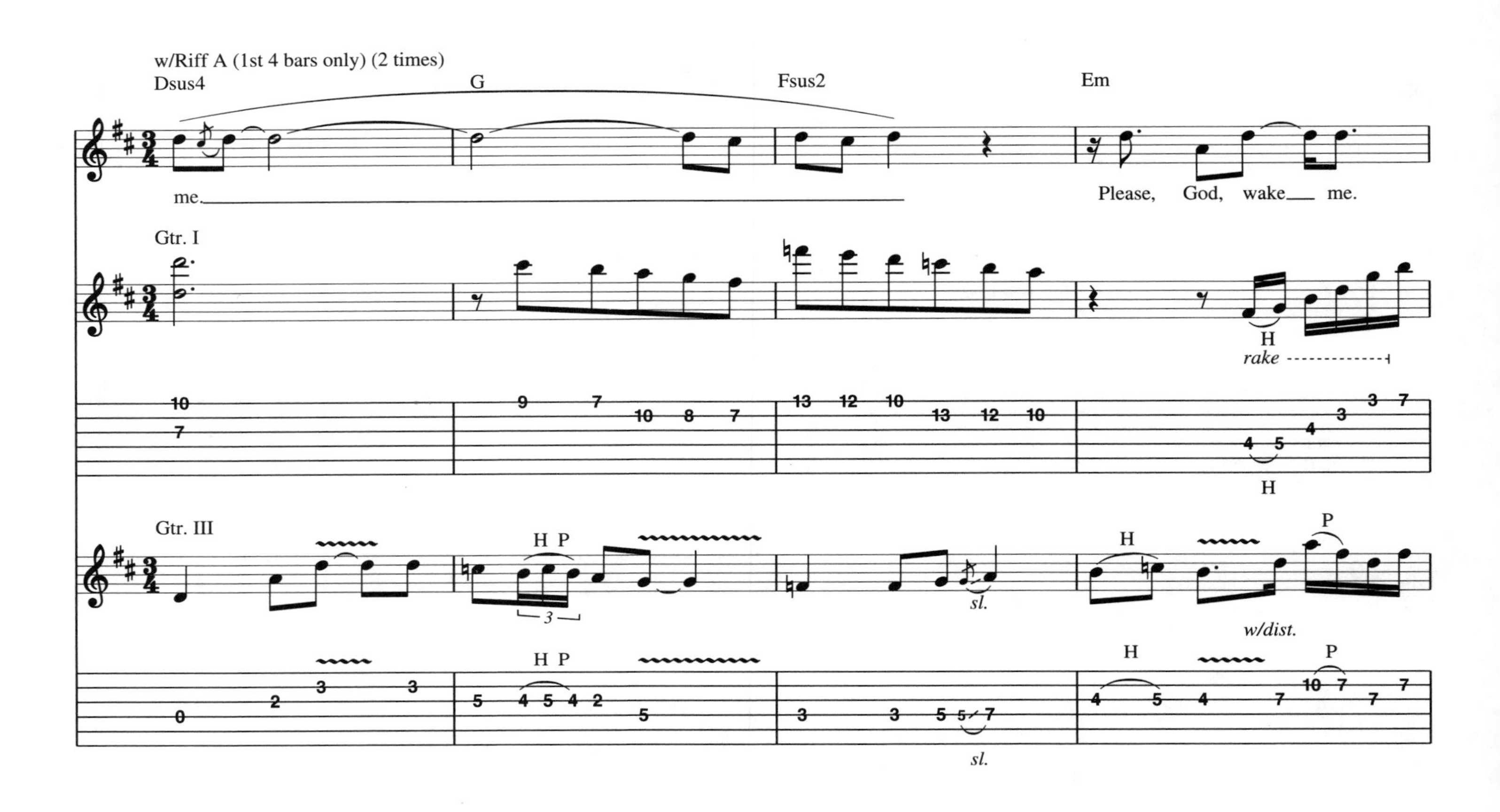
w/Riff A (1st 4 bars only) (2 times)
Dsus4
G
Fsus2
Em
me.___ Please, God, wake_ me.
Gtr. I
rake
Gtr. III
sl.
w/dist.

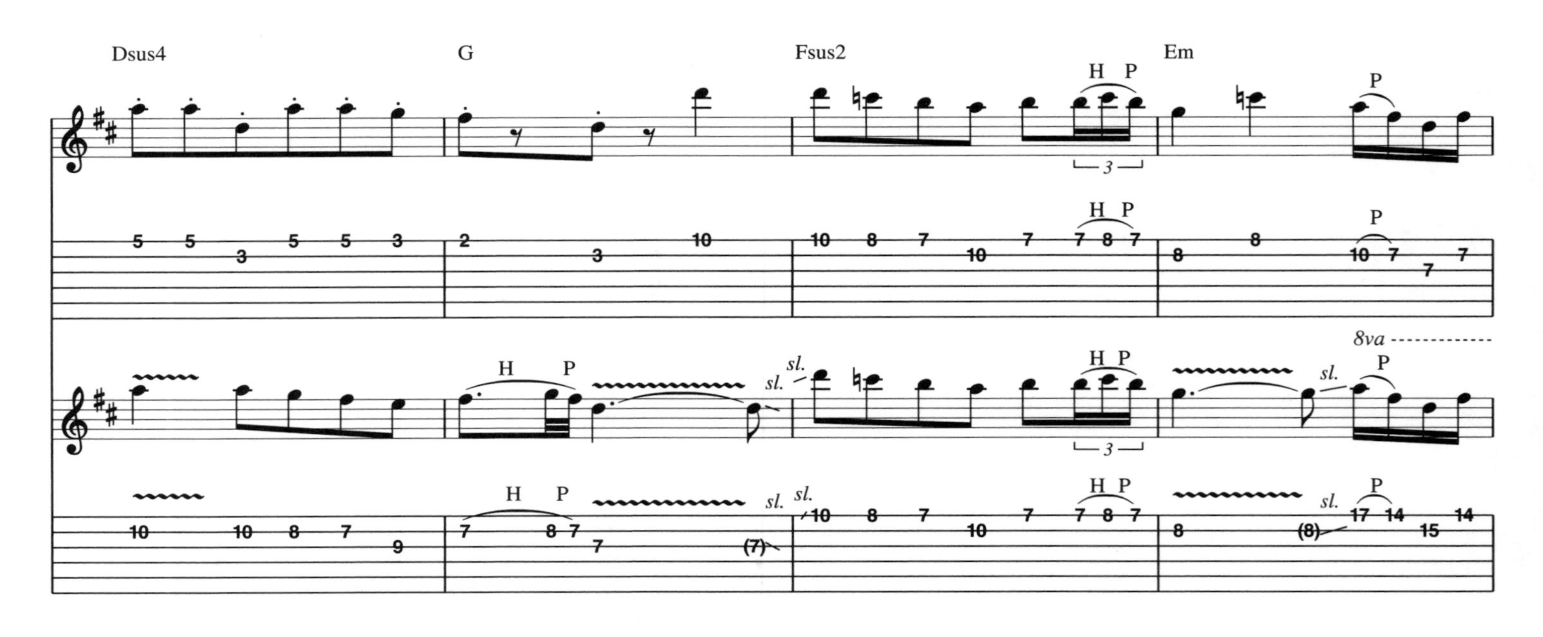
Dsus4
G
Fsus2
Em
8va
sl.

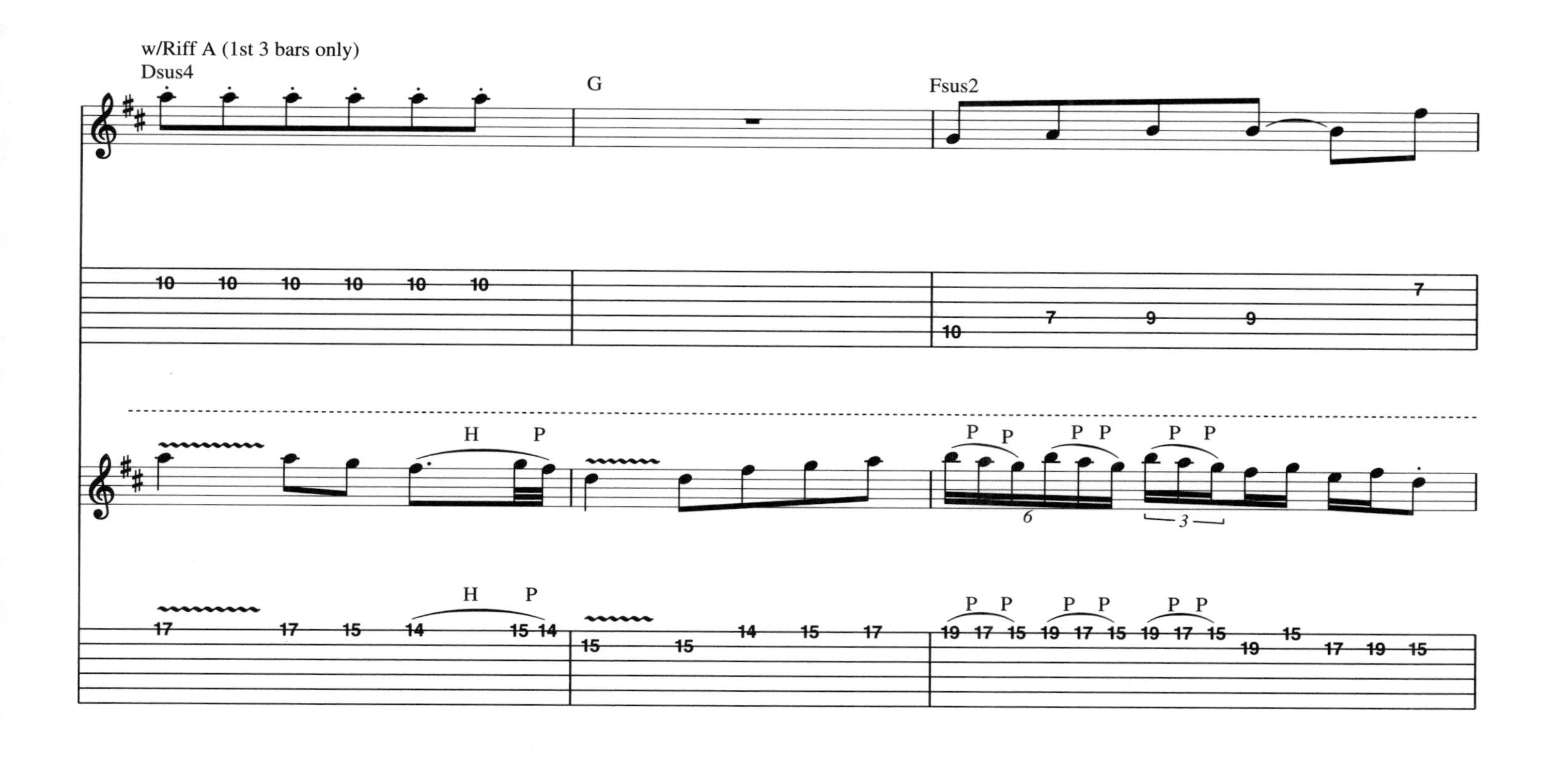
w/Riff A (1st 3 bars only)
Dsus4
G
Fsus2
H P
P P P P P P
6
3

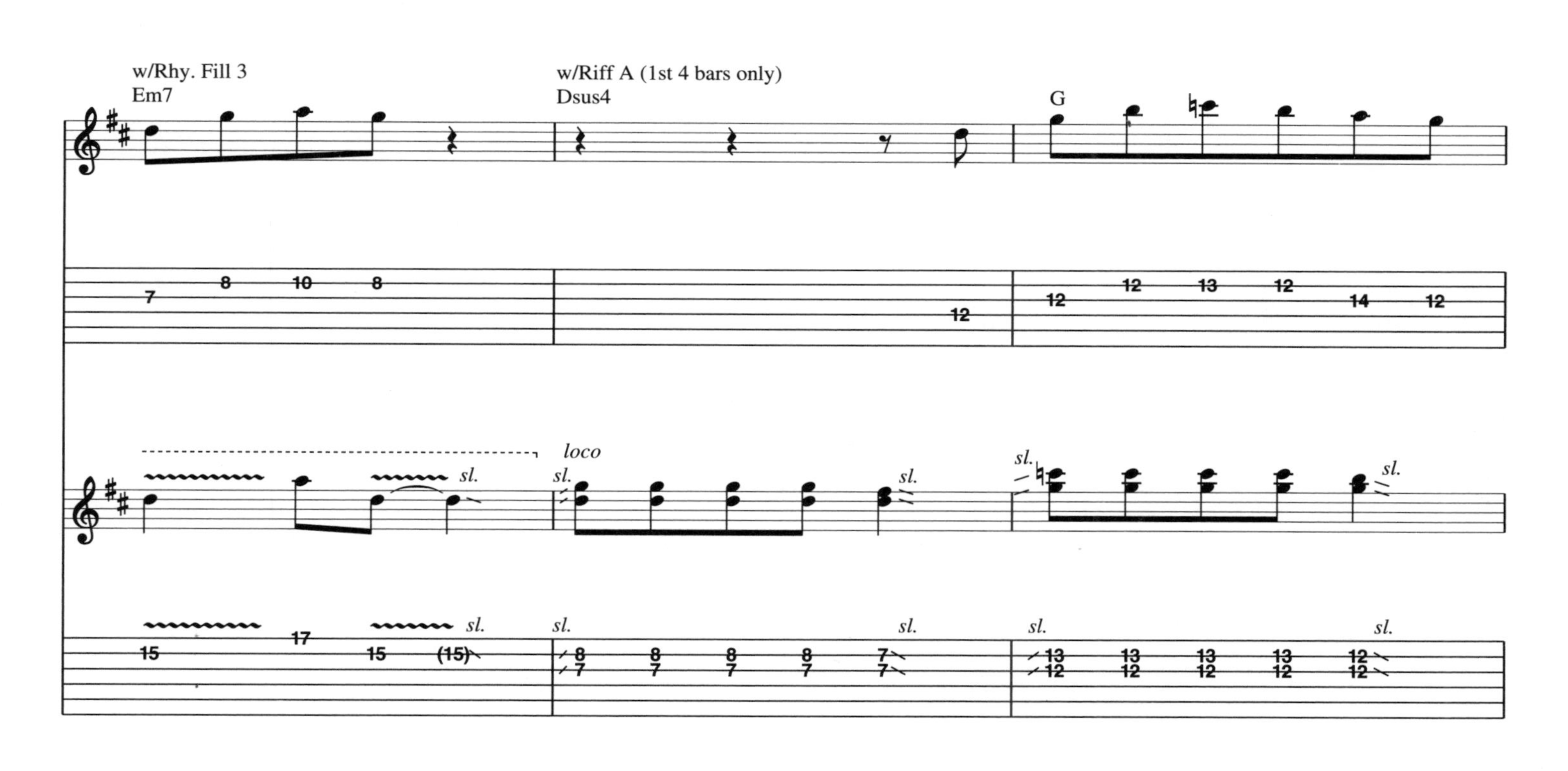
w/Rhy. Fill 3
Em7
w/Riff A (1st 4 bars only)
Dsus4
G
loco
sl.

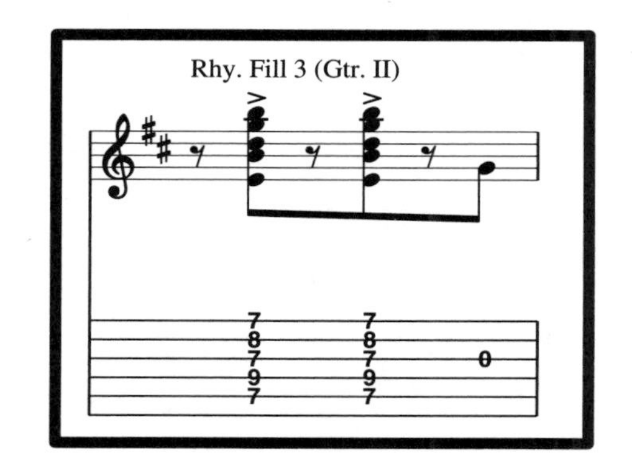
Rhy. Fill 3 (Gtr. II)

Fsus2
Em
8va
sl.
loco
trem. pick
G5 A5 B5 A5 G5 F♯5 G5 A5 B5 C♯5 B5 A5 B5 C♯5
Now the world is gone, I'm just one.
Oh God, help me.
Gtrs. II & III
loco
P.M.
(w/dist.)
G5 A5 B5 A5 G5 B5 G5 A5 B5 C♯5 B5 A5 B5 C♯5 G5 A5 B5 A5 G5 F♯5 B5
Hold my breath as I wish for death.
Oh please, God, help me.
Help me!

Am
Gtr. I
G
B5
C5
Gtr. II
sl.
Rhy. Fig. 4 (Gtr. III)
(end Rhy. Fig. 4)
P.M.

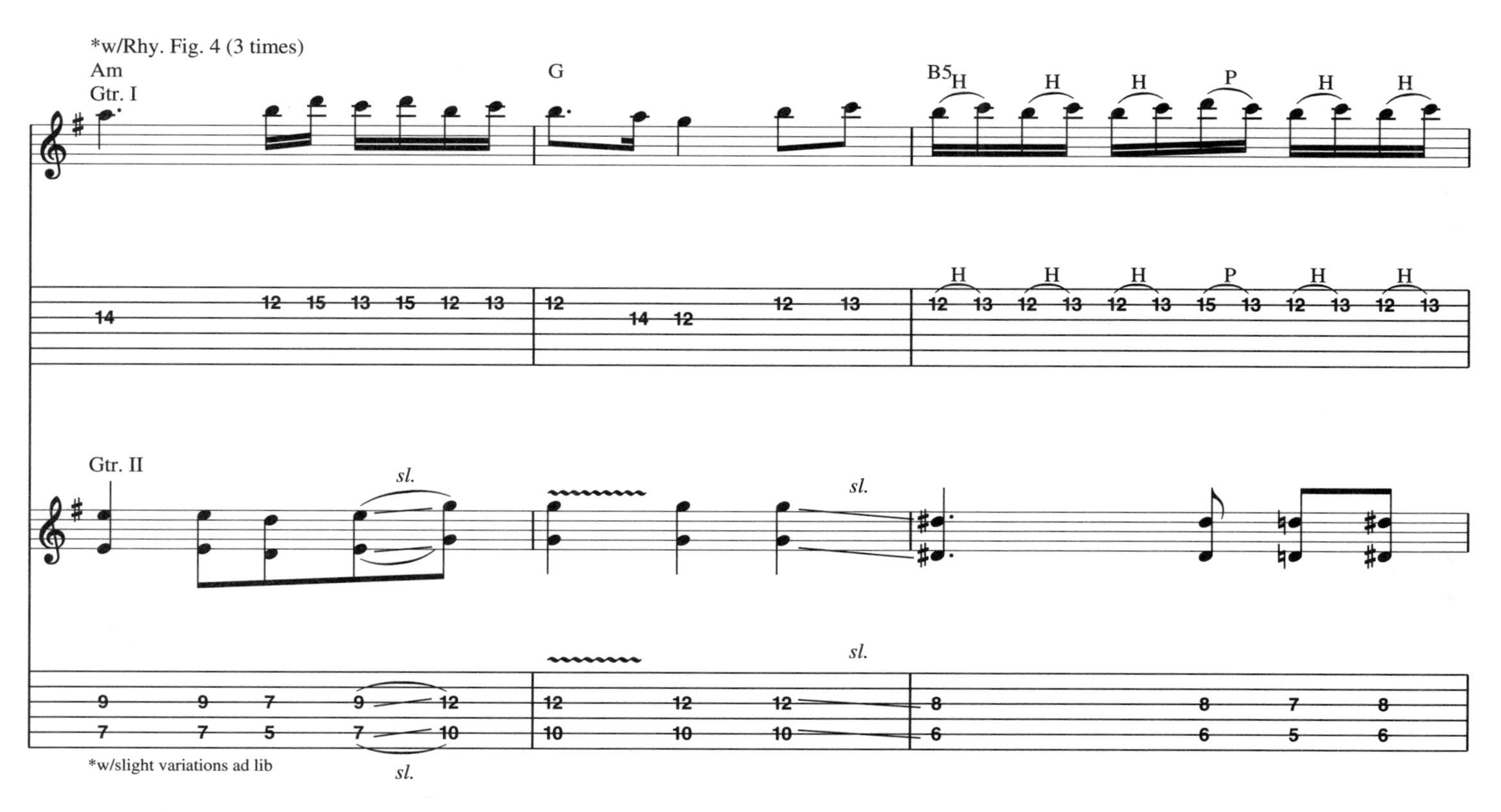
*w/Rhy. Fig. 4 (3 times)
Am
Gtr. I
G
B5
H
P
Gtr. II
sl.
*w/slight variations ad lib

C5
Am
G
Gtr. II
B5
C5
Am
G
B5
C5
H
P
sl.

Em
Gtr. I
D
B5
C5
Gtr. II
P.M.
sl.
Gtr. III

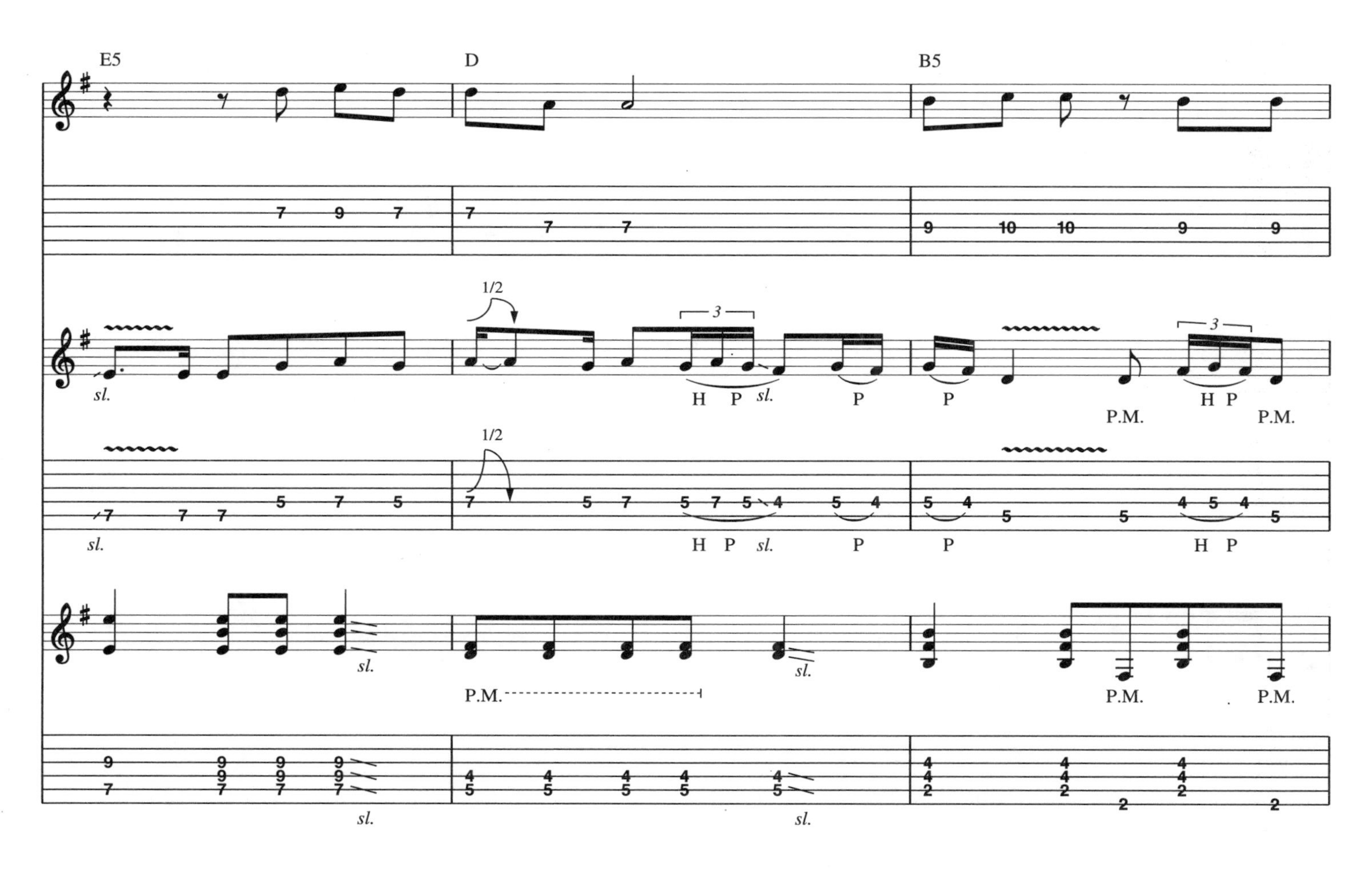
E5
D
B5
1/2
H P sl.
P
P.M.
sl.

C5
E5
Gtrs. I & IV
Gtr. I
C/E
Gtr. IV
(Gtr. IV out)
*
sl.
P
sl.
1/2
P.M.
*Gtr. I to left of slash in TAB.
Gtr. I
Gtrs. II & III
P.M.

P.M.
Bridge
E5
F5
Darkness imprisoning me, all that I see, absolute horror!
Rhy. Fig. 5

E5
F5
I can-not live! I can-not die! Trapped in my - self, bod - y, my hold - ing
(end Rhy. Fig. 5)
P.M.
N.C.
cell!
sl.

Gtr. I
8va
Gtr. II
P.M.
sl.
Gtr. III
w/Rhy. Fig. 5
E5
F5
Land - mine has tak - en my sight, tak - en my speech, tak - en my hear - ing,
tak - en my arms, tak - en my legs, tak - en my soul, left me with life in
loco

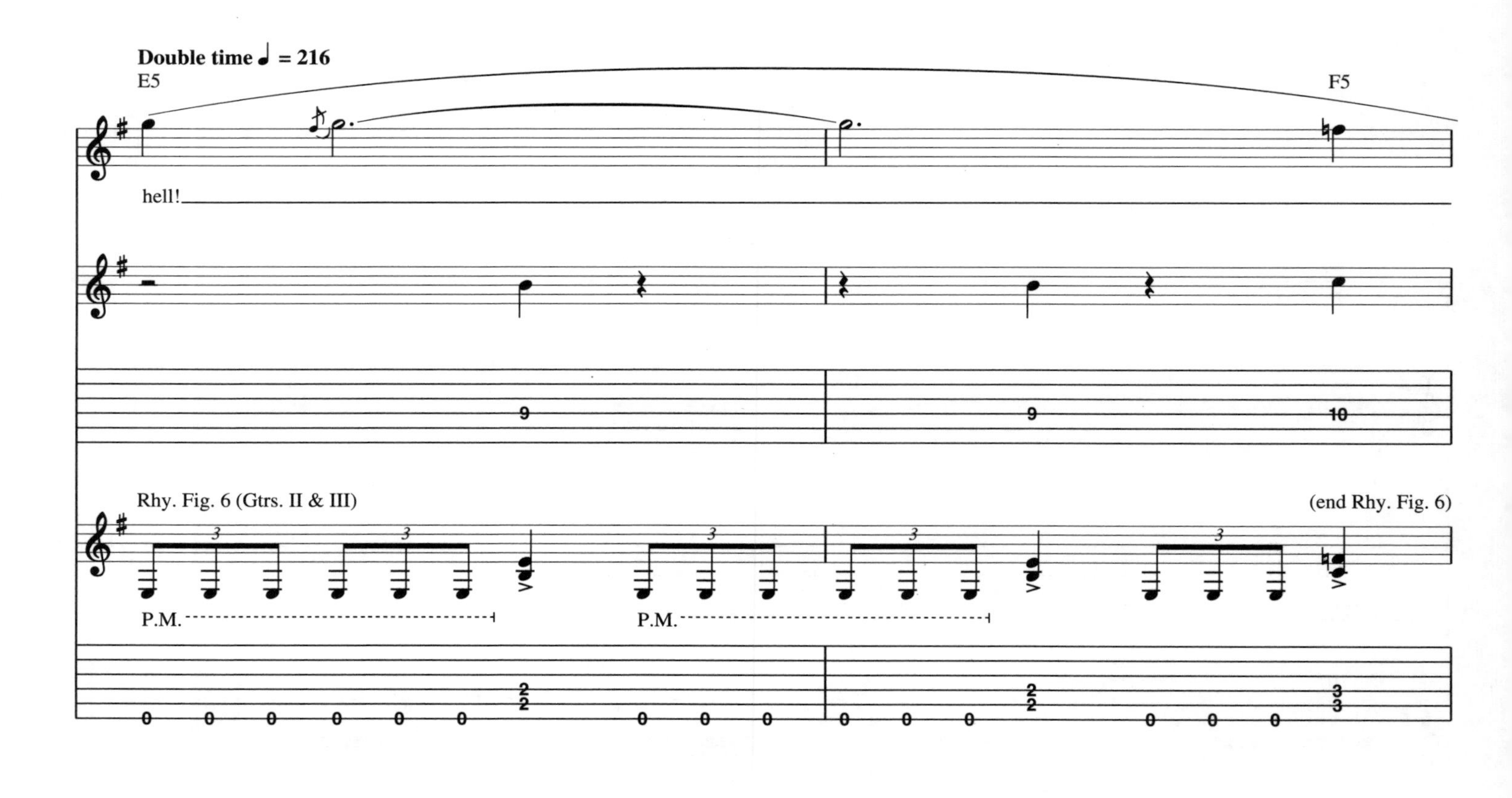
Double time ♩ = 216
E5
F5
hell!
Rhy. Fig. 6 (Gtrs. II & III)
(end Rhy. Fig. 6)
P.M.
P.M.

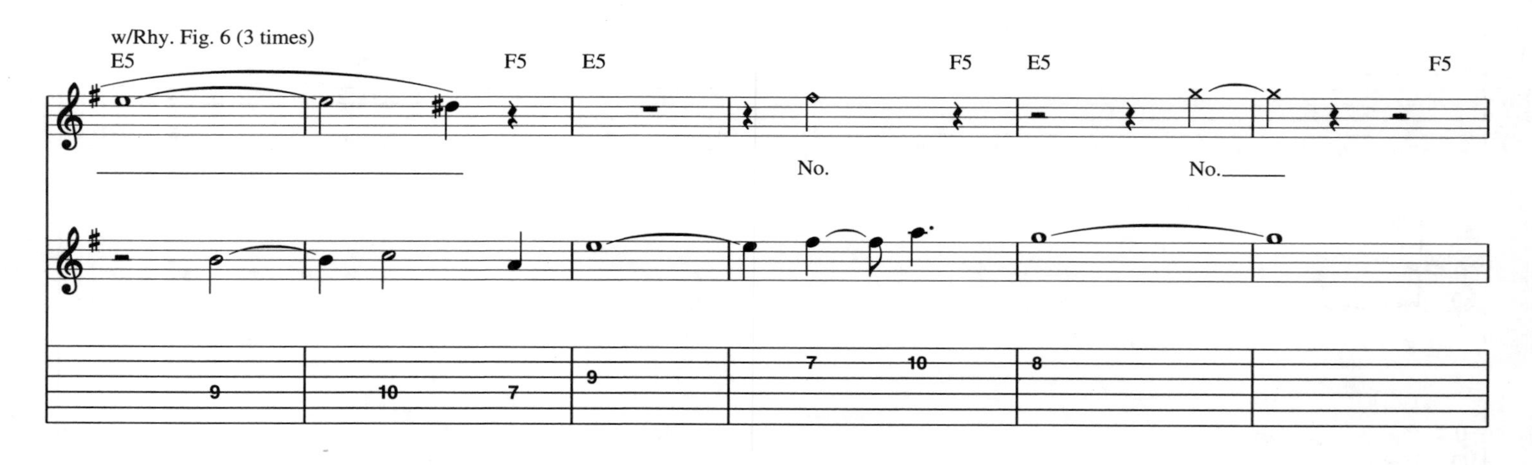
w/Rhy. Fig. 6 (3 times)
E5
F5
E5
F5
E5
F5
No.
No.

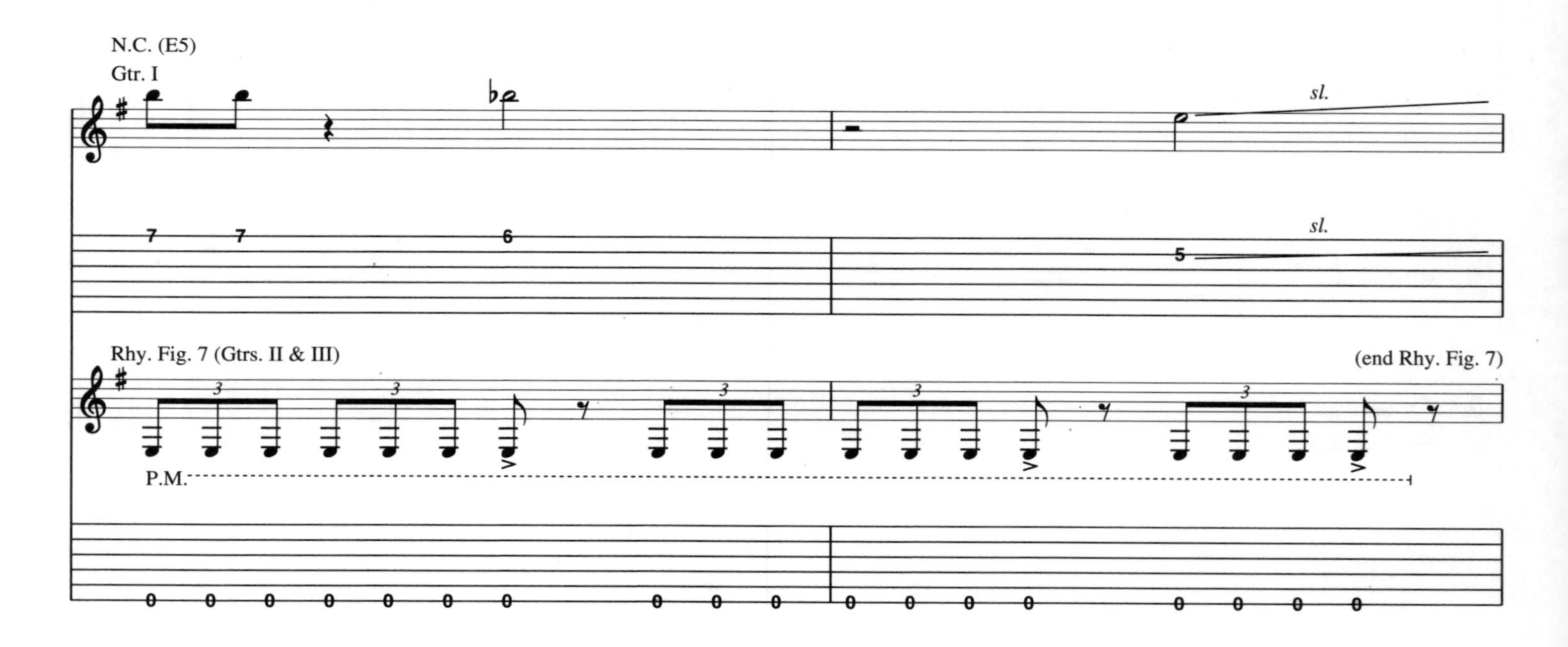
N.C. (E5)
Gtr. I
sl.
sl.
Rhy. Fig. 7 (Gtrs. II & III)
(end Rhy. Fig. 7)
P.M.

No, no, no, no, no!
Rhy. Fig. 8
(end Rhy. Fig. 8)
P.M.
w/Rhy. Fig. 6
E5
Play 4 times
F5
w/Rhy. Fig. 7
N.C.(E5)
w/Rhy. Fig. 8
Oh please, God, help me.

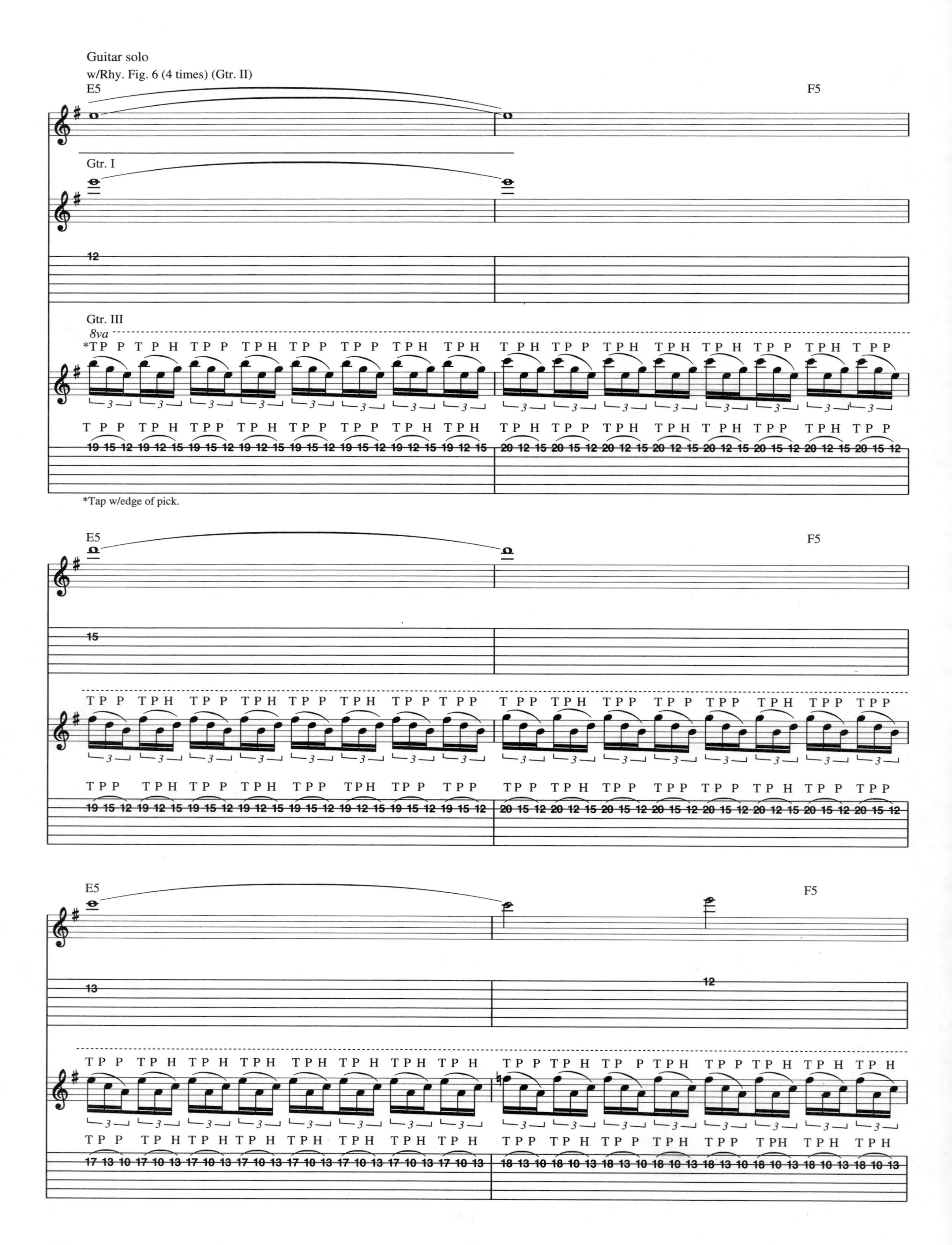
Guitar solo
w/Rhy. Fig. 6 (4 times) (Gtr. II)
E5
F5
Gtr. I
Gtr. III
8va
*Tap w/edge of pick.

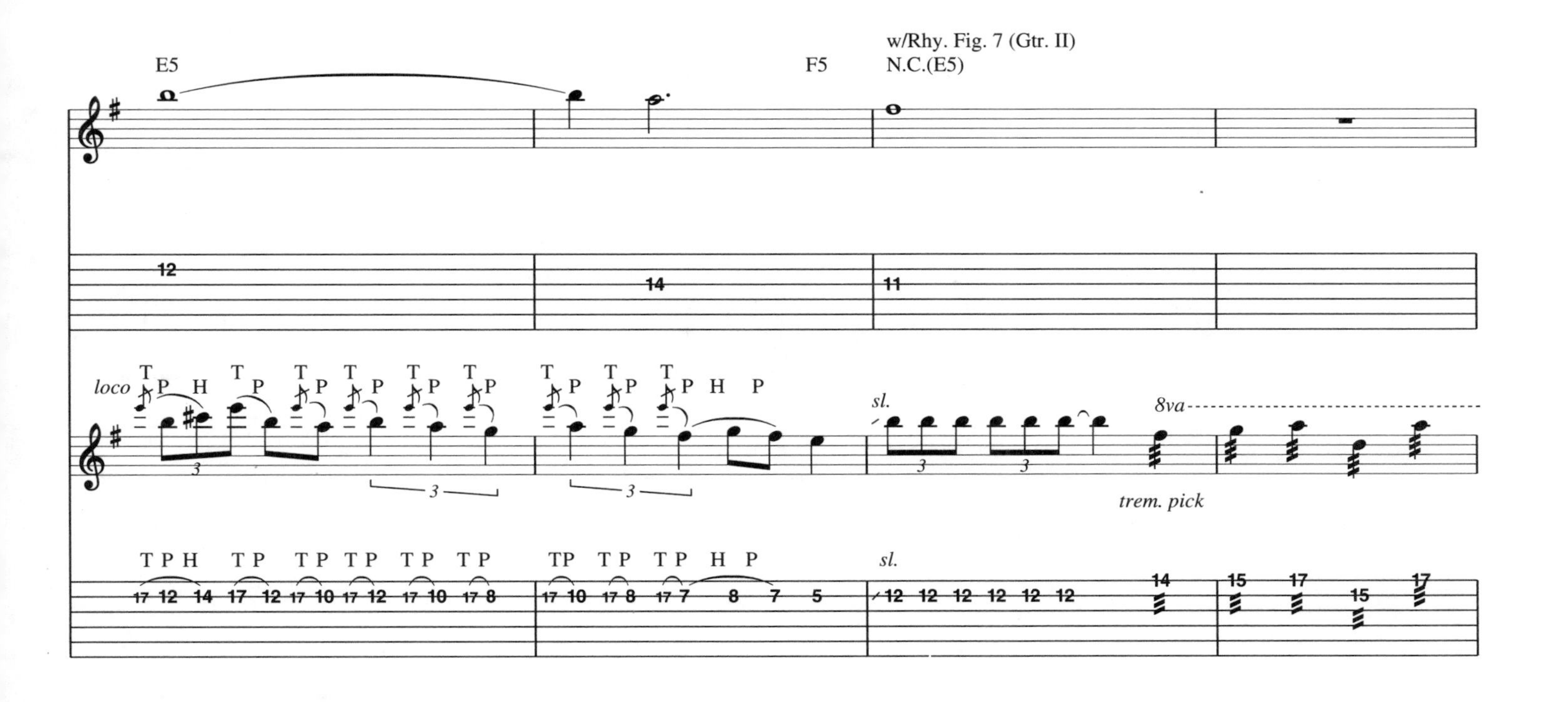
w/Rhy. Fig. 7 (Gtr. II)
E5
F5
N.C.(E5)
loco
sl.
8va
trem. pick

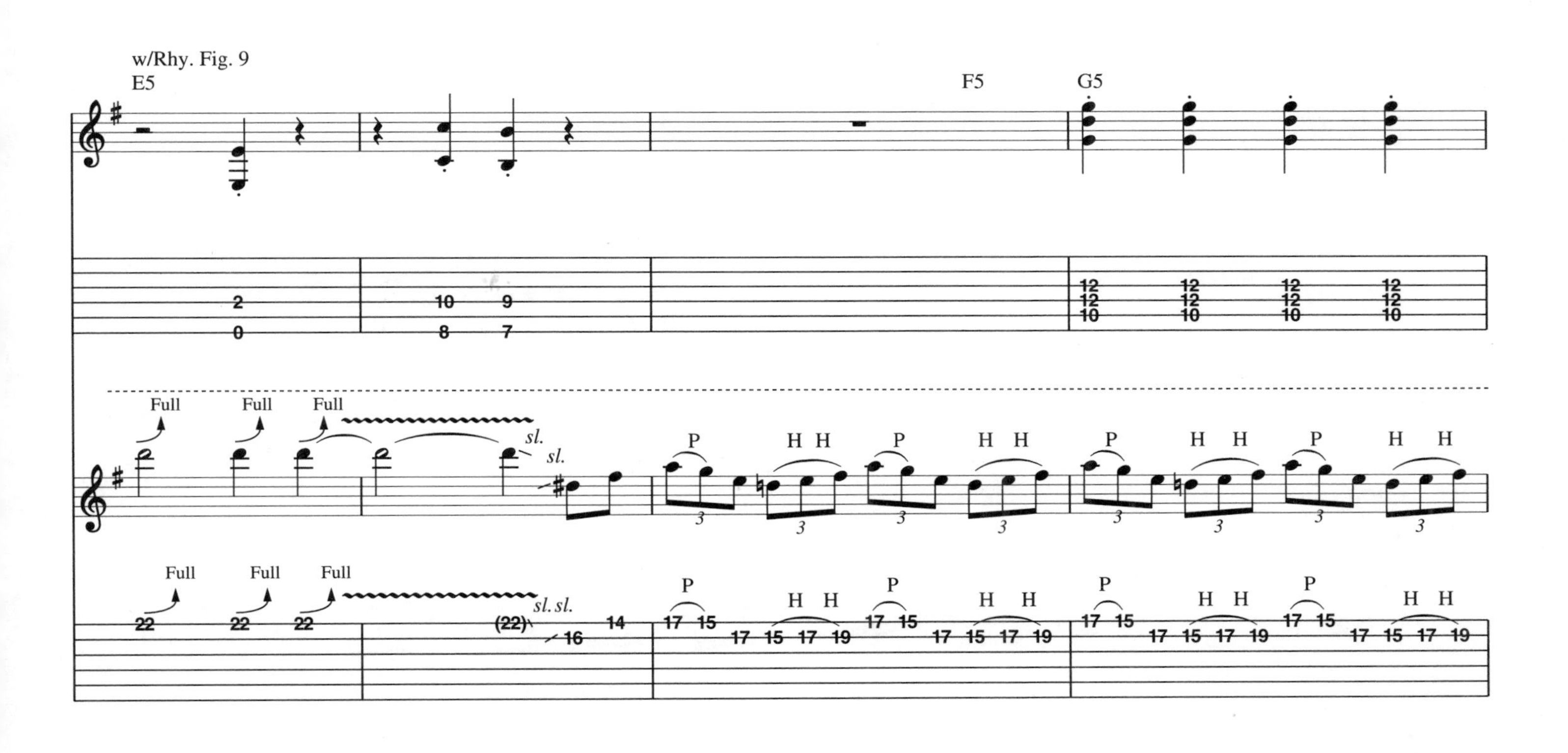
w/Rhy. Fig. 9
E5
F5
G5
Full
sl.

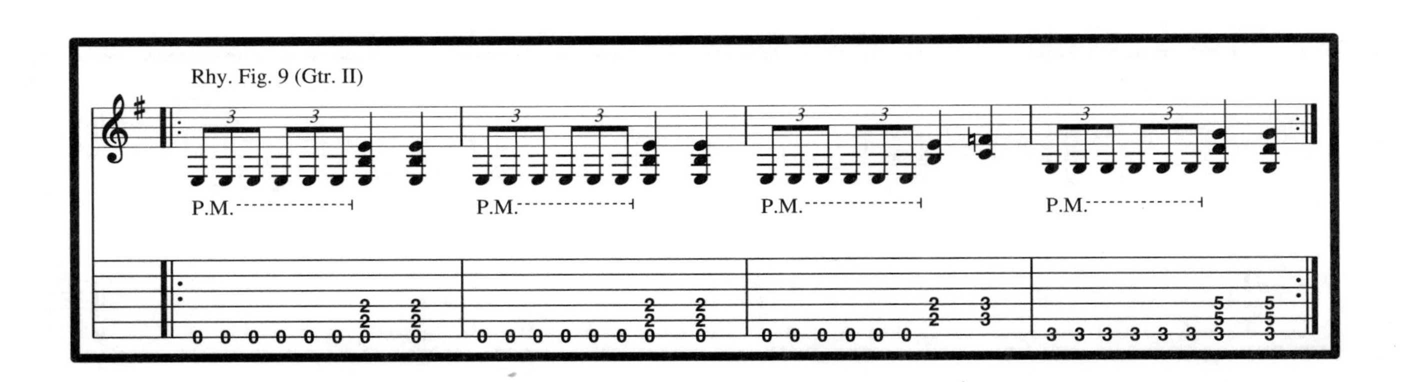
Rhy. Fig. 9 (Gtr. II)
P.M.

E5
(Gtr. I out)
F5
G5
Gtr. III
Full
w/Rhy. Fig. 10
A♭5
1/2
sl.
F5
loco
G5
A♭5
F5
Rhy. Fig. 10 (Gtr. II)
P.M.

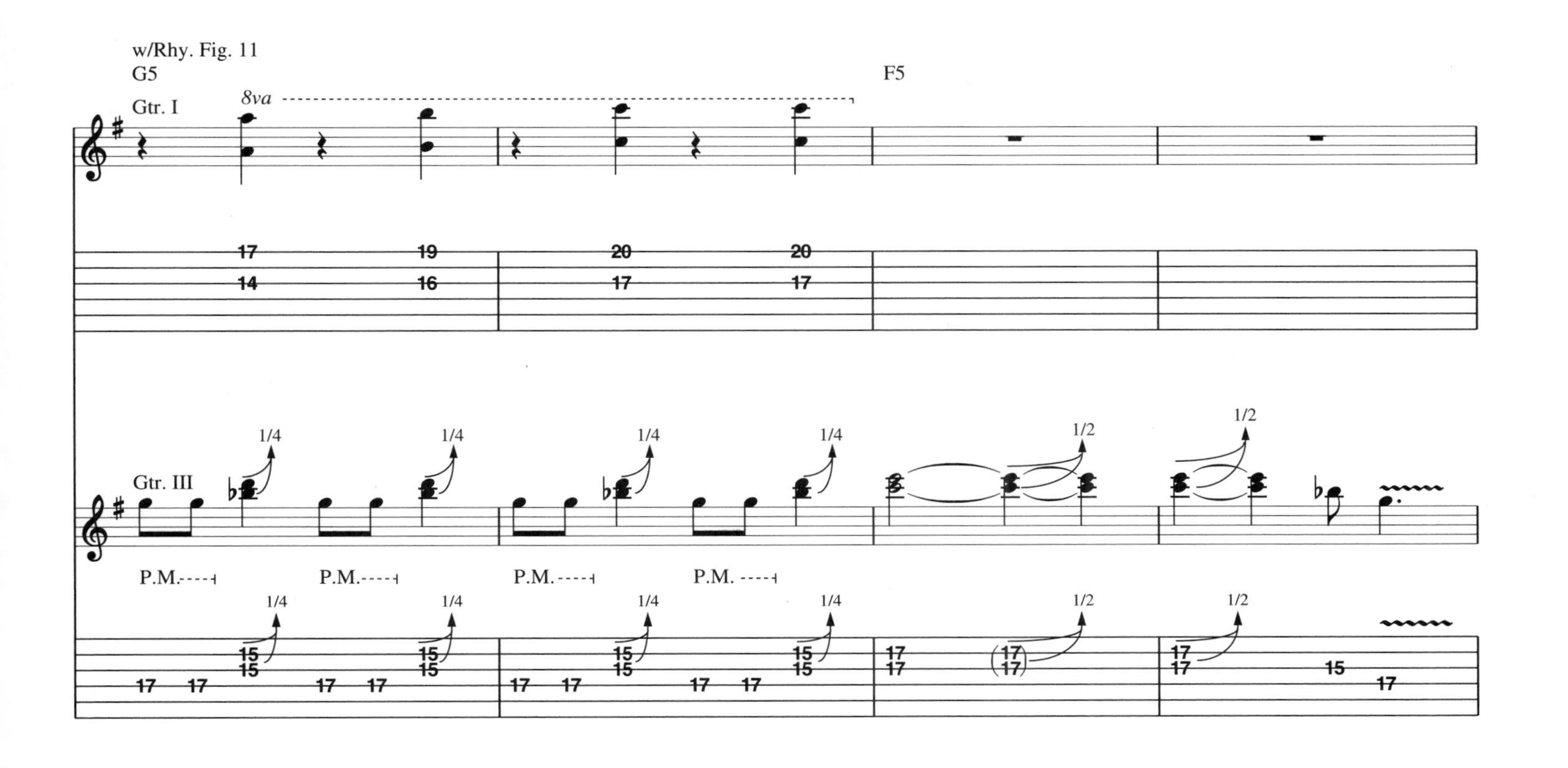
w/Rhy. Fig. 11
G5
F5
Gtr. I
8va
Gtr. III
1/4
1/2
P.M.

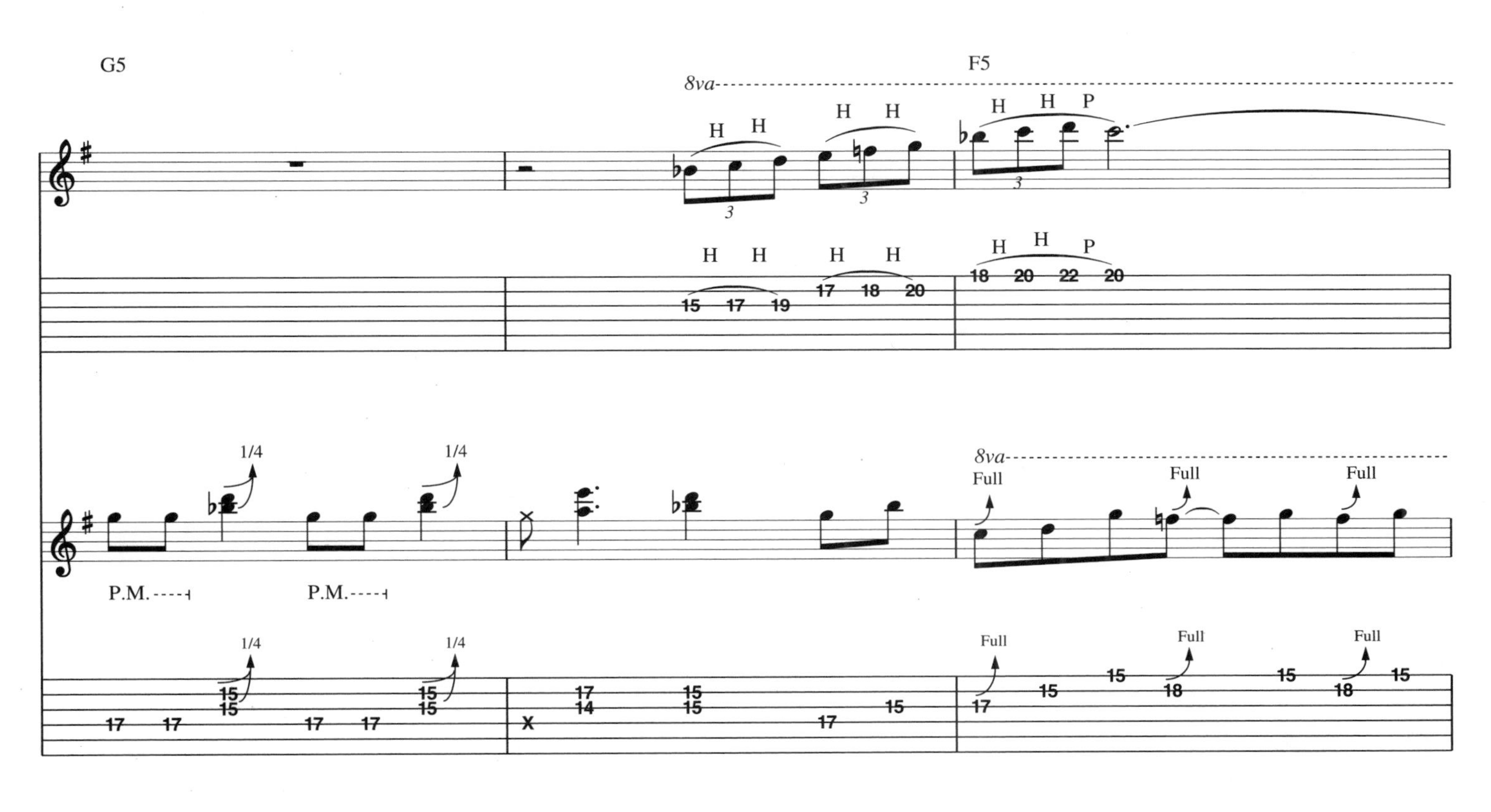
G5
F5
8va
H H
H H
H H P
1/4
Full
P.M.

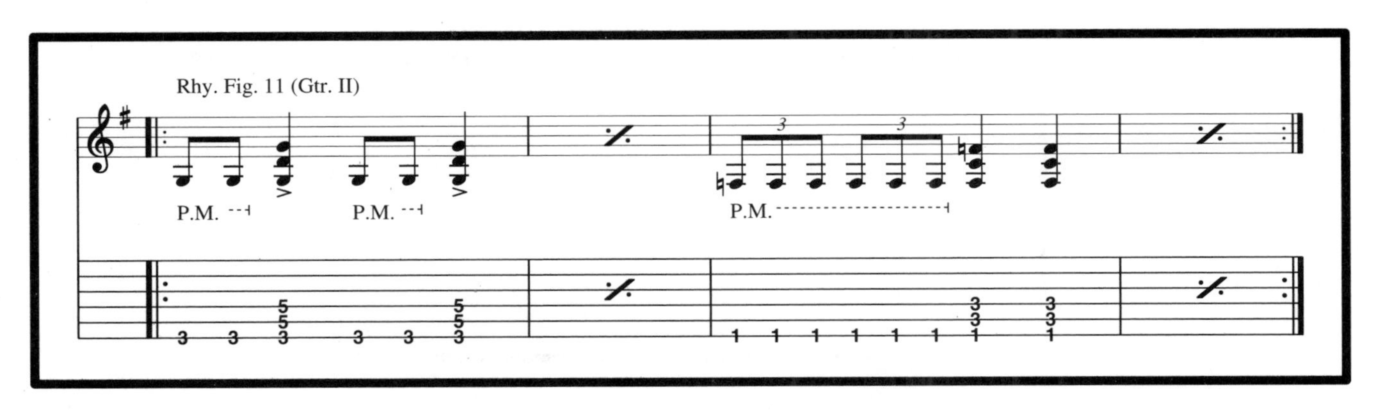
Rhy. Fig. 11 (Gtr. II)
P.M.

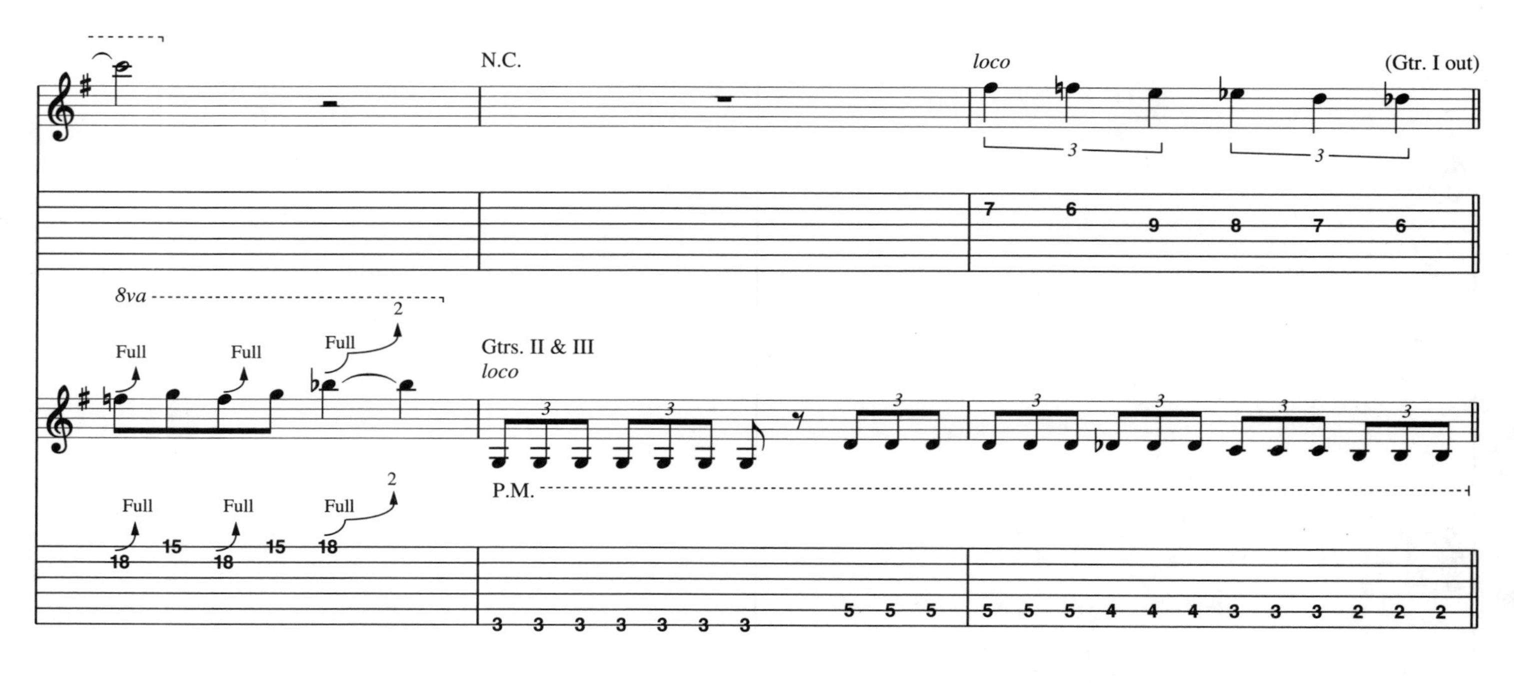
N.C.
loco
(Gtr. I out)
8va
Full
Full
Full
2
Gtrs. II & III
loco
P.M.

4th time w/Fill 1
E5
Gtrs. II & III
Play 4 times
F5
N.C.
P.M.

N.C.
Riff B1 (Gtr. III)
(end Riff B1)
P sl.
Riff B (Gtr. II)
(end Riff B)
P P

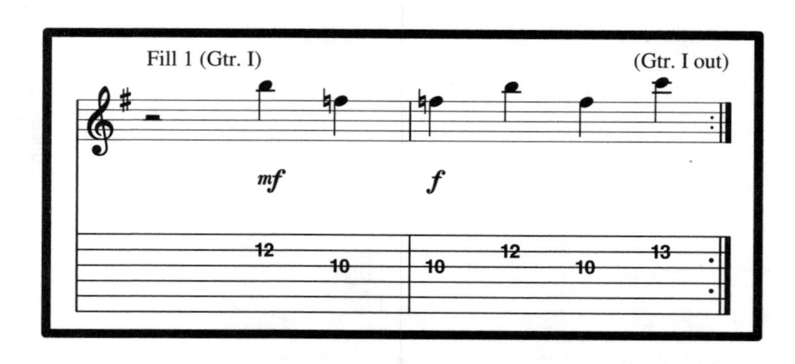
Fill 1 (Gtr. I)
(Gtr. I out)
mf
f

Gtr. I
Gtr. III
Gtr. II
w/Riffs B & B1 (both 2 times)
(Gtr. I out)
Outro
E5
F5
Please, God, help me.
Hey! Hey!
(end Fill 2)
(cont. on lower staff)
Fill 2 (Gtr. I)
Rhy. Fig. 12 (Gtrs. II & III)
(end Rhy. Fig. 12)
P.M.
Full
1/2

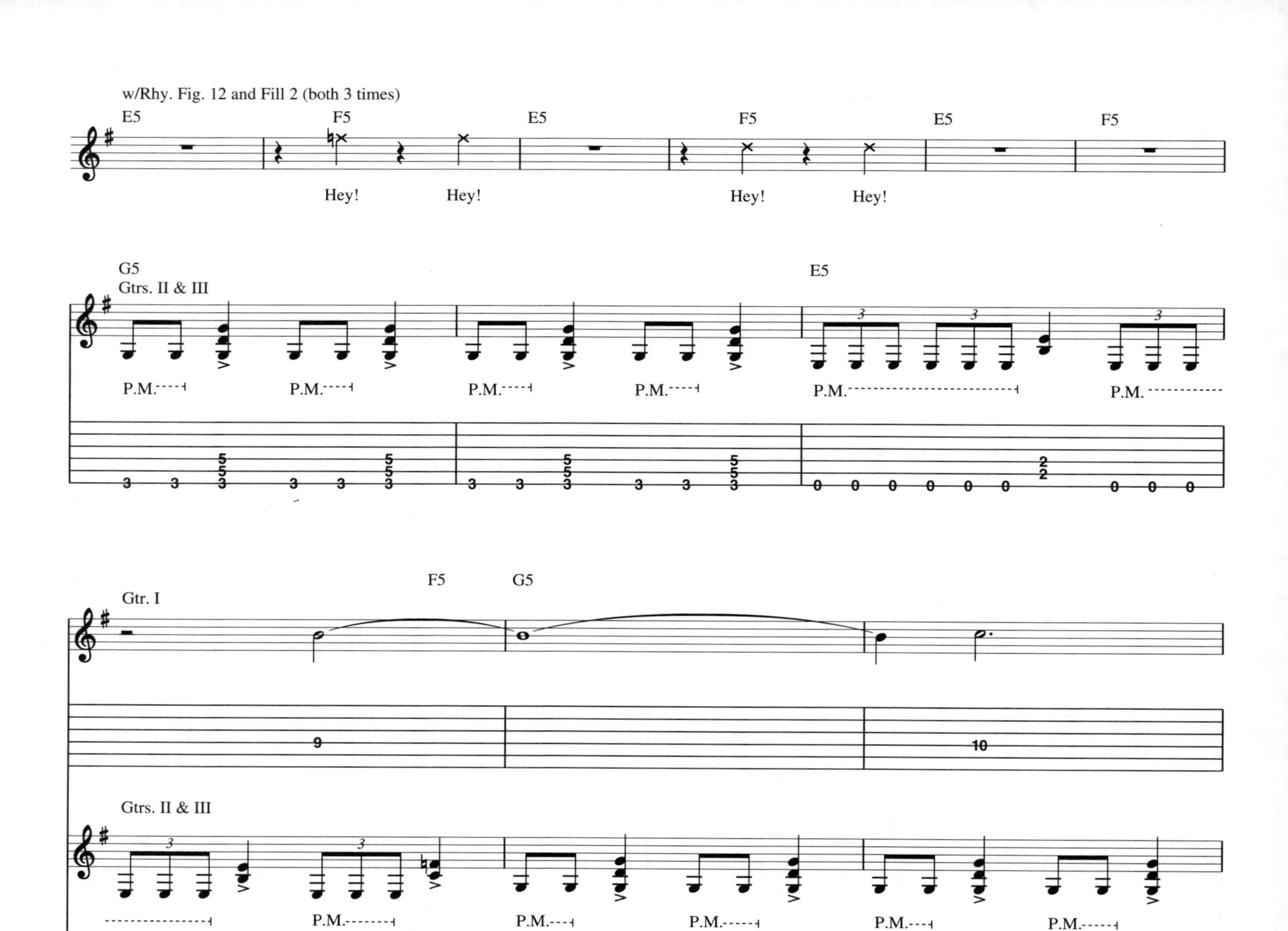
w/Rhy. Fig. 12 and Fill 2 (both 3 times)
E5
F5
E5
F5
E5
F5
Hey!
Hey!
Hey!
Hey!
G5
Gtrs. II & III
E5
P.M.
Gtr. I
F5
G5
Gtrs. II & III
P.M.

E5
F5
E5
F5
Hey!
Hey!
Hey!
Hey!
P.M.

*Gtr. II to left of slash in TAB.
**P.M. refers to Gtr. III only.

ENTER SANDMAN

Words and Music by James Hetfield,
Lars Ulrich and Kirk Hammett

Gtr. I
f
P.M.
sl.
A5
E5
⑤ 1fr.
B♭
Rhy. Fig. 1
P
H

(cont. in notation)
Bb A5
E5
Yeah.
N.C.
E5
G5
F#5
Oh, yeah.
Let loose, man.
Rhy. Fig. 2 (Gtrs. II & IV)
(end Rhy. Fig. 2)
P.M.
sl.
8va

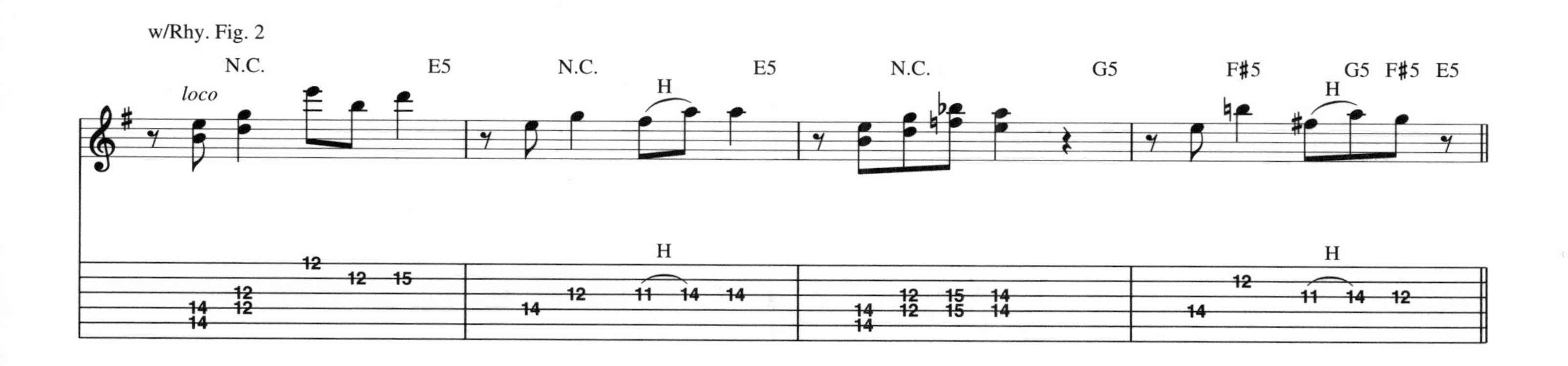
w/Rhy. Fig. 2
N.C. E5 N.C. E5 N.C. G5 F#5 G5 F#5 E5
loco
H
H
H
H

1st Verse
N.C. F5 N.C. F5 N.C. G5
Say your prayers, lit - tle one. Don't for - get, my son, to in - clude ev - 'ry - one.
Rhy. Fig. 3 (Gtrs. II & IV)
P.M.
P.M.
P.M.

F#5 G5 F#5 E5 N.C. F5 N.C. F5
I tuck you in, warm with - in, keep you free from sin
Gtr. I
sl.
sl.
P.M.
P.M.

Half time feel
Pre-chorus
N.C.
G5
F#5
G5 F#5 N.C.
till the sand-man, he comes,
ah.
Sleep with one
sl.
(end Rhy. Fig. 3)
Rhy. Fig. 4
P.M.
eye o - pen,
grip-ping your pil - low tight.
(end half time feel)
P
H P
(end Rhy. Fig. 4)

Chorus
F#5
B5
F#5
B5
F#5
B5
E5
Ex - it: light.__ (Spoken:) What is it? (Audience:) (En - ter: night.)__
H sl.
sl.
Gtr. I
*P.M.
Rhy. Fig. 5B (Gtr. IV)
Rhy. Fig. 5
(Gtr. IV cont. on upper staff)
(end Rhy. Fig. 5)
Rhy. Fig. 5A (Gtr. II)
*P.M. applies to Gtr. IV only.
F#5
B5
E5
G5
F#5
G5
F#5
E5
Take__ my hand.__ We're off to nev - er - nev - er land.__
*P.M.
(end Rhy. Fig. 5B)
(end Rhy. Fig. 5A)
P.M.
sl.
*P.M. applies to Gtr. IV only.

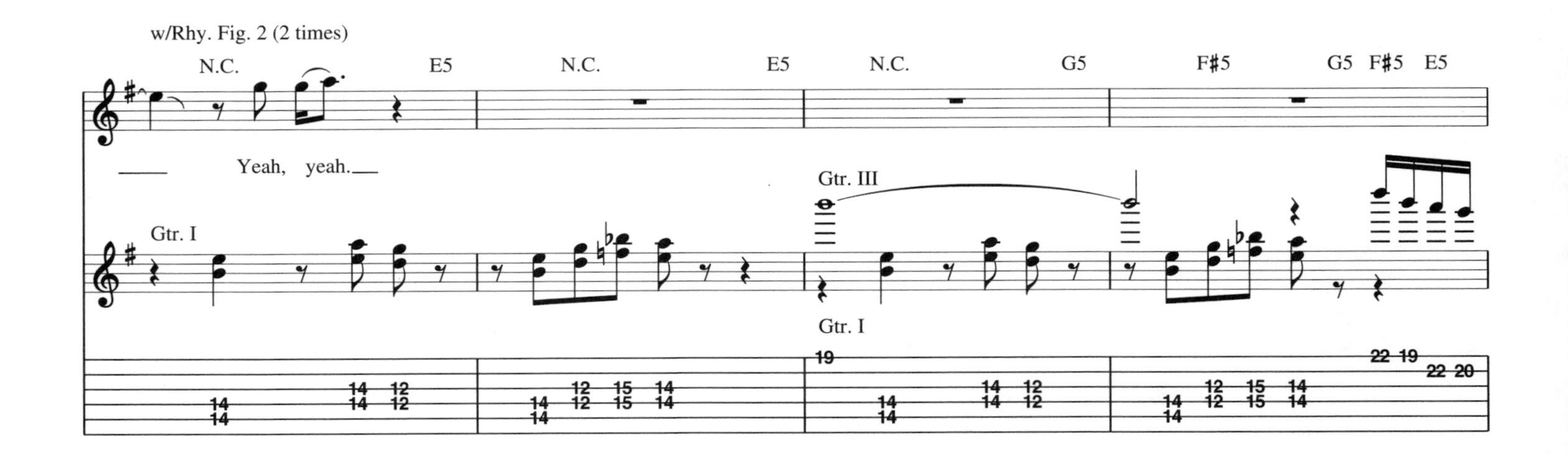
w/Rhy. Fig. 2 (2 times)
N.C.
E5
N.C.
E5
N.C.
G5
F#5
G5 F#5 E5
Yeah, yeah.
Gtr. III
Gtr. I
Gtr. I

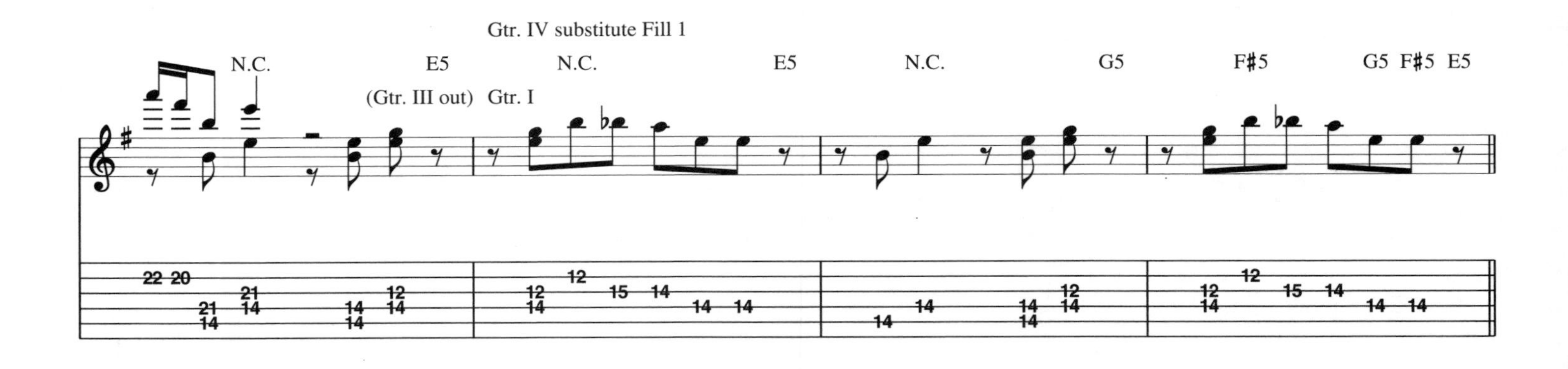
Gtr. IV substitute Fill 1
N.C.
E5
(Gtr. III out) Gtr. I
N.C.
E5
N.C.
G5
F#5
G5 F#5 E5

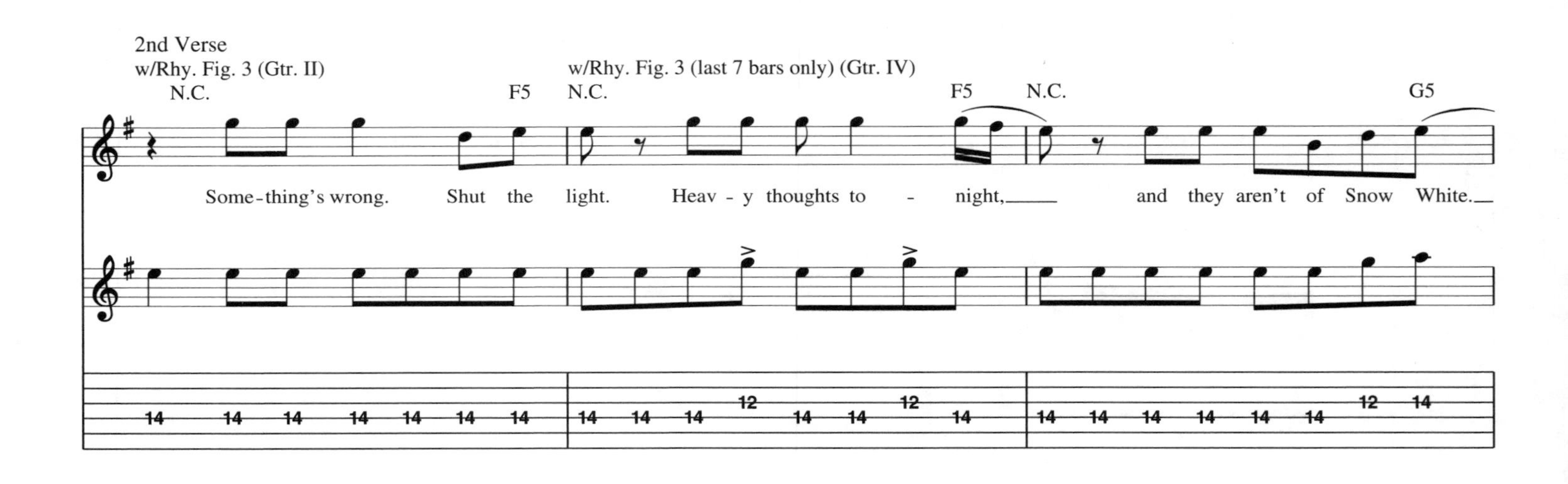
2nd Verse
w/Rhy. Fig. 3 (Gtr. II)
N.C.
F5
w/Rhy. Fig. 3 (last 7 bars only) (Gtr. IV)
N.C.
F5
N.C.
G5
Some-thing's wrong. Shut the light. Heav - y thoughts to - night, and they aren't of Snow White.

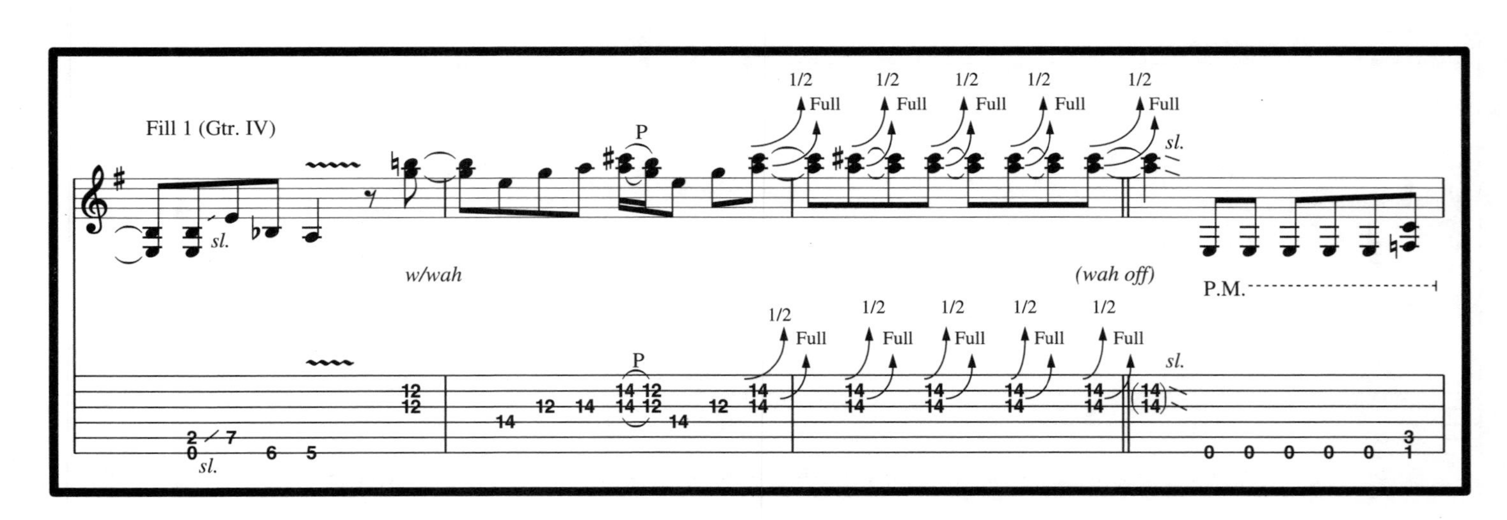
Fill 1 (Gtr. IV)
sl.
w/wah
P
1/2
Full
(wah off)
P.M.

Gtr. IV substitute Fill 2
F#5
G5
F#5
E5
N.C.
F5
N.C.
F5
Dreams of war, dreams of liars, dreams of drag - on's fire
N.C.
G5
F#5
G5 F#5 N.C.
Half time feel
Pre-chorus
w/Rhy. Fig. 4
and the things that will bite,
yeah.
Sleep with one
Riff B
8va
sl.
eye o - pen,
grip - ping your pil - low tight.
(end half time feel)
(end Riff B)

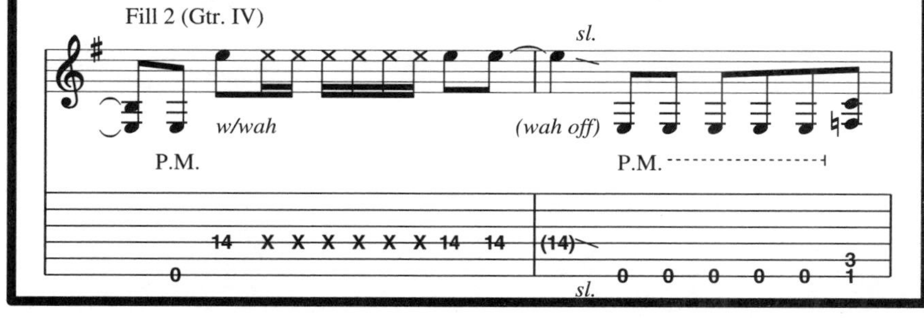

Fill 2 (Gtr. IV)
w/wah
(wah off)
sl.
P.M.
P.M.

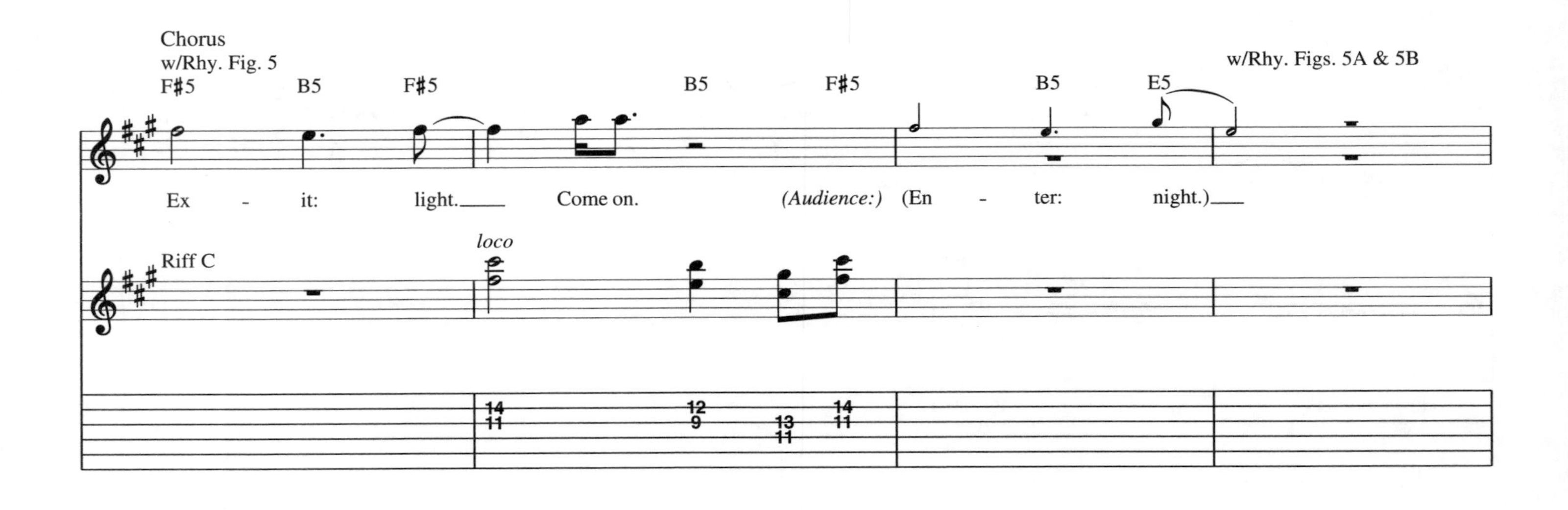
Chorus
w/Rhy. Fig. 5
w/Rhy. Figs. 5A & 5B
F♯5 B5 F♯5 B5 F♯5 B5 E5
Ex - it: light. Come on. (Audience:) (En - ter: night.)
Riff C
loco
14 11 12 9 13 11 14 11

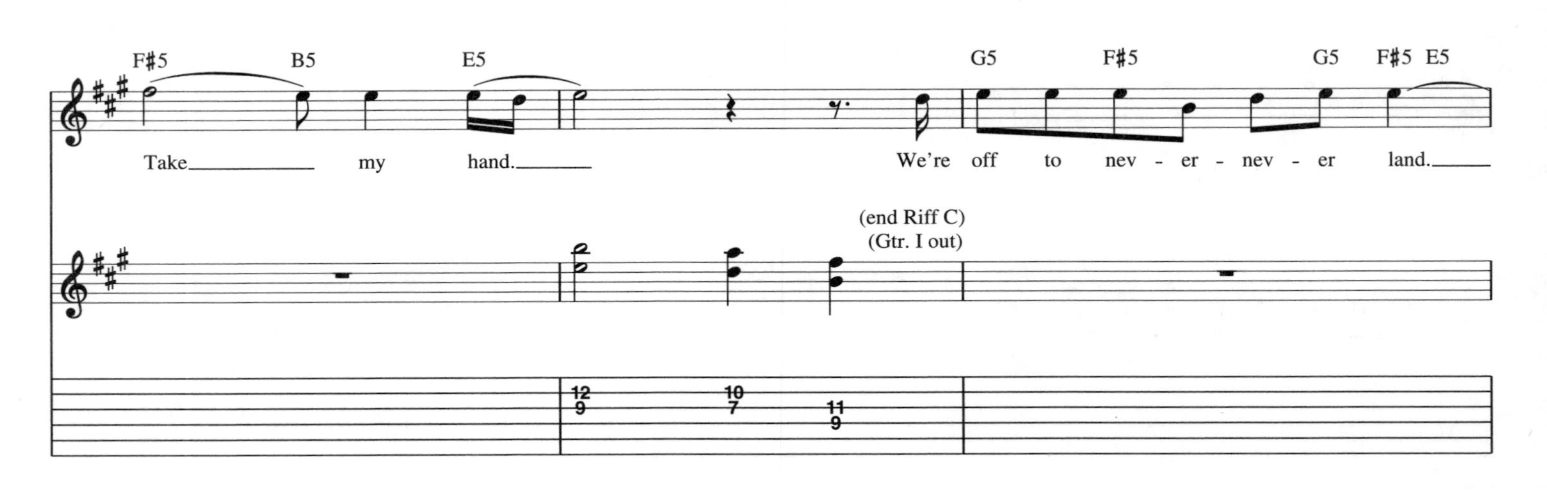
F♯5 B5 E5 G5 F♯5 G5 F♯5 E5
Take my hand. We're off to nev - er - nev - er land.
(end Riff C)
(Gtr. I out)
12 9 10 7 11 9

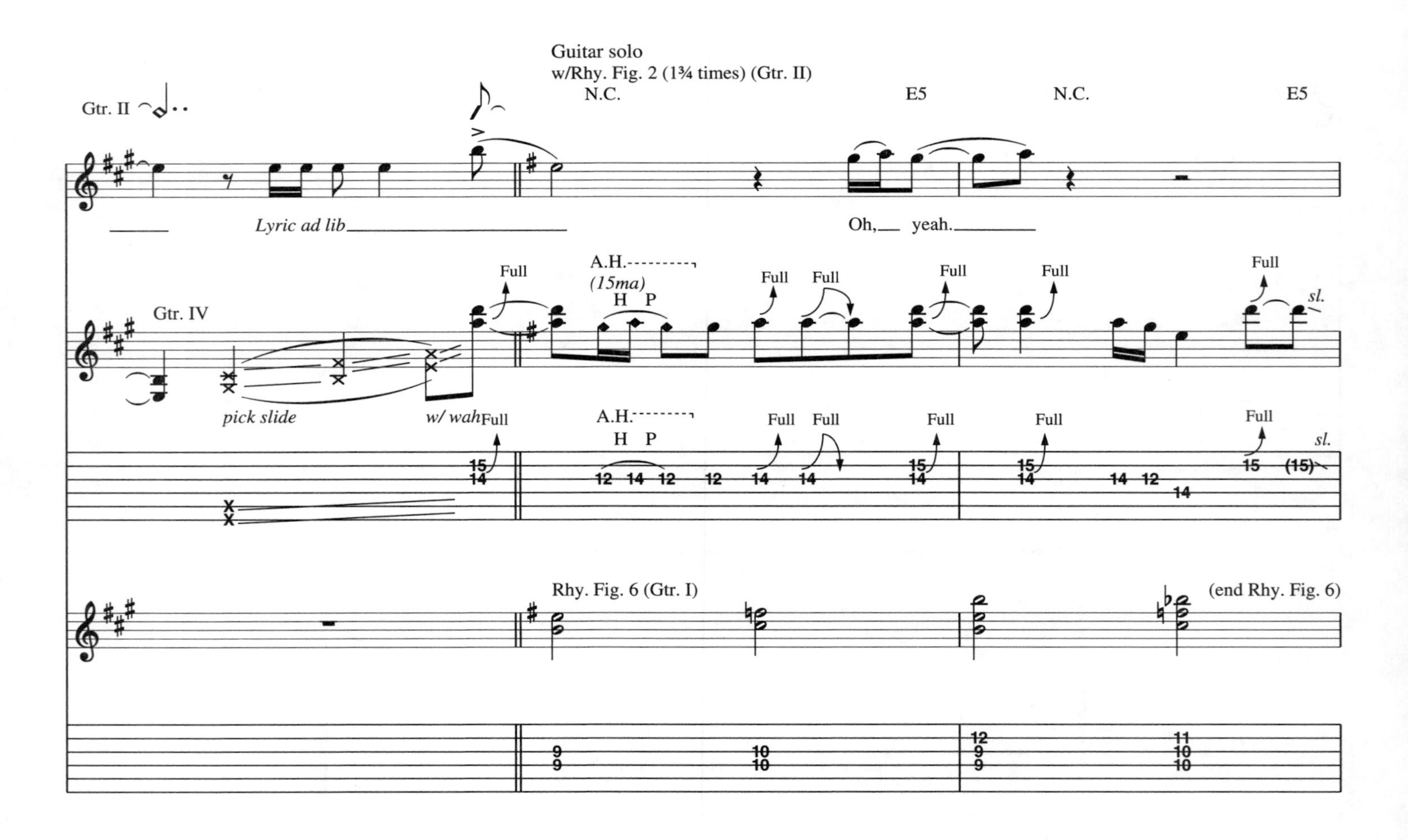
Guitar solo
w/Rhy. Fig. 2 (1¾ times) (Gtr. II)
N.C. E5 N.C. E5
Gtr. II
Lyric ad lib
Oh, yeah.
Gtr. IV
Full
A.H.
(15ma)
H P
sl.
pick slide
w/ wah
Rhy. Fig. 6 (Gtr. I)
(end Rhy. Fig. 6)

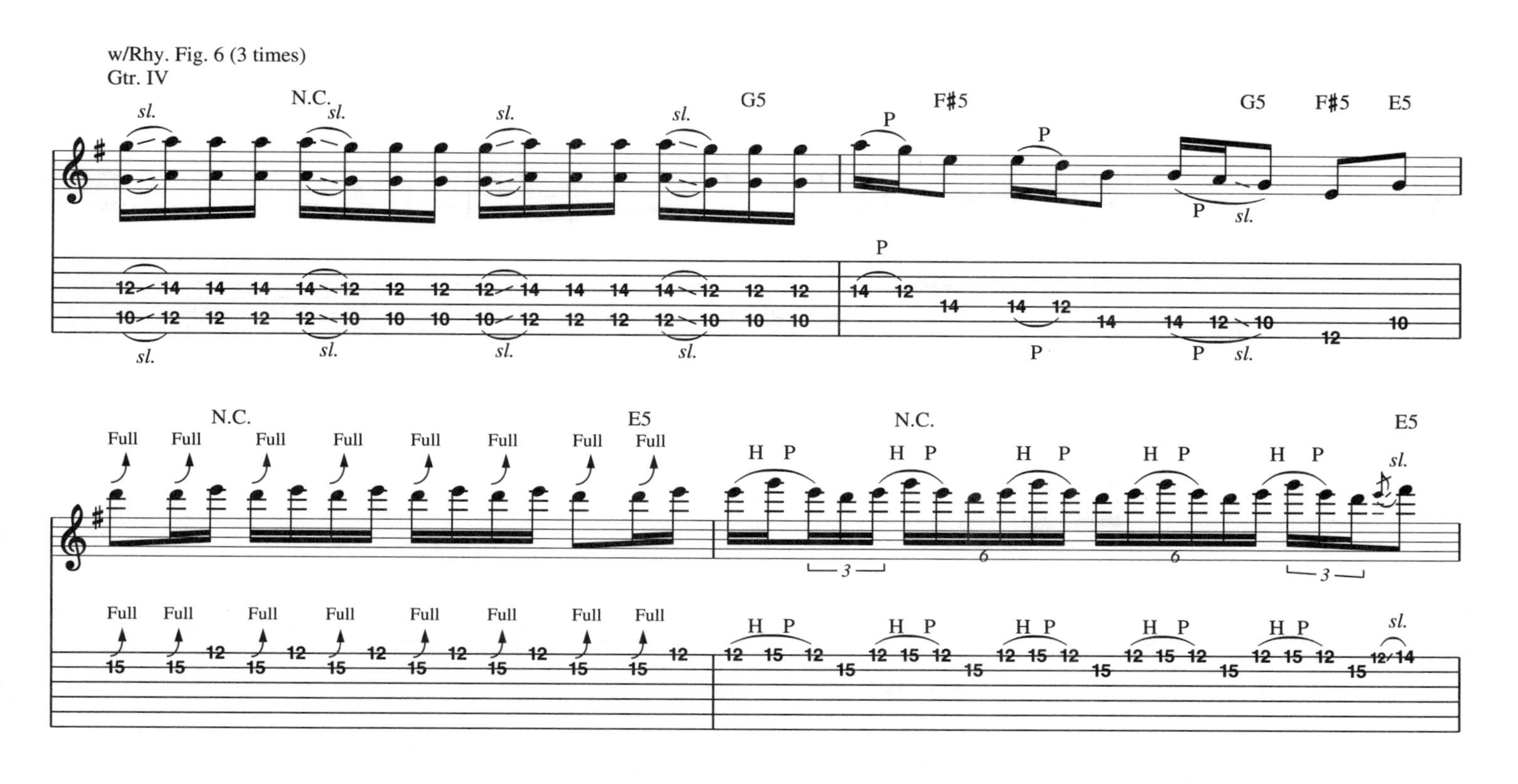
w/Rhy. Fig. 6 (3 times)
Gtr. IV
N.C.
G5
F#5
G5
F#5
E5
N.C.
E5
N.C.
E5

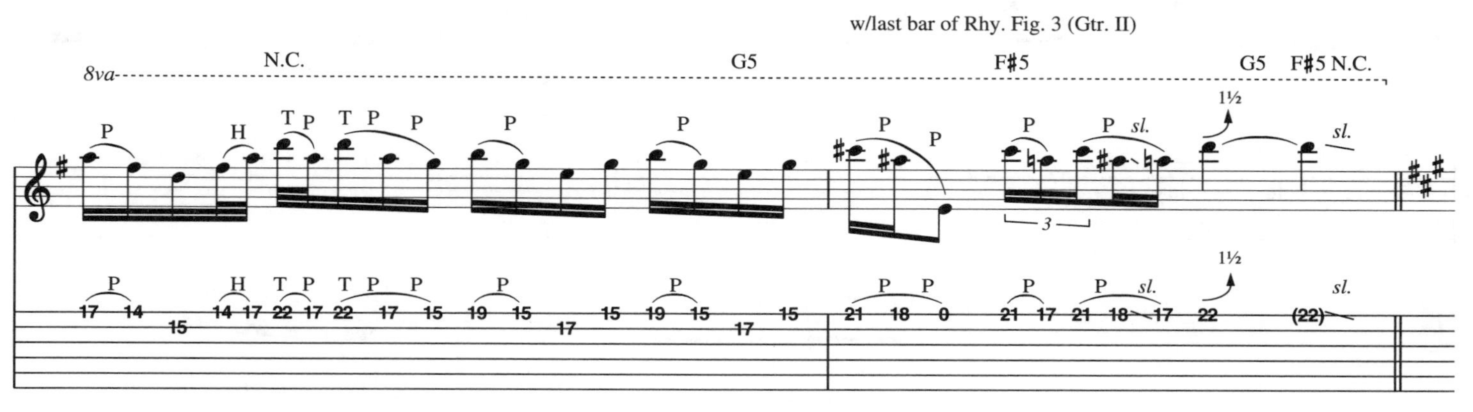
w/last bar of Rhy. Fig. 3 (Gtr. II)
8va
N.C.
G5
F#5
G5
F#5 N.C.

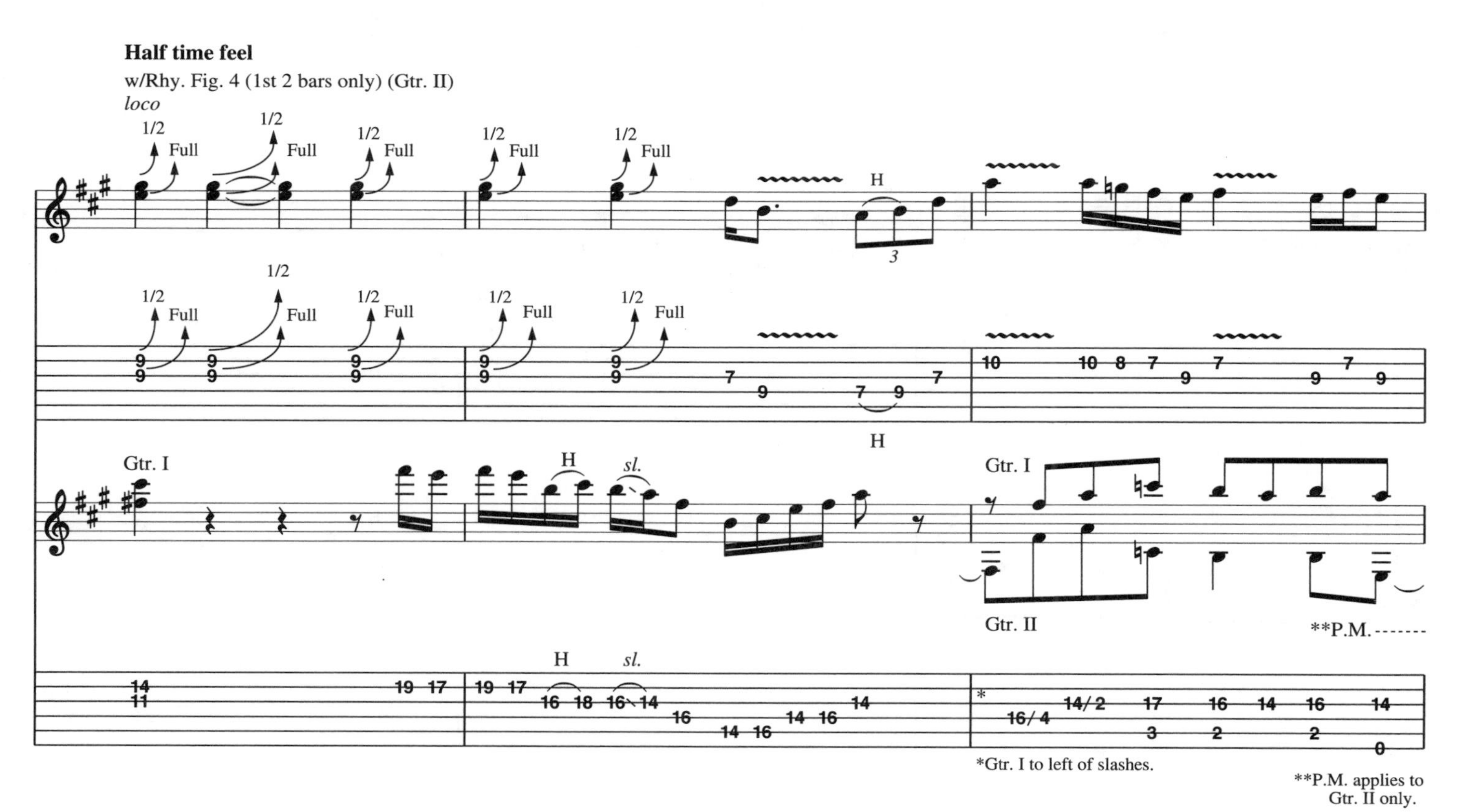
Half time feel
w/Rhy. Fig. 4 (1st 2 bars only) (Gtr. II)
loco
Gtr. I
Gtr. II
**P.M.
*Gtr. I to left of slashes.
**P.M. applies to Gtr. II only.

w/Rhy. Fig. 5 (Gtr. II)
(end half time feel)
Gtr. I
w/Rhy. Fig. 5A (1st 2 bars only)
trem. bar
N.C.
loco
Gtr. II *P.M.
(Gtr. II out)
*P.M. applies to Gtr. II only.

Put your hands to - geth - er.
A.H.
(8va)
(Gtr. IV out)
trem. bar
H
(wah off)
A.H. pitches: F♯
F♯
Gtr. I
Gtr. II
mf
clean tone
w/Riff A (6 times)
N.C.
(Spoken:) Now I lay me down to sleep.
(Child:) Now I lay me down to sleep.
Pray the Lord my soul
(Gtr. I)
(Gtr. II)
to keep.
Pray the Lord my soul to keep.
If I die before I wake,
If I die before

w/1st bar of Rhy. Fig. 4 (4 times) (Gtr. II)
N.C.
pray the Lord my soul to take.
I wake, pray the Lord my soul to take.
Hush, lit - tle ba - by. Don't
Gtr. I
Gtr. II
say a word.
And nev - er mind that noise you heard.
w/Rhy. Fig. 4 (Gtr. II)
w/Riff B
It's just the beasts un - der your bed, ah, in your clos - et, in your head.
Chorus
*w/Rhy. Fig. 5
w/Riff C
w/Rhy. Figs. 5A & 5B
(both 1st 3 bars only)
F#5 B5 F#5 B5 F#5 B5 E5
Ex - it: light. Come on.
(Audience:) (En - ter: night.)
*Resume f and dist. tone.
w/Rhy. Fig. 5
F#5 B5 E5 F#5 B5 F#5 B5 F#5
Grain of sand, ah. Ex - it: light.

w/Rhy. Figs. 5A & 5B
B5
E5
F#5
B5
E5
En - ter: night.
Take my hand.
Oo, we're
H P
H P
14
11
13
12
9
11
11
10
12
13
12
11
12
14
12
9
11
G5
F#5
G5
F#5
E5
w/Rhy. Fig. 7 (7 times)
Gtr. II
off to nev - er - nev - er land.
Yeah,
mf
Rhy. Fig. 7 (Gtr. I)
Gtr. IV
Fdbk.
Gtr. IV
Fdbk.
12
9
12
9
9
11
10
10
3
hey, hey.
(cont. on lower staff)

(Gtr. II out)
N.C.
Gtr. I
mp
Gtr. IV
Fdbk.
(8va)
Fdbk.
(Gtr. IV out)
Fdbk.
Fdbk.
Fdbk. pitch: A
N.C.
Gtr. I
mf
Gtr. II
E5
f
Outro
w/Rhy. Fig. 1 (4 times) (Gtr. II)
N.C.
E5
Gtr. IV
E5
w/Rhy. Fig. 1 (2 times) (Gtr. IV)
N.C.
E5
N.C.
E5
Oo!
Hey, yeah.
Rhy. Fig. 8
8va
(end Rhy. Fig. 8)
f
w/Rhy. Fig. 2
w/Rhy. Fig. 8 (2 times)
N.C.
E5
N.C.
E5
N.C.
G5
F#5
G5
F#5
E5
Woh,
yeah.
No,
whoa,

N.C.
F5
N.C.
F5
w/Rhy. Fig. 9 (10 times)
N.C.
F5
N.C.
F5
huh.
(We're off to nev - er - nev - er land.
Gtrs. II & IV
Rhy. Fig. 9
P.M.
sl.
Take my hand, uh.
We're off to nev - er - nev - er - land.
Riff D (Gtr. I)
(end Riff D)
w/Riff D
Take my hand,
uh.
We're off to nev - er - nev - er land.)
w/last bar of Riff D
w/Rhy. Fig. 10 (11 times)
Gtr. II substitute Rhy. Fill 1
Uh!
Rhy. Fig. 10 (Gtrs. II & IV)
Gtr. I
H
Rhy. Fill 1 (Gtr. II)

*P.M. applies to Gtr. IV only (next 5 bars).

Free time
Em
Gtr. II
trem. pick
A.H.
(8va)
F♯5
G5 F♯5
(Gtr. I cont. on lower staff)
Gtr. IV
w/wah
Full
P.M.
A.H. pitch: B
Gtr. I
(cont. in slashes)
P
H
1½

A.H.
(8va)
Full
sl.
A.H. pitches: F♯ G♯ F♯ G♯ F♯ G♯ F♯ G♯
In time ♩. = 140
(cont. in notation)
P
1/2
Harm.
trem. bar
(wah off)
N.C.
D5
E
P.M.
Gtr. I
Gtr. II
H P H P
*P.M. applies to Gtr. II only (till end).

• Tablature Explanation/Notation Legend •

TABLATURE: A six-line staff that graphically represents the guitar fingerboard. By placing a number on the appropriate line, the string and the fret of any note can be indicated. For example:

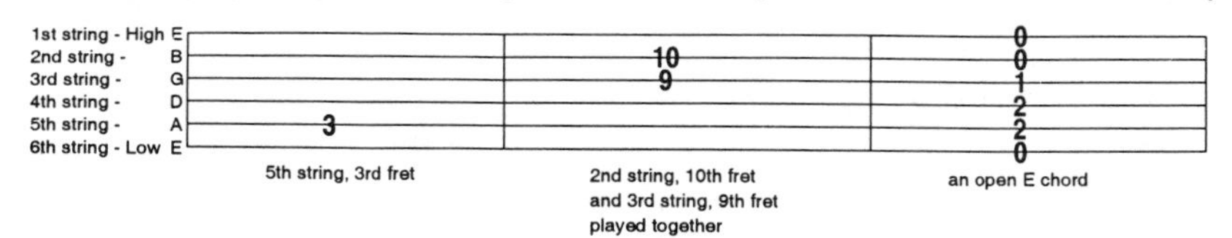

Definitions for Special Guitar Notation

BEND: Strike the note and bend up a half step (one fret).

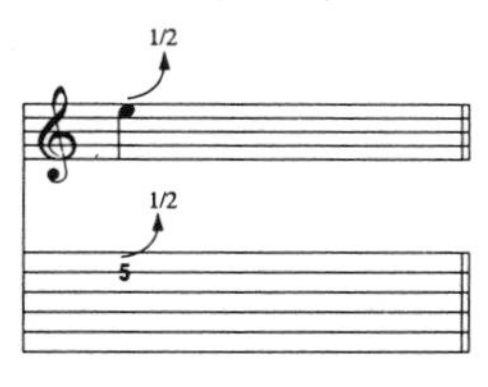

BEND: Strike the note and bend up a whole step (two frets).

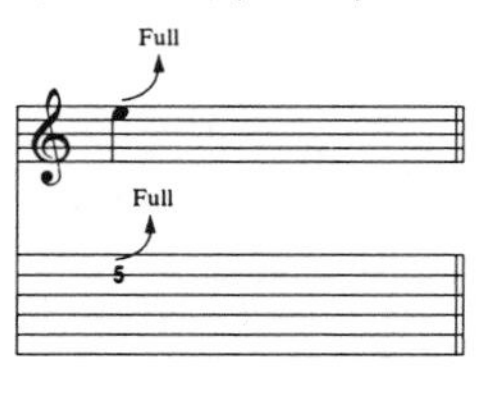

BEND AND RELEASE: Strike the note and bend up a half (or whole) step, then release the bend back to the original note. All three notes are tied; only the first note is struck.

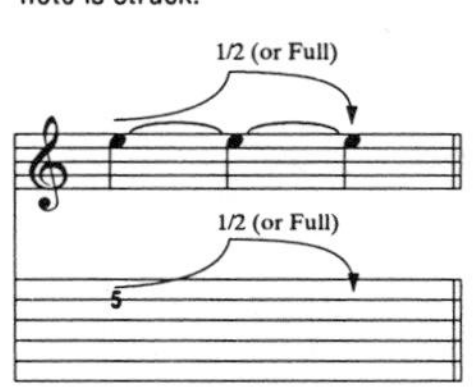

PRE-BEND: Bend the note up a half (or whole) step, then strike it.

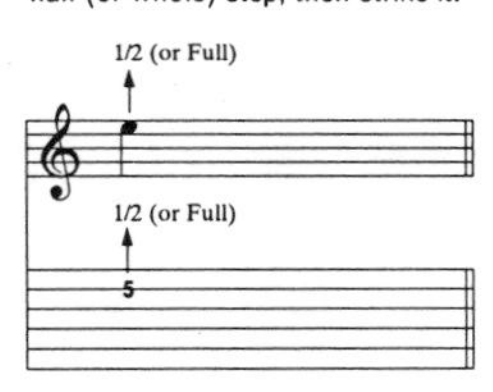

PRE-BEND AND RELEASE: Bend the note up a half (or whole) step, strike it and release the bend back to the original note.

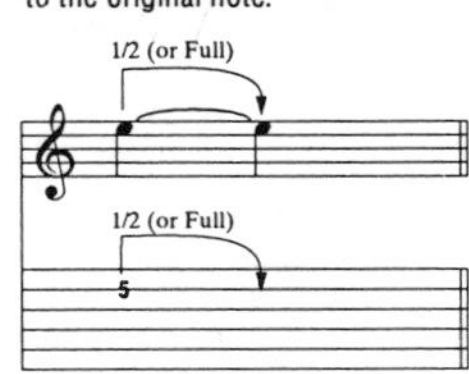

UNISON BEND: Strike the two notes simultaneously and bend the lower note to the pitch of the higher.

VIBRATO: Vibrate the note by rapidly bending and releasing the string with a left-hand finger.

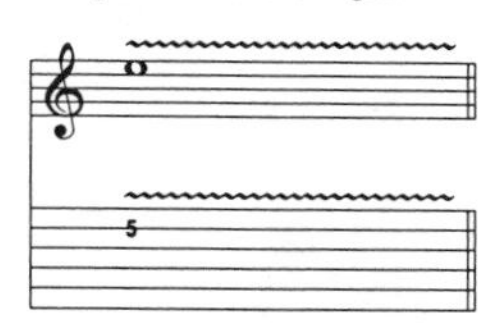

WIDE OR EXAGGERATED VIBRATO: Vibrate the pitch to a greater degree with a left-hand finger or the tremolo bar.

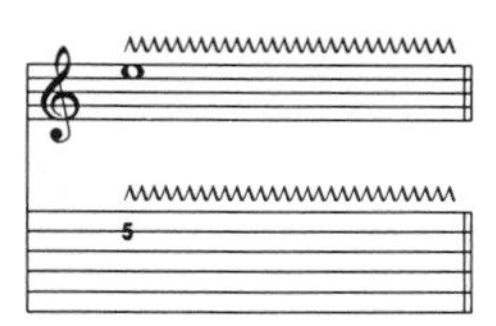

SLIDE: Strike the first note and then with the same left-hand finger move up the string to the second note. The second note is not struck.

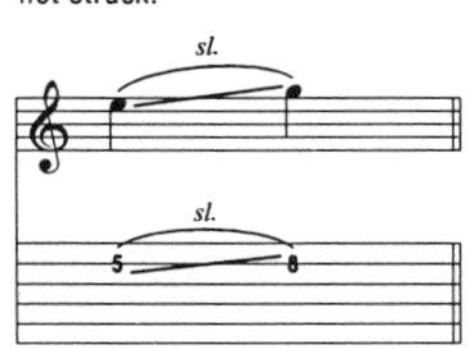

SLIDE: Same as above, except the second note is struck.

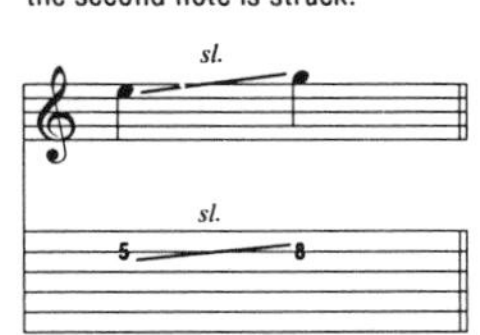

SLIDE: Slide up to the note indicated from a few frets below.

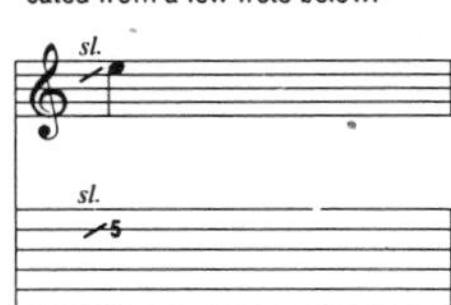

HAMMER-ON: Strike the first (lower) note, then sound the higher note with another finger by fretting it without picking.

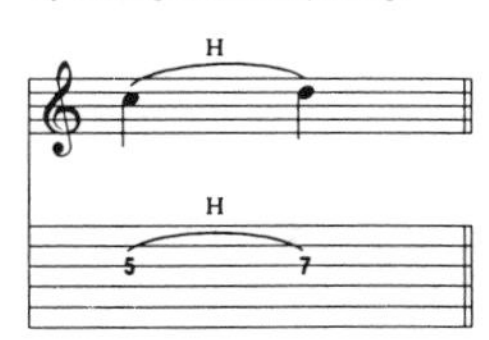

PULL-OFF: Place both fingers on the notes to be sounded. Strike the first (higher) note, then sound the lower note by pulling the finger off the higher note while keeping the lower note fretted.

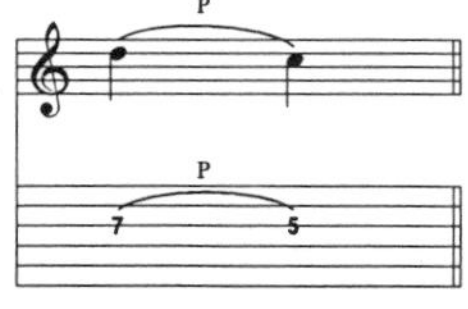

TRILL: Very rapidly alternate between the note indicated and the small note shown in parentheses by hammering on and pulling off.

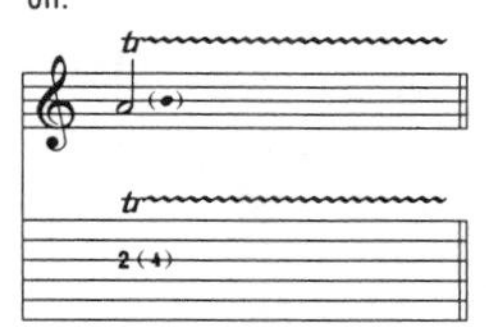

TAPPING: Hammer ("tap") the fret indicated with the right-hand index or middle finger and pull off to the note fretted by the left hand.

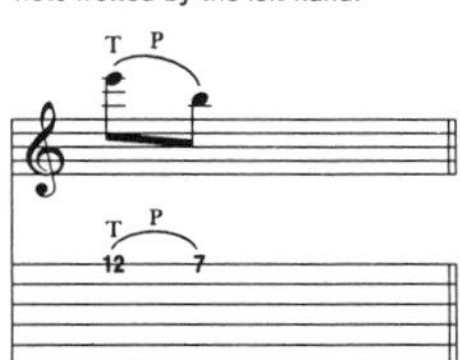

NATURAL HARMONIC: With a left-hand finger, lightly touch the string over the fret indicated, then strike it. A chime-like sound is produced.

ARTIFICIAL HARMONIC: Fret the note normally and sound the harmonic by adding the right-hand thumb edge or index finger tip to the normal pick attack.

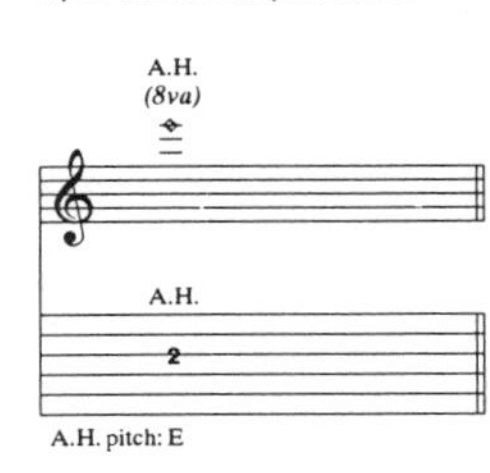

TREMOLO BAR: Drop the note by the number of steps indicated, then return to original pitch.

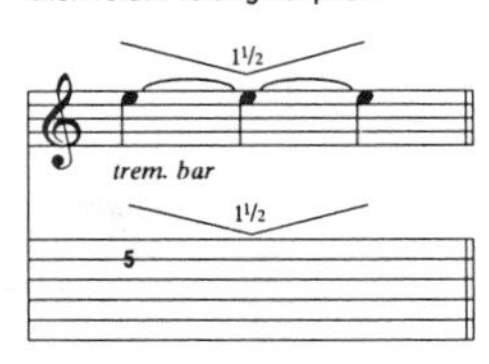

PALM MUTE: With the right hand, partially mute the note by lightly touching the string just before the bridge.

MUFFLED STRINGS: Lay the left hand across the strings without depressing them to the fretboard; strike the strings with the right hand, producing a percussive sound.

PICK SLIDE: Rub the pick edge down the length of the string to produce a scratchy sound.

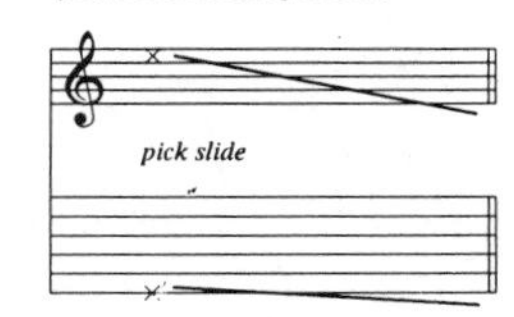

TREMOLO PICKING: Pick the note as rapidly and continuously as possible.

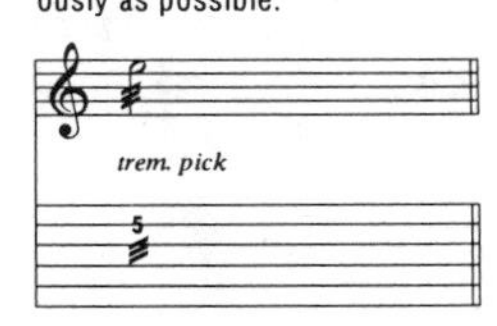

RHYTHM SLASHES: Strum chords in rhythm indicated. Use chord voicings found in the fingering diagrams at the top of the first page of the transcription.

SINGLE-NOTE RHYTHM SLASHES: The circled number above the note name indicates which string to play. When successive notes are played on the same string, only the fret numbers are given.

THE HOTTEST TAB SONGBOOKS AVAILABLE FOR GUITAR & BASS!

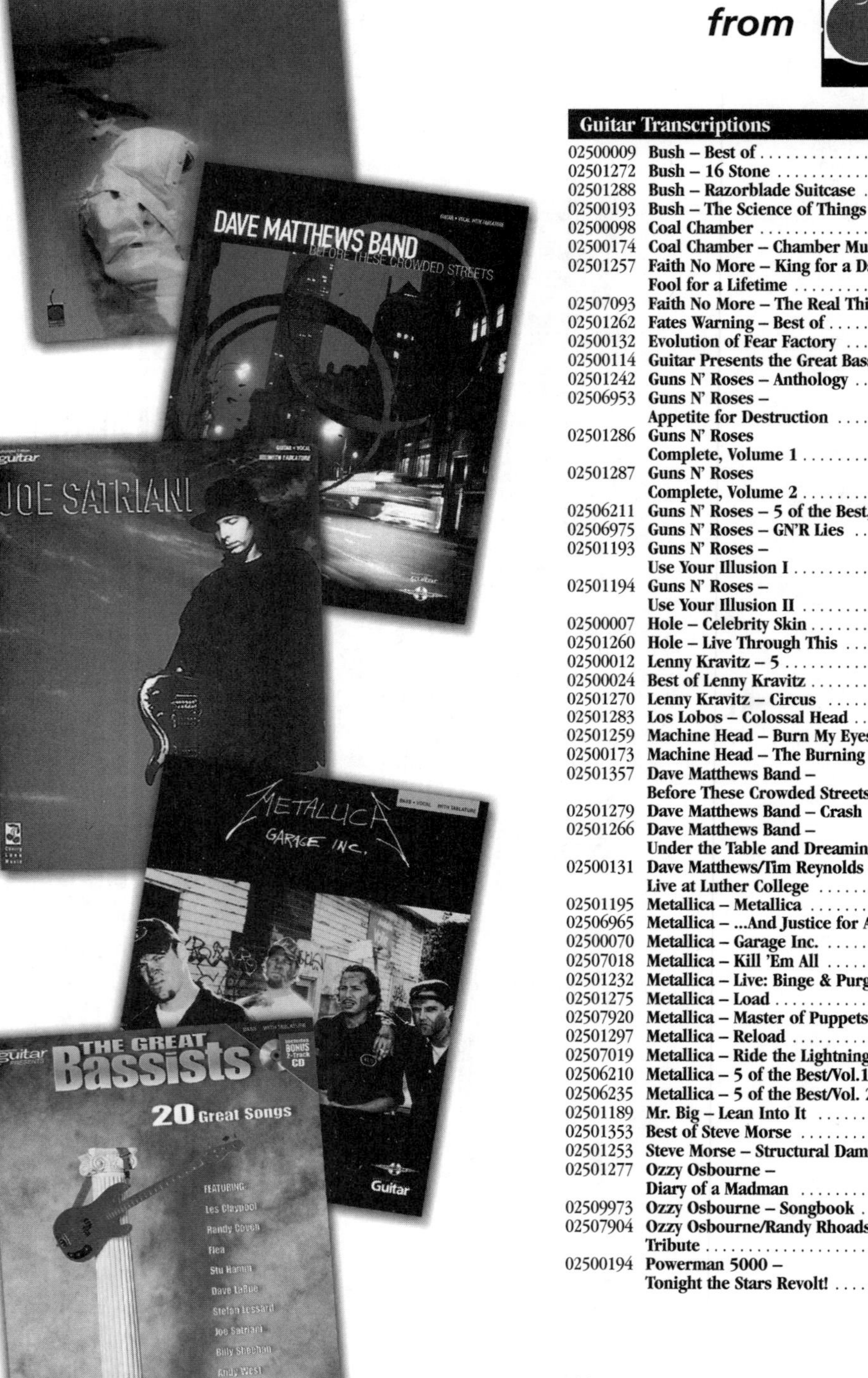

from  CHERRY LANE MUSIC COMPANY™
Quality in Printed Music

Guitar Transcriptions

02500009 Bush – Best of $19.95
02501272 Bush – 16 Stone $21.95
02501288 Bush – Razorblade Suitcase $21.95
02500193 Bush – The Science of Things $19.95
02500098 Coal Chamber $19.95
02500174 Coal Chamber – Chamber Music $19.95
02501257 Faith No More – King for a Day/ Fool for a Lifetime $19.95
02507093 Faith No More – The Real Thing $19.95
02501262 Fates Warning – Best of $21.95
02500132 Evolution of Fear Factory $19.95
02500114 Guitar Presents the Great Bassists $16.95
02501242 Guns N' Roses – Anthology $24.95
02506953 Guns N' Roses – Appetite for Destruction $22.95
02501286 Guns N' Roses Complete, Volume 1 .... $24.95
02501287 Guns N' Roses Complete, Volume 2 .... $24.95
02506211 Guns N' Roses – 5 of the Best, Vol. 1 .... $12.95
02506975 Guns N' Roses – GN'R Lies $19.95
02501193 Guns N' Roses – Use Your Illusion I $24.95
02501194 Guns N' Roses – Use Your Illusion II $24.95
02500007 Hole – Celebrity Skin $19.95
02501260 Hole – Live Through This $19.95
02500012 Lenny Kravitz – 5 .... $16.95
02500024 Best of Lenny Kravitz $19.95
02501270 Lenny Kravitz – Circus $19.95
02501283 Los Lobos – Colossal Head $19.95
02501259 Machine Head – Burn My Eyes $19.95
02500173 Machine Head – The Burning Red $19.95
02501357 Dave Matthews Band – Before These Crowded Streets $19.95
02501279 Dave Matthews Band – Crash $19.95
02501266 Dave Matthews Band – Under the Table and Dreaming $19.95
02500131 Dave Matthews/Tim Reynolds – Live at Luther College $19.95
02501195 Metallica – Metallica $22.95
02506965 Metallica – ...And Justice for All $22.95
02500070 Metallica – Garage Inc. $24.95
02507018 Metallica – Kill 'Em All $19.95
02501232 Metallica – Live: Binge & Purge $19.95
02501275 Metallica – Load $24.95
02507920 Metallica – Master of Puppets $19.95
02501297 Metallica – Reload $24.95
02507019 Metallica – Ride the Lightning $19.95
02506210 Metallica – 5 of the Best/Vol.1 .... $12.95
02506235 Metallica – 5 of the Best/Vol. 2 .... $12.95
02501189 Mr. Big – Lean Into It $19.95
02501353 Best of Steve Morse $19.95
02501253 Steve Morse – Structural Damage $22.95
02501277 Ozzy Osbourne – Diary of a Madman $19.95
02509973 Ozzy Osbourne – Songbook $24.95
02507904 Ozzy Osbourne/Randy Rhoads Tribute $22.95
02500194 Powerman 5000 – Tonight the Stars Revolt! $17.95
02500025 Primus Anthology – A-N (Guitar/Bass) $19.95
02500091 Primus Anthology – O-Z (Guitar/Bass) $19.95
02501255 Best of Joe Satriani $19.95
02501268 Joe Satriani $22.95
02501299 Joe Satriani – Crystal Planet $24.95
02501205 Joe Satriani – The Extremist $22.95
02506236 Joe Satriani – 5 of the Best/Vol. 2 .... $12.95
02507029 Joe Satriani – Flying in a Blue Dream $22.95
02507074 Joe Satriani – Not of This Earth $19.95
02506959 Joe Satriani – Surfing with the Alien $19.95
02501226 Joe Satriani – Time Machine 1 .... $19.95
02501227 Joe Satriani – Time Machine 2 .... $19.95
02500088 Sepultura – Against $19.95
02501239 Sepultura – Arise $19.95
02501240 Sepultura – Beneath the Remains $19.95
02501238 Sepultura – Chaos A.D. $19.95
02501271 Sepultura – Roots $19.95
02501241 Sepultura – Schizophrenia $19.95
02500188 Best of the Brian Setzer Orchestra $19.95
02500177 Sevendust $19.95
02500176 Sevendust – Home $19.95
02501246 Slayer – Decade of Aggression $19.95
02501358 Slayer – Diabolus in Musica $21.95
02501244 Slayer – Divine Intervention $19.95
02501229 Slayer – Haunting the Chapel $14.95
02501167 Slayer – Hell Awaits $19.95
02501264 Primal Slayer for Guitar $19.95
02501215 Slayer – Reign in Blood $19.95
02501179 Slayer – Seasons in the Abyss $19.95
02501282 Slayer – Undisputed Attitude $19.95
02500090 Soulfly $19.95
02501250 Best of Soundgarden $19.95
02501198 Soundgarden – Badmotorfinger $19.95
02501274 Soundgarden – Down on the Upside $21.95
02501230 Soundgarden – Superunknown $19.95
02500167 Best of Steely Dan for Guitar $19.95
02500168 Steely Dan's Greatest Songs $19.95
02501263 Tesla – Time's Making Changes $19.95
02501251 Type O Negative – Bloody Kisses $19.95
02501154 Ugly Kid Joe – America's Least Wanted $19.95
02506972 Steve Vai – Songbook $19.95
02500104 WWF: The Music, Vol. 3 .... $19.95

Bass Transcriptions

02500008 Best of Bush $16.95
02505920 Bush – 16 Stone $19.95
02506966 Guns N' Roses – Appetite for Destruction $19.95
02500013 Best of The Dave Matthews Band $16.95
02505911 Metallica – Metallica $19.95
02506982 Metallica – ...And Justice for All $19.95
02500075 Metallica – Garage, Inc. $24.95
02507039 Metallica – Kill 'Em All $19.95
02505919 Metallica – Load $19.95
02506961 Metallica – Master of Puppets $19.95
02505926 Metallica – Reload $21.95
02507040 Metallica – Ride the Lightning $17.95
02505925 Ozzy Osbourne – Diary of a Madman $17.95
02500025 Primus Anthology – A-N (Guitar/Bass) $19.95
02500091 Primus Anthology – O-Z (Guitar/Bass) $19.95
02505918 Best of Sepultura for Bass $18.95
02505924 Primal Slayer for Bass $16.95
02505917 Best of Soundgarden $16.95

Prices, contents and availability subject to change without notice.

FOR MORE INFORMATION, SEE YOUR LOCAL MUSIC DEALER, OR WRITE TO:

HAL•LEONARD® CORPORATION
7777 W. BLUEMOUND RD. P.O. BOX 13819 MILWAUKEE, WI 53213

0500

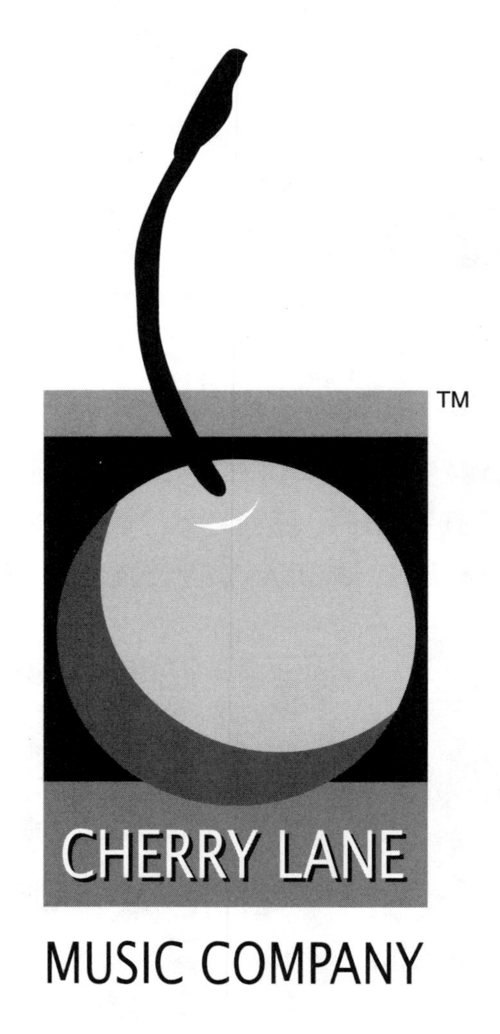

QUALITY IN PRINTED MUSIC